5.00
9/10

the food of
INDIA

the food of
INDIA

Location photography by Jason Lowe
Recipe photography by Alan Benson
Recipes by Priya Wickramasinghe
and Carol Selva Rajah

MURDOCH
BOOKS

JAMMU & KASHMIR

China (Tibet)

HIMACHAL PRADESH

Pakistan

PUNJAB

HARYANA

Delhi

Nepal

ARUNACHAL PRADESH

SIKKIM Bhutan

ASSAM

NAGALAND

MEGHALAYA

RAJASTHAN

UTTAR PRADESH

BIHAR

Bangladesh

MANIPUR

WEST BENGAL

TRIPURA MIZORAM

GUJARAT

MADHYA PRADESH

Myanmar (Burma)

MAHARASHTRA

ORISSA

Kolkata (Calcutta)

Mumbai (Bombay)

Hyderabad

Bay of Bengal

KARNATAKA

ARABIAN SEA

Goa

ANDHRA PRADESH

ANDAMAN AND NICOBAR ISLANDS

Chennai (Madras)

Kochi (Cochin)

TAMIL NADU

KERALA

Sri Lanka

LAKSHADWEEP ISLANDS

CONTENTS

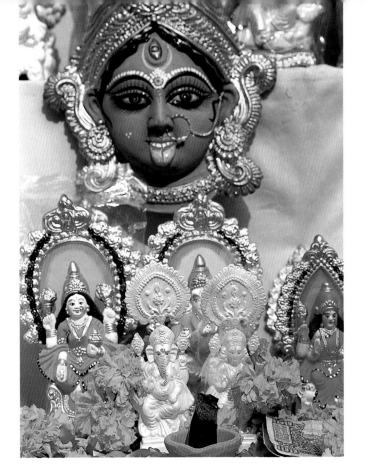

the food of
INDIA

INDIA IS A VERY COMPLEX COUNTRY CULTURALLY, GEOGRAPHICALLY AND FROM A CULINARY POINT OF VIEW. COOKING STYLES VARY NOT ONLY FROM STATE TO STATE AND TOWN TO TOWN BUT ALSO FROM SUBURB TO SUBURB.

Modern India is one of the most diverse countries in the world. It is made up of 25 states and 7 territories and its people use 18 major (and over 1600 minor) languages and practice 7 major religions. Despite this, and its history of constant invasion and change, India has kept a strong sense of national identity and has used outside influences to its advantage.

INFLUENCES

Historically, Indian cuisine has had many influences, one of the biggest being vegetarianism, brought about by religious beliefs. Buddhism and Jainism came to India around the 6th century BC and though they faded as major religions in India, they were particularly successful in converting people to a way of life in which living beings are considered to be sacred. Hinduism predated both these religions but early Hindu texts such as the Mahabharata show that meat was not originally prohibited. Meat is still occasionally eaten by some Hindus. Over time, vegetarianism slowly pervaded Indian culture and today it is practiced by many people, particularly in the South. The sacred status of the cow, a Vedic idea from before Hinduism, also remains to this day.

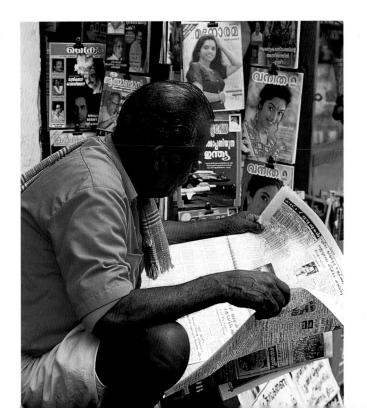

In 1525, the Moghul emperors arrived and brought with them their own style of cooking, architecture and living, which affirmed their religion, Islam, and its Arabic heritage. Muslims had periodically been invading India since the 10th century but this later time was the period of their greatest influence and at one stage they ruled nearly the whole subcontinent. Pork was taboo but meats such as lamb and chicken were eaten as long as they were killed according to Muslim law.

Hindu deities are on display at festival times. Old buildings in Chennai (Madras) present a range of architectural styles, all built for coolness in the heat of the day. Reading is a popular pastime in Kerala where the literacy rate officially runs at 100 per cent. Tea is the national drink; a woman sits in her doorway in Hyderabad; vegetables, pappadams and sweets can be bought on the streets.

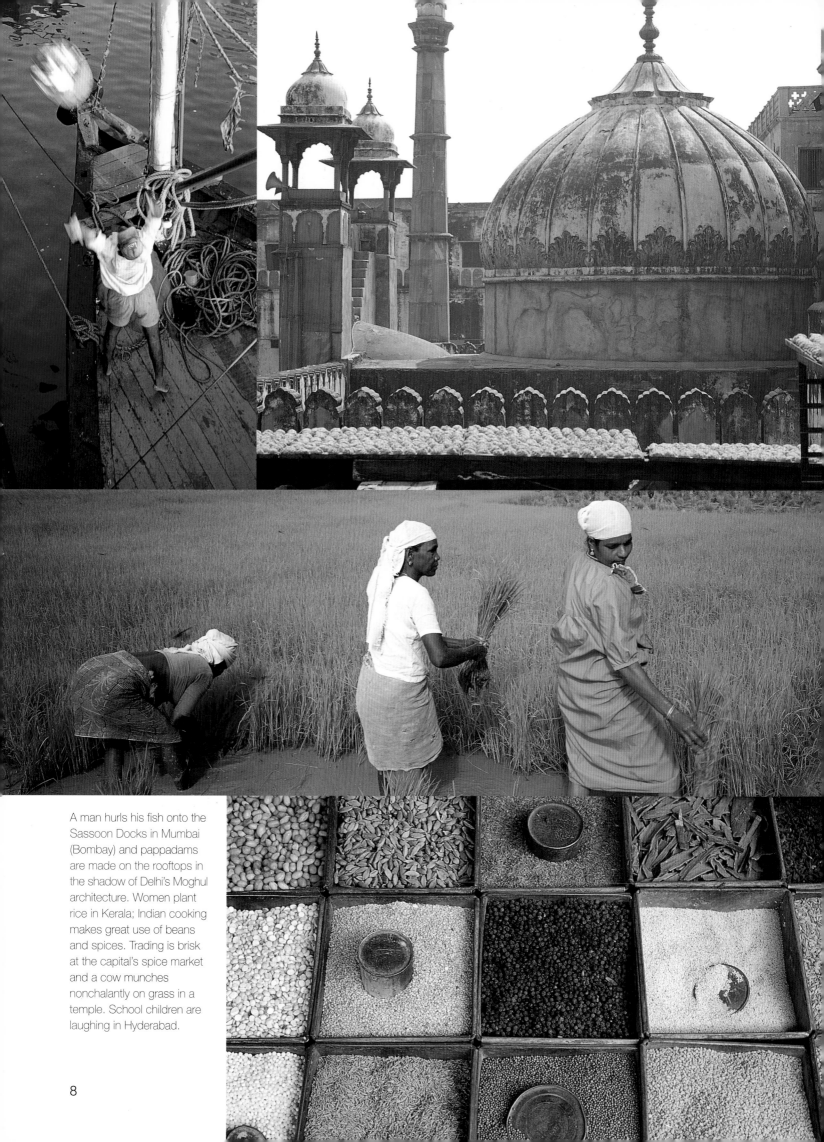

A man hurls his fish onto the Sassoon Docks in Mumbai (Bombay) and pappadams are made on the rooftops in the shadow of Delhi's Moghul architecture. Women plant rice in Kerala; Indian cooking makes great use of beans and spices. Trading is brisk at the capital's spice market and a cow munches nonchalantly on grass in a temple. School children are laughing in Hyderabad.

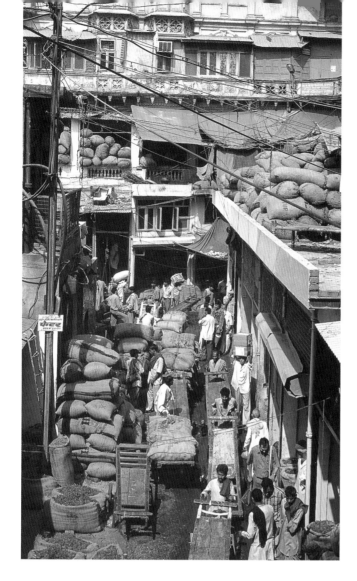

Many dishes were a product of the court chefs, trained in Central Asian, Persian and Afghani culinary styles. Money was no object and imagination was boundless. The Moghuls incorporated some of their favorite foods such as almonds, cream and dried fruits into Indian cuisine and introduced cold weather fruit such as peaches, cherries and apricots to the orchards of Kashmir. The use of saffron and gold and silver leaf reflects the opulence of Moghul cuisine, especially in sweets. These influences are most apparent in northern India and in areas such as Hyderabad, the site of an ancient court, where there were Muslim settlements.

China, another ancient culture, had also long had an association with India via its maritime and overland trading routes. The karhai and wok are extremely similar in appearance, though which came first is impossible to say. Chinese-style bowls are used to serve soups and foods thought to have come from China. Some words, such as 'chiniani' meaning peach, start with 'chin'. The Chinese word for tea, 'cha', also became incorporated into the language when the British began to cultivate tea in India.

Influences from further afield can be seen in Goa and Kerala where the Portuguese established ports, in Chennai (Madras) where the British set up the East India Company, in Pondicherry, a French enclave, and in Kolkata (Calcutta), the center of the British Raj. With the Europeans came more widespread Christianity (St Thomas had arrived in AD 52) and new styles of cooking to add to the established Muslim and Hindu ways. Foods such as potatoes, tomatoes, peppers and chiles, imported from the New World via Europe, were gradually incorporated into local cuisines until in some cases, as with the chile, they became ubiquitous.

The British influence on Indian cuisine was much less than the Indian impact on British food. For example, the British encouraged the idea of frequently nibbling on tiffin, which are little snacks. Also the Indian cooks of the British Empire, urged on by their memsahibs, learned to make cakes, yeasted bread and curries, which were more suited to the British palate. The British developed a liking for spicy food and transported the idea back home where it was Anglicized.

INDIAN FOOD MYTHS

The type of Indian food found in the majority of Indian restaurants is based on a very successful menu formula. The original versions of these restaurants were run by Punjabis in India where they served a mixture of Punjabi cuisine, such as tandoori, and Moghul dishes such as korma and biryani. As the popularity of the cuisine grew, the "menu" was established, then replicated in new restaurants. This menu represents a tiny section of Indian cuisine.

In India, there is no such thing as a curry. The word is of English origin, based on the Tamil word kari meaning black pepper, and is a term used to denote all kinds of Indian dishes, particularly those in a sauce. Dishes in India are named either for the combination of spices used (rogan josh), for the cooking method (korma, biryani, do piaza), or for their main ingredients (saag, aloo gobi). Curry powder does not exist within India, the closest equivalent being masala (spice mix). There are hundreds of masala combinations. In northern India, they tend to be dry mixtures using ground spices such as garam masala and in the southern areas, wet ones, such as coconut masala, using fresh spices. Indian food is not universally hot. Some dishes contain lots of chiles, others none at all.

EATING

Meat or vegetarian dishes are never the main part of the meal. They are always an accompaniment to rice or breads and are eaten alongside relishes, chutneys and other dishes such as dal. Yogurt or curd is also served with meals and is particularly useful for cooling hot or spicy food. The types of dishes eaten vary according to religious group. Hindus tend to eat vegetable dishes and dals served with plain boiled rice. Muslims serve meat and seafood dishes, breads, and fried snacks such as samosas, but dal does not play such an important part. So generally, Indian meals consist of a couple of vegetable dishes (and meat or fish where appropriate), some relishes or chutneys, yogurt, rice, breads and a dessert, usually all served at the same time. Sometimes, samosas or other deep-fried snacks are included.

Meals are often served on thalis, which are large, flat plates, made from banana leaves or metal. Though more prevalent in southern areas and in Gujarat, they are a common element of Indian cuisine, used by all strata of society. The leaf or plate is covered with either small mounds of food or metal bowls called katoris which hold the food. The food, eaten with the fingertips of your right hand, is replenished as you eat.

Paan is a collection of spices and aromatics often served at the end of the meal to freshen the breath and act as a digestive. A betel leaf is folded around pieces of betel nut, and either lime paste, red katha paste, chewing tobacco or mitha masala (spices). The whole lot is chewed before being either spat out, or in the case of mitha masala, swallowed.

Food is all encompassing in India. A small boy carries his lunch in a tiffin carrier; pickles and samosas are sold on the street and a man fishes in peace from a tank in Kolkata (Calcutta). The pace of life on the roads, whether on two wheels or more, is in direct contrast to the leisurely sale of paan, banana leaves and fish by food vendors. Kolkata's (Calcutta) New Market is busy all day.

11

Tandoori is popular all over the northern areas, as are Moghul-style pulaos. Delicious fruit chaat is sold on the streets alongside pistachios, amla and pomegranates. Holy cows wander the streets of Delhi as rice from around the country is unloaded at the market. The Jama Masjid (Friday mosque) is a focus for Delhi's Muslims while Hindus sell puris during Divali.

12

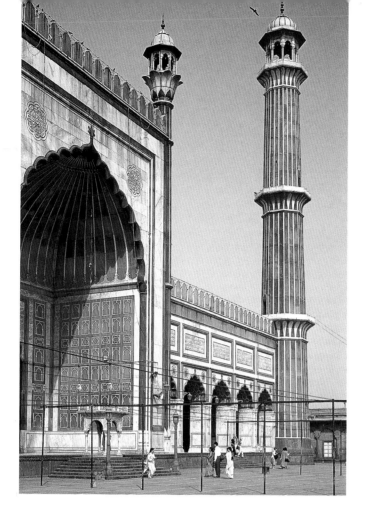

THE FOOD OF THE NORTH

The cuisines in the north of India cover a wide range of food styles, the main influences coming from the cooking of the Moghuls and Punjabs, as well as from the land, which produces a diverse range of grains. Traditionally, rice was not eaten in large quantities as the climate of the area meant it could not be easily grown. However, in Jammu and Kashmir, and in Dera Dun, rice is grown on terraces in the Himalayan foothills. Basmati, the king of rices, comes from Dera Dun and is prized throughout India.

As breads are a staple, there is a huge range to choose from. In Kashmir and Jammu, the kulcha and sheermal are Middle Eastern in style, in the Punjab and Haryana, naan are cooked in tandoors, and parathas, puris, chapatis and roti are widely eaten. Breads are usually served with dishes which have a thick sauce that is easily scooped up. Dishes with a more liquid sauce are generally served with rice.

Dairy products such as malai (cream), paneer and yogurt appear at almost every meal in some guise or other. Butter appears in the form of ghee or makhan (white butter). Dishes are thickened and enriched with cream and in the Punjab butter is used both as a condiment and as a flavoring. Rajasthani cuisine contains many dishes cooked in buttermilk, milk or butter. This cooking style evolved because water was scarce and its use as a cooking medium had to be avoided. Northern dishes are often cooked in sealed pots in very little liquid, a method known as dum.

Meat is a feature of northern cuisine. This is a reflection of Moghul influences as well as those of other communities such as the Parsis and Sikhs. Lamb is popular meat though game is also favored in the Punjab and Rajasthan. Beans and legumes are commonly eaten and a dal of some sort, often well spiced, will accompany every meal.

Spices in these areas tend to be based on 'hot mixes'. This means warmly flavored spices rather than heat from chiles. Many spices are dry-roasted before being used, in order to add depth to their flavor. The best-known is garam masala which is used to temper dishes at the end of cooking.

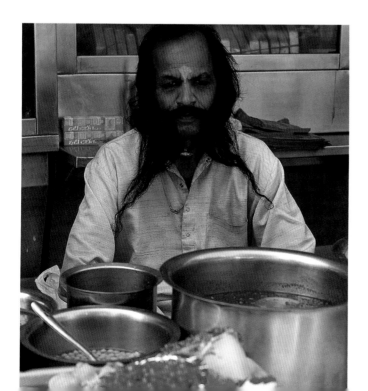

The custom of cooking in community ovens or tandoors prevails in rural areas, especially in the Punjab. The ovens are used to cook breads and roast meats, something which is not possible in homestyle kitchens, where cooking pots are set above open fires.

THE FOOD OF THE CENTER

Central India has an eclectic mix of foods which can be roughly divided into East (Bengal), West (Gujarat and Maharashtra) and Central (Hyderabad) styles. Fish feature heavily on both coasts while Hyderabad has a cuisine with Moghul overtones and a diet rich in meat.

Fish, both coastal and those from inland waterways, appear in many Bengali, Assamese and Orissan dishes, hilsa being a particular favorite. Smaller fish are made into soupy johl or deep-fried with spices. Larger ones are covered with thick spice pastes and steamed or fried. On the opposite coast, the fish market on Mumbai's (Bombay) Sassoon Docks is the busiest in India and caters to the varied communities of Mumbai (Bombay), as well as national and international buyers. The Parsi people in Mumbai (Bombay) and Gujarat use fish for more elaborate dishes such as patra ni machi, which is traditionally served at weddings.

Spices are varied in their use. Seed spices such as cumin and coriander grow in Gujarat, as do turmeric and chiles. These are all used extensively in the mainly vegetarian cuisine of the area. In Bengal, a spice mix called panch phoron dominates and mustard seeds and mustard oil are a common combination. Hyderabad, further south, uses southern spices and aromatics, such as curry leaves and tamarind, blended with a Moghul style of cooking.

Rice is eaten as a staple across most of the Center. Red patni rice, with its chewy texture and nutty aroma, grows in the Center and West, especially in coastal areas, and is thought to be good for giving energy. In Hyderabad, rice is cooked with saffron and spices and transformed into biryani and pulao, or added to lentils to make khichhari, which is a favorite breakfast dish eaten with pappadams and kheema.

Dairy-based sweets such as rossogollas, gulab jamun and sandesh are found all over Bengal but especially in the capital, Kolkata (Calcutta), where there are numerous sweet shops. Gujarat produces jaggery, a raw sugar made from sugar cane. This is eaten as a sweetmeat and is also added in small quantities to bean and vegetable dishes.

Tea is grown all along the Brahmaputra valley in Assam, the main tea-producing area of India. It is here that the first tea gardens were established by the British in the 19th century. India's finest tea, however, is grown in Darjeeling, a hill station in the foothills of the Himalayas in West Bengal.

Children play on the streets in Kolkata (Calcutta). Beans and vegetables are eaten across the central states. Fish are popular in Bengal and Maharashtra. Tea is grown in Assam. On the west coast in Mumbai (Bombay), people gather on Chowpatty beach at sunset to walk, talk and eat chaat. Bhajis are fried on request. In Hyderabad the selection of pickles is incomparable.

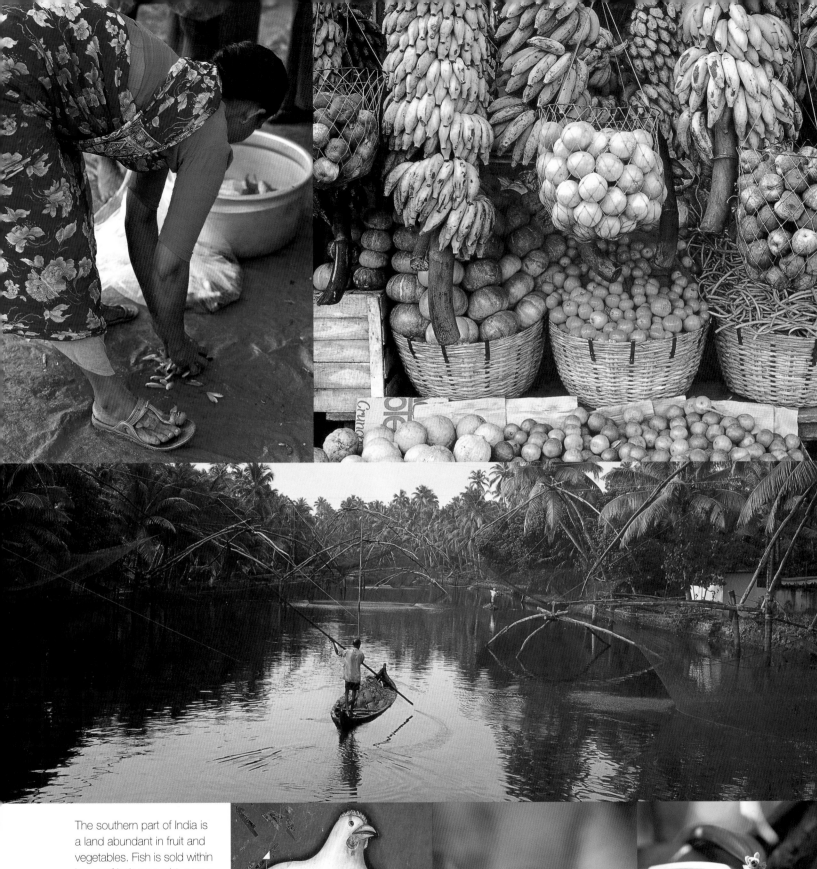

The southern part of India is
a land abundant in fruit and
vegetables. Fish is sold within
hours of being caught, some
coming from the Chinese
fishing nets in the backwaters
of Kerala. Chicken is popular
as are turmeric and
coconuts, while vanilla
is grown for the international
market. Elephants carry
their own lunch to work
and masks hang on a wall
in Kochi (Cochin).

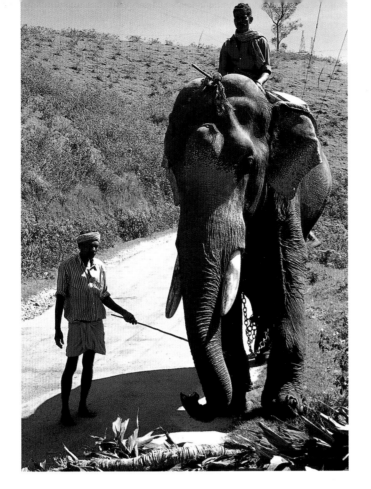

THE FOOD OF THE SOUTH

The food of southern India has a lighter, fresher flavor than that of the northern parts. It is often more pungent because of its use of chiles and souring agents such as lime juice, kokum and tamarind. Freshly grated coconut is used in abundance and coconut milk is a common cooking liquid.

Along the west coast in Goa, Karnataka and Kerala, there are culinary influences from the Portuguese who lived in the area for 500 years, the Syrian Christians, and the Jews of Kochi (Cochin). Commercial coconut cultivation was encouraged by the Portuguese, tea was planted around the hill stations in the Nilgiris by the British, and coffee, which is grown across the South, a legacy of Arab merchants, is more popular than tea. The chile, which was to have a profound effect on the cuisine of India, arrived in Kerala with the Portuguese.

The spice center of India is Kochi (Cochin) in Kerala and it is here that the Indian Spices Board has its headquarters. Cardamom, turmeric, vanilla, pepper and ginger grow in abundance in the Cardamom Hills and are sold locally and internationally via the spice market in Kochi.

Rice is the main staple, along with beans and legumes, and dishes are flavored with wet (fresh) spice and herb mixtures, and coconut. Many dishes are tempered with a final seasoning (tarka), usually a combination of mustard seeds, dried chiles and curry leaves heated in oil and stirred into the dish. Beans are eaten as dals and also ground into flours to make pappadams and other deep-fried snacks. Appams, idlis and dosas are common across southern India and are eaten with chutneys and stew-like dishes, or in the case of the dosa, holding a spicy potato filling.

Pork and beef are sold and eaten in Goa and Kerala, supported by a high level of religious tolerance. Vindaloo and bafath are popular pork dishes with European styles of cooking using local ingredients. Lamb dishes are eaten by the Mappilas, the Muslims of the Malabar coast, descendants of Arab traders. Moghul-style recipes such as korma are cooked using southern flavors including coconut and curry leaves. In contrast, Karnataka and Tamil Nadu both have a strong vegetarian bent to their cuisine.

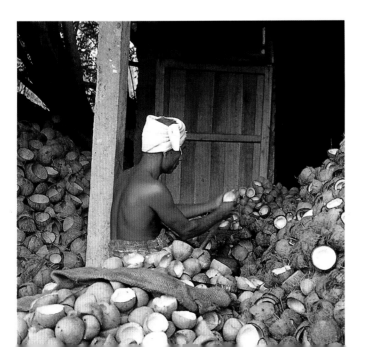

Both the coast and waterways of the area provide many types of fish and shellfish. In Kerala, there are Chinese fishing nets used for catching fish in the backwaters.

TIFFIN

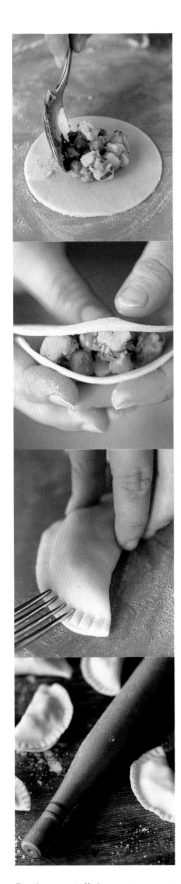

Don't overstuff the samosas or they will burst when cooked. Seal them and use a fork to press the edges together firmly.

SAMOSAS

THESE CRISP, DEEP-FRIED PASTRIES ARE THE MOST POPULAR SAVORY SNACK IN INDIA. THIS RECIPE HAS A DELICIOUS SPICY VEGETABLE FILLING BUT IF YOU PREFER A MEAT SAMOSA, YOU CAN USE THE SINGHARA FILLING ON PAGE 46. SAMOSAS ARE USUALLY SERVED WITH CHUTNEY.

PASTRY
3 1/2 cups maida or all-purpose flour
1 teaspoon salt
4 tablespoons oil or ghee

FILLING
3/4 lb. potatoes, cut into quarters
1/2 cup peas
1 1/2 teaspoons cumin seeds
1/2 teaspoon coriander seeds
2 tablespoons oil
1/2 onion, finely chopped
1/4 teaspoon ground turmeric
1/2 teaspoon garam masala
   (page 284)
2 green chiles, chopped
1 inch piece of ginger, chopped
1 1/2 tablespoons lemon juice
2 tablespoons chopped cilantro
   leaves

oil for deep-frying

MAKES 30

TO MAKE the pastry, sift the maida and salt into a bowl, then rub in the oil or ghee until the mixture resembles bread crumbs. Add 3/4–1 cup warm water, a little at a time, to make a pliable dough. Turn out onto a floured surface and knead for 5 minutes, or until smooth. Cover and allow to rest for 15 minutes. Don't refrigerate or the oil will harden.

TO MAKE the filling, cook the potatoes in simmering water for 10 minutes, or until tender. Drain and cut into small cubes. Cook the peas in simmering water for 2 minutes. Drain and refresh in cold water.

PLACE a small frying pan over low heat, dry-roast the cumin seeds until aromatic, then remove. Dry-roast the coriander seeds. Grind 1/2 teaspoon of the cumin and all the coriander to a fine powder in a spice grinder or pestle and mortar.

HEAT the oil in a heavy-bottomed saucepan over low heat and fry the onion until light brown. Stir in all the cumin, the coriander, turmeric and garam masala. Add the potatoes, chiles, ginger and and stir for 1 minute. Mix in the lemon juice and cilantro leaves and salt to taste, then allow to cool.

ON a floured surface, roll out a third of the pastry to an 11 inch circle, about 1/8 inch thick. Cut 10 circles with an 3 inch cutter and spoon 1/2 tablespoon of filling onto the center of each. Moisten the edges with a little water, then fold over and seal with a fork into a semicircle. Repeat to use all the filling and pastry. Cover until ready to fry.

FILL a karhai or heavy-bottomed saucepan a third full with oil and heat to 350°F (a cube of bread will brown in 15 seconds). Fry a few samosas at a time until lightly browned. Turn them over and brown them on the other side. Drain on a wire rack for 5 minutes before draining on paper towels. Serve warm or cold.

PORK TIKKA

ENCRUSTED IN SPICES AND MOUTHWATERINGLY TENDER ON THE INSIDE, PORK TIKKA IS POPULAR IN PUNJABI DHABAS (ROADSIDE RESTAURANTS) AND AT STREET STANDS. IT IS OFTEN SERVED WITH CHAPATIS, ROTI OR NAAN AND CHUTNEY ON THE SIDE.

MARINADE
1 onion, roughly chopped
3 garlic cloves, roughly chopped
2 inch piece of ginger, roughly
   chopped
1/2 tablespoon ground cumin
1 teaspoon ground coriander
1/2 tablespoon garam masala
   (page 284)
1/4 teaspoon chili powder
1/2 pinch ground black pepper
1 cup plain yogurt (page 280)

1 lb. center-cut pork tenderloin,
   cut into 1 inch cubes

SAUCE
1 large red onion, roughly chopped
1 garlic clove, roughly chopped
1 inch piece of ginger, roughly
   chopped
1 green chile, roughly chopped
1/2 cup cilantro leaves

1/2 cup oil
1 tablespoon garam masala
   (page 284)

SERVES 4

TO PREPARE the marinade, finely chop the onion, garlic and ginger in a food processor or, if you don't have a processor, with a knife. Add the spices and yogurt to the paste and mix through.

PUT the pork in a bowl, add the marinade and mix well. Cover and marinate in the fridge for 2 hours or overnight.

TO MAKE the sauce, finely chop the onion, garlic, ginger, chile and cilantro in a food processor or, if you don't have a processor, with a knife.

HEAT the oil in a heavy-bottomed frying pan, large enough to fit the meat in a single layer, until sizzling but not smoking. Add the sauce and stir over medium heat for 2 minutes, or until softened but not brown. Increase the heat to high and add the pork with the marinade. Stir constantly for 5 minutes, then reduce the heat to medium and let the meat and its juices bubble away for 15–20 minutes, or until the liquid has completely evaporated. The meat and the dryish sauce will be a rich dark brown.

SEASON with salt, to taste, and sprinkle with the garam masala. Cook for another 2 minutes to allow the added seasoning to be absorbed.

A Punjabi dhaba in Mumbai (Bombay) sells specialty snacks.

Chapatis are cooked on a large tava at a street stand.

TANDOORI PANEER

10 oz. paneer (page 279)
2 green peppers
1 onion
2 firm tomatoes
1¹/4 cups plain yogurt (page 280)
1 teaspoon ground turmeric
1 inch piece of ginger, grated
4 garlic cloves, crushed
1¹/2 tablespoons lemon juice
2 tablespoons chopped mint leaves
1 tablespoon chopped cilantro
　　leaves
2 tablespoons oil

SERVES 4

CUT the paneer into pieces measuring about
³/4 x ¹/2 inch. Cut the peppers into squares, the
onion into chunks and the tomatoes into cubes.
Mix the yogurt, turmeric, ginger, garlic and lemon
juice, together with a little salt, in a large bowl. Stir
in the herbs. Add the paneer and vegetables to
the marinade, cover and refrigerate for 3 hours.

PREHEAT the broiler. Using eight skewers, thread
onto each 5 pieces of paneer and some pepper,
onion and tomato, dividing the vegetables equally.
Brush with the oil, season with salt and roast on
all sides for 3–4 minutes, or until the paneer and
vegetables are cooked and slightly charred
around the edges. Serve with roti (page 220)
and a salad such as laccha (page 233).

NIMKI

NIMKI

THESE ARE SMALL, DEEP-FRIED PIECES OF DOUGH SERVED AS A SNACK. THE KALONJI GIVE THESE

TIDBITS A PUNGENT, DISTINCTIVE TASTE AND AROMA. IN INDIA, THEY ARE SOLD AT SWEET SHOPS

WHERE THEY ALSO SELL NUTS AND OTHER SAVORY SNACKS SUCH AS SINGHARAS.

2 cups maida or all-purpose flour
1 teaspoon salt
1 teaspoon kalonji (nigella seeds)
1 tablespoon ghee
oil for deep-frying

MAKES 60

SIFT the maida and salt into a bowl and add the
kalonji. Rub in the ghee until the mixture resembles
bread crumbs. Add ¹/2 cup water, a little at a time,
to make a pliable dough. Turn the dough out onto
a floured surface and knead for 5 minutes, or until
smooth, then cover and rest it for 10 minutes.
Don't refrigerate or the ghee will harden.

DIVIDE the dough into two portions and roll out
each portion until about 1¹/4 inches thick. Cut
into ¹/2 inch wide strips, then into diamonds
1¹/4 inches long, by making diagonal cuts along
the strips. Prick the diamonds with a fork.

FILL a karhai or heavy-bottomed saucepan
a third full with oil and heat to about 325°F
(a cube of bread will brown in 20 seconds).
Fry the nimki in batches until light golden and
crisp. Drain on paper towels. Serve with mint
and cilantro chutney (page 250).

CHUCUMBER

A VERY HEALTHY NORTH INDIAN SNACK OFTEN SERVED AS AN APPETIZER IN RESTAURANTS, OR WITH DRINKS. MANY OF THE INGREDIENTS CAN BE INCREASED OR DECREASED ACCORDING TO PERSONAL TASTE. THE COMBINATION OF CUCUMBER AND FRESH CILANTRO IS VERY REFRESHING.

1 red onion, finely chopped
2 small cucumbers (7 oz.), finely chopped
1/2 cup ripe tomatoes, finely chopped
3 tablespoons finely chopped cilantro
1 red chile, finely chopped
1 green chile, finely chopped
1 1/2 tablespoons lemon juice
1 teaspoon oil
3/4 cup unroasted peanuts, roughly chopped
1 teaspoon salt
1/2 teaspoon ground black pepper
1 1/2 teaspoons chaat masala (page 284)

SERVES 4

STIR together in a bowl the onion, cucumbers, tomatoes, cilantro, chiles and lemon juice.

HEAT the oil in a heavy-bottomed frying pan over high heat, add the peanuts and salt and fry for 1 minute. Sprinkle with the pepper and chaat masala and stir. Fry for 2 minutes. Remove from the heat and add to the onion mixture. Season with more salt to taste, just before serving. The seasoning is added at the end to prevent the ingredients from releasing too much juice before serving.

SERVE in small bowls. Chucumber can be eaten with a spoon or scooped up in pieces of roti (page 220) or pappadams.

Chili powder and turmeric marry well with small fish to make both spicy snacks and curries.

SPICY WHITEBAIT

AS A DELICIOUS SNACK TO ENJOY WITH DRINKS, SMALL FISH CAUGHT IN RIVERS AND WATERWAYS IN INDIA ARE QUICKLY DEEP-FRIED AND SEASONED WITH SALT AND SPICES. THIS WORKS PARTICULARLY WELL WITH WHITEBAIT. YOU CAN VARY THE STRENGTH OF THE SEASONING ACCORDING TO TASTE.

3/4 lb. whitebait
1/2 teaspoon chili powder
1/4 teaspoon cayenne pepper
1/2 teaspoon ground turmeric
oil for deep-frying

SERVES 4

RINSE the whitebait and dry them thoroughly on paper towels. Mix the chili powder, cayenne pepper and turmeric together and toss the whitebait in the seasoning until well coated.

FILL a karhai or heavy-bottomed saucepan a third full with oil and heat to 375°F (a cube of bread will brown in 10 seconds). Fry the fish in batches until crisp, drain on paper towels and sprinkle with salt. Serve hot and crisp.

SPICY WHITEBAIT

GOLDEN EGG CURRY

8 eggs
oil for deep-frying
2 ripe tomatoes
1 1/2 tablespoons ghee
1 onion, finely chopped
1 garlic clove, finely chopped
1 2/3 cups coconut milk (page 283)
1 teaspoon ground turmeric
1/2 teaspoon cayenne pepper
6 curry leaves

SERVES 4

PUT the eggs in a saucepan of water and bring to a boil. Boil for 6 minutes, until medium-hard, then cool quickly in a bowl of cold water. Peel them. You can now deep-fry the eggs if you wish. Fill a karhai or heavy-bottomed saucepan a third full with oil and heat to 325°F (a cube of bread will brown in 20 seconds). Fry the eggs in batches until golden and crisp. Drain on paper towels. Cut each egg in half if you prefer.

SCORE a cross in the top of each tomato. Plunge into boiling water for 20 seconds, then drain and peel away from the cross. Roughly chop the tomatoes, discarding the cores and seeds.

MELT the ghee in a karhai or heavy-bottomed frying pan over low heat, add the onion and garlic and cook until soft and golden. Add the tomatoes and cook until soft. Gradually stir in the coconut milk, then the turmeric, cayenne and season with salt. Bring to a boil and simmer for 2–3 minutes, until the sauce thickens slightly. Add the eggs and heat gently for 2–3 minutes. Garnish with curry leaves.

PARSI SCRAMBLED EGGS

PARSI SCRAMBLED EGGS

WHEN THE PARSIS CAME TO INDIA FROM PERSIA, THEY BROUGHT CULINARY IDEAS WITH THEM, INCLUDING THE USE OF SAFFRON. THIS EGG RECIPE IS ALSO KNOWN AS AKOORI OR EKOORI.

2 tablespoons oil or ghee
1 red onion, finely chopped
1 garlic clove, finely chopped
3/4 inch piece of ginger, grated
1 teaspoon garam masala
  (page 284)
pinch of chili powder
4 strands saffron soaked in
  2 tablespoons hot milk
6 eggs
2 green chiles, finely chopped
4 slices of toast
chopped cilantro leaves

SERVES 4

HEAT the oil or ghee in a heavy-bottomed saucepan over low heat, add the onion and garlic and fry for 4–5 minutes, until soft. Add the ginger and stir for 2 minutes, or until soft. Add the garam masala, chili powder and saffron and cook for 1 minute. Season with salt.

WHISK the eggs and add them to the saucepan. Cook over low heat, scraping the egg from the side of the saucepan into the center until the mixture is soft and creamy. Remove from the heat to prevent the eggs from cooking further. Sprinkle the chopped chiles over the egg, then fold in. Pile onto hot toast, sprinkle with chopped cilantro and serve.

BHEL PURI

BHEL PURI IS A MIXTURE OF SAVORY MORSELS, INCLUDING CRISP PUFFED RICE, POTATOES AND GREEN

MANGO, TOSSED WITH A TART TAMARIND CHUTNEY AND MINT CHUTNEY. SERVED FRESHLY MADE IN

BOWLS, IT IS A FAVORITE SNACK AT SUNSET ON CHOWPATTY BEACH IN MUMBAI (BOMBAY).

A bhel puri seller prepares potatoes on Chowpatty beach.

MINT CHUTNEY
1¹/₂ cups cilantro leaves
2¹/₂ cups mint leaves
6 garlic cloves, chopped
3 red chiles, chopped
¹/₂ red onion, chopped
3 tablespoons lemon juice

TAMARIND CHUTNEY
¹/₄ cup fennel seeds
1³/₄ cups tamarind paste
  (page 280)
3 oz. ginger, sliced
1¹/₃ cups jaggery or light brown
  sugar
1 teaspoon chili powder
1 tablespoon ground cumin
1 tablespoon chaat masala
  (page 284)
1 teaspoon black salt

3 potatoes
1 tomato
2 cups puffed rice
2 oz. sev noodles
1 green unripe mango, sliced
  into thin slivers
1 onion, finely chopped
4 tablespoons finely chopped
  cilantro or mint leaves
1 teaspoon chaat masala
  (page 284)
12 crushed puri crisps (page 219)

cilantro leaves

SERVES 6

TO MAKE the mint chutney, blend the ingredients together in a food processor or pestle and mortar. Transfer to a saucepan and bring to a boil. Remove from the heat, allow to cool, then season with salt.

TO MAKE the tamarind chutney, place a small frying pan over low heat and dry-roast the fennel seeds until aromatic. Mix together the tamarind, ginger and sugar with 1 cup water in a saucepan. Cook over low heat until the tamarind blends into the mixture and the sugar completely dissolves.

STRAIN the ginger mixture, discard the ginger, and cook the remaining mixture to a thick pulp. Add the fennel seeds, chili powder, cumin, chaat masala and black salt. Season with salt and reduce, stirring occasionally, over medium heat until thickened to a dropping consistency (it will fall in sheets off the spoon). Allow to cool.

TO MAKE the bhel puri, cook the potatoes in boiling water for 10 minutes or until tender, then cut into small cubes. Score a cross in the top of the tomato. Plunge into boiling water for 20 seconds, then drain and peel. Roughly chop the tomato, discarding the core and seeds and reserving any juices.

PUT the puffed rice, noodles, mango, onion, chopped coriander, chaat masala and puri crisps in a large bowl and toss them together. When well mixed, stir in a little of each chutney. Vary the chutney amounts depending on the flavor you want to achieve. The tamarind chutney has a tart flavor and the mint chutney is hot. Serve in small bowls and garnish with cilantro leaves.

LEFTOVER MINT chutney can be eaten with samosas (page 20) or pakoras (page 41) but cannot be stored. Store unused tamarind chutney in a jar in the fridge. It will keep for several weeks.

LAMB KOFTA

THESE MINIATURE MEATBALLS ARE OFTEN SERVED AS A SNACK IN HOMES AND RESTAURANTS. THEY
ARE A TYPICAL EXAMPLE OF A DISH THAT MIGRATED FROM PERSIA TO INDIA. THE MEATBALLS ARE SOFT
AND SUCCULENT INSIDE BECAUSE THE MIXTURE IS THOROUGHLY KNEADED BEFORE COOKING.

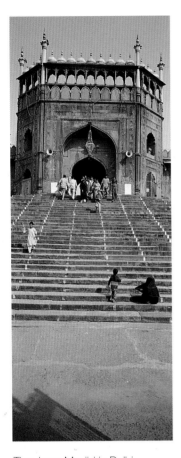

The Jama Masjid in Delhi.

1 small onion, roughly chopped
2 inch piece of ginger, roughly
   chopped
2 garlic cloves, roughly chopped
2 green chiles, seeded and
   roughly chopped
1/4 cup cilantro leaves
2 tablespoons plain yogurt
   (page 280)
1 lb. ground lamb
2 1/2 teaspoons ground cumin
1 1/2 teaspoons ground coriander
2 teaspoons garam masala
   (page 284)
1/4 teaspoon chili powder
2 1/2 teaspoons salt
1/2 teaspoon ground black pepper
3–4 tablespoons oil

SERVES 6

BLEND the onion, ginger, garlic, chopped chiles
and the cilantro leaves together in a food
processor until they form a paste. If you don't
have a food processor, use a pestle and mortar,
or finely chop everything together with a knife.
Add the yogurt to the paste and mix well.

PUT the ground lamb in a bowl, add the paste
and mix by hand, kneading the ingredients into
the meat until thoroughly combined. Add all the
spices, and the salt and pepper, and mix again
to distribute evenly. Cover and refrigerate for
1–2 hours to allow the flavors to develop and
also to make the mixture firmer and therefore
easier to handle.

WET YOUR hands and roll small handfuls (about
a heaping tablespoon) of the lamb mixture into
small balls (wetting your hands prevents the
mixture from sticking to your hands). You should
have about 30–40 meatballs.

HEAT 1 tablespoon of the oil in a large, heavy-
bottomed frying pan. When hot but not smoking,
add 10 meatballs in a single layer. Brown on all
sides by gently shaking the pan for 2–3 minutes.
Don't be tempted to turn them over with a spoon
or they may break up. Test a kofta by breaking
it open. If it is cooked through, there should be
no pink meat inside. If the meat is still pink, cook
for another minute or two. Remove and drain
on paper towels. Repeat with the remaining
meatballs. Serve with wooden skewers or
toothpicks for picking them up. Mint and cilantro
chutney (page 250) is the perfect side dish but
other chutneys are also suitable.

PANI PURI also called gol gappa or puchkas, these are deep-fried puffs of bread often filled with potatoes, chickpeas and spiced tamarind or cumin water. Eaten as one highly flavored mouthful.

KALA CHANA black chickpeas which have been sprouted are sold in bags or paper cones, dressed with a combination of lime juice, chili powder and chopped onion.

CUCUMBER peeled cucumbers are sold as a cool refreshing snack which is almost as thirst-quenching as a drink. They are often dipped in salt to add a bit of flavor.

PINEAPPLE beautifully peeled pineapples are sold by the roadside. They are cut into chunks and wrapped in banana leaves to be eaten on hot, dusty car journeys.

PEANUT BHUJIYA peanuts that are coated in chickpea batter and deep-fried until crunchy. The green snack is vantana, or deep-fried green peas which are tossed in salt and spices.

SAMOSAS are deep-fried crispy pastries filled with a spicy vegetable mixture, a spicy meat and pea mixture, or, sometimes, paneer. They can be eaten hot or carried away to be eaten cold.

MOONGPHALI peanuts roasted under hot coals are a popular snack to nibble at on Mumbai's beaches. The portion to be sold is placed under the pan of coals until it roasts.

BHEL PURI Mumbai's (Bombay) renowned snack is made from sev (besan flour) noodles, puffed rice, chopped onions, tomatoes, potatoes and spices all tossed with tamarind and mint chutney.

CHANA MASALA green unripe chickpeas (choliya) are cooked with spices before being sold garnished with onions, tomatoes, lemon juice and some fresh cilantro leaves.

ROASTED CORN corn cobs are cooked directly on glowing charcoal in karhais until they start to blacken. The type of corn used in India is paler in color than sweetcorn.

CHOLE CHAAT white chickpeas are cooked with potatoes in a spicy sauce and garnished with chopped onions, tomatoes and cilantro leaves. Shown here in a disposable leaf bowl.

TANDOORI PANEER cubes of paneer, a type of fresh cheese, are threaded onto long skewers with vegetables, and are cooked for a few minutes in the intense heat of a tandoori oven.

STREET FOOD is available at all hours of the night and day and ranges from a simple bag of fried peanuts or lentils sold by a wandering vendor, or pakoras fried to order, to a pani puri filled with spiced tamarind water or a more elaborate plate of dal and rice and bhaji. A delicious variety of snacks is sold not just at breakfast, lunch or dinner, but all day long.

STREET FOOD

IN INDIA, THERE ARE FOOD CARTS, TEA STANDS AND MOBILE SNACK VENDORS ON ALMOST EVERY STREET CORNER. EATING THROUGHOUT THE DAY IS A WAY OF LIFE AND THE DIVERSITY OF FRESHLY MADE SNACKS TO CHOOSE FROM ASTOUNDING.

Street food, part of the culture in India, came about after mass migration to the cities. It provides not just delicious food but a way of life, including an opportunity to socialize. Eating street food starts as early as breakfast time when men in suits snack on their way to work. They visit again at lunchtime when they take a quick break for a nourishing dish of rice and dal. In the evening, families and young couples stroll in parks, or on beaches, and nibble on chickpea crackers or pistachio kulfi (ice cream). At other times of the day, there is room for a refreshing glass of lassi (whipped yogurt drink), a pani puri (deep-fried stuffed bread) or a quick sandwich made from dubble roti (sliced bread).

Some vendors have permanent fixtures for their stand or cart. Others (komcha-wallahs) carry baskets of prepared foods on their heads or around their waists, or set up karhais (cooking pots) filled with bubbling oil to deep-fry morsels, such as samosas, to order. The vendor with the longest line is likely to have the best reputation and the tastiest snacks.

The food sold on the street varies regionally and is an indication of the cuisine that is popular with the locals. In the south, idlis (steamed rice cakes) and dosas (rice pancakes)

ALOO KI TIKKI

THESE ARE SMALL POTATO PATTIES SOLD AT STREET FOOD STANDS IN NORTHERN INDIA. THERE ARE MANY VARIATIONS, SOME OF WHICH INCLUDE GROUND MEAT, AND THEY ARE SERVED WITH A VARIETY OF CHUTNEYS SUCH AS TAMARIND OR MINT AND CILANTRO. THEY ARE A GOOD APPETIZER OR SNACK.

1 lb. potatoes, cut into pieces
1 cup fresh or frozen peas
4 tablespoons oil
2 green chiles, finely chopped
1/2 red onion, finely chopped
3/4 inch piece of ginger, grated
1 teaspoon ground turmeric
1 teaspoon ground cumin
1 teaspoon ground coriander
1/2 teaspoon garam masala
   (page 284)
2 tablespoons besan flour
1 tablespoon lemon juice

MAKES 24

COOK the potatoes in boiling water for 15 minutes, or until tender enough to mash. Drain well until they are dry but still hot. Cook the peas in boiling water for 4 minutes, or until tender, then drain.

MASH the potatoes in a large bowl and add the peas. Put 1 tablespoon of the oil in a small saucepan and fry the chiles, onion, ginger and spices for 1 minute, or until aromatic. Add them to the potatoes with the besan flour and mix. Mix in the lemon juice and some salt. Divide the potatoes into portions the size of golf balls and shape into patties.

HEAT the remaining oil in a heavy-bottomed frying pan (nonstick if you have one) and add the potato patties in batches. Fry them on each side until crisp and golden brown. Serve hot or cold in small dishes.

ALOO CHAAT

ALOO CHAAT IS A SAVORY SNACK THAT CAN BE SERVED AS A POTATO SALAD OR A LIGHT MEAL. SALAD POTATOES OR OTHER WAXY POTATOES ARE USED BECAUSE THEY HOLD THEIR SHAPE WELL. THE TANGY FLAVORS OF THE CHAAT MASALA AND THE TAMARIND MAKE THE SALAD QUINTESSENTIALLY INDIAN.

ALOO CHAAT

2 lb. small salad potatoes,
   unpeeled
1/2 cup tamarind paste (page 280)
4 green chiles, seeded and finely
   chopped
4 tablespoons chopped cilantro
   leaves
2 teaspoons chaat masala
   (page 284)

SERVES 4

BOIL the potatoes in their skins for 15 minutes, or until just tender. Peel the potatoes and slice them into small rounds. Put them in a serving bowl.

MIX the tamarind paste with 1/4 cup of water. Mix all the other ingredients with the tamarind, then season with salt.

GENTLY toss the potato rounds with the tamarind mixture and serve as a snack or as a refreshing salad on a very hot day.

KACHORIS

A SPECIALTY FROM GUJARAT, WHERE A LOT OF SEED SPICES ARE GROWN, THESE LITTLE FRIED BREADS STUFFED WITH SPICY DAL ARE SOMEWHAT TIME-CONSUMING TO MAKE BUT THE RESULT IS WELL WORTH THE EFFORT. THEY ARE PERFECT WITH A CHUTNEY FOR A VEGETARIAN APPETIZER.

Try to keep the kachoris in their semicircular shape, folding and rolling gently so the filling doesn't ooze out. Fry until they puff up.

FILLING
1/2 cup urad dal
1 1/2 tablespoons oil
1 teaspoon cumin seeds
1/4 teaspoon ground turmeric
1/4 teaspoon asafoetida
3 green chiles, finely chopped
  (optional)
3/4 inch piece of ginger, grated

DOUGH
2 cups atta (chapati flour), or
  2/3 cup wholewheat flour, mixed
  with 3/4 cup maida or all-purpose
  flour
1 teaspoon kalonji (nigella seeds)
2 teaspoons oil or ghee

oil for deep-frying

MAKES 20

TO MAKE the filling, begin by soaking the dal in 2 cups of cold water for 2 hours. Drain and chop in a food processor for a few seconds to form a coarse paste. If you don't have a food processor, grind the dal in a pestle and mortar. Heat the oil over medium heat in a saucepan, add the cumin seeds, then cover and allow the seeds to pop. Add the turmeric, asafoetida, chiles and ginger and stir until well mixed. Add the dal paste and 1/2 cup water and cook over low heat, stirring constantly until the liquid has evaporated. Add salt to taste. Spread on a plate and leave until cold.

TO MAKE the dough, sift the atta and a little salt into a bowl and add the kalonji. Rub in the oil or ghee until the mixture resembles bread crumbs. Add 1/2–2/3 cup warm water, a little at a time, to make a pliable dough. Turn out onto a floured surface and knead for 5 minutes, or until the dough is smooth. Cover and set aside for 15 minutes. Don't refrigerate or the oil will harden.

DIVIDE the dough into 20 balls. Roll one out on a floured surface to resemble a thin pancake 3–4 inches in diameter. Place 1 heaping teaspoon of the dal mixture in the center, then fold over the dough to form into a semicircle. Pinch the edges together to seal securely. Gently roll out on a floured surface, taking care that the filling doesn't escape. Try to retain the semicircular shape. Repeat to use all the dough and filling.

FILL a karhai or heavy-bottomed saucepan a third full with oil and heat to 350°F (a cube of bread will brown in 15 seconds). Lower a kachori into the hot oil and, when it rises to the surface, gently push it down using the back of a spoon, to keep it submerged until it puffs up. Turn it over and cook until the other side is lightly browned. Drain on a wire rack and keep the cooked kachori warm while you cook the rest.

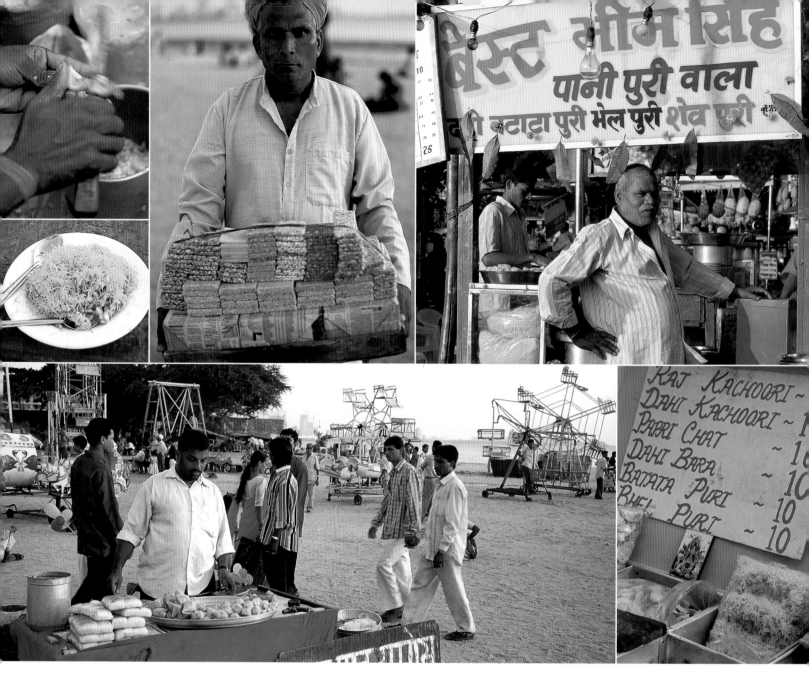

CHOWPATTY BEACH is the place where all of Mumbai (Bombay) gathers to eat chaat (snacks) and take in the sea air at dusk. Families, couples and groups of friends buy snacks and stroll around, while children play on the mini fairground with its hand-cranked rides. As the sun sets, the lights come on and the bustle around the stands increases as ingredients are prepared and chaat are mixed and served.

feature heavily, as do vada (deep-fried doughnut shapes made of ground lentils or semolina). Samosas (filled pastries) are dunked into tamarind chutneys, and bondas (deep-fried balls of urad dal batter) are served with coconut chutney. In the north, you find meat kebabs wrapped in roti (bread), pakoras (fritters) and bhaji (deep-fried tidbits).

Indians love to enjoy a variety of chaat when relaxing and socializing. Chaat are little spicy nibbles made from a diverse range of foods ranging from fruit to puffed rice. The most famous chaat, bhel puri, appeals to all your tastebuds at once. Chaat sellers make up each type to a basic recipe, or to your specification. They add a selection of either chiles for heat, tamarind chutney for sourness, yogurt for cooling and chaat masala for flavor. These are spooned onto aloo ki tikki (potato cakes), stuffed into puris (puffed fried breads), sprinkled on fruit or tossed with sev noodle and lentils.

ALOO KI TIKKI

ALOO KI TIKKI these fried potato cakes, made of potatoes mashed with turmeric, chiles and spices, are drizzled with a tamarind chutney *(above left)*. Each is then garnished with a small pile of sev (besan flour) noodles *(center left)*. The whole lot is doused in a spicy, tart chickpea stew *(center right)* which is garnished with cilantro. At this stand, aloo ki tikki is served with chopped onions *(right)*.

PAV BHAJI

PAV BHAJI For this, tomatoes, onions, cilantro and chiles are fried together on a tawa *(above left)*. Chickpeas *(center left)* and potatoes are added along with some chili powder. The mixture is roughly mashed *(center right)* before being garnished with fresh cilantro and served with a side dish of chopped onions, lime pieces for squeezing, and a bun called a pav or pao *(right)* which has been fried on the tawa.

BHUJIYA

CRUNCHY mixes such as those above are eaten with drinks or as a snack in between meals. They vary from roasted chana (chickpeas) and moong dal to chana chor (chickpea chips) and besan flour noodles. Nuts, raisins, deep-fried peas, puffed rice and seasonings such as chaat masala are added in different quantities to vary the mixes. Some are sweet, others are hot or sweet-sour.

DAHI BATATA PURI

RAGDA PAT

SHRIMP PAKORAS

PAKORAS, KNOWN AS BHAJIS IN SOME AREAS, ARE VERSATILE SNACKS THAT CAN BE MADE USING SHRIMP, FISH PIECES OR CHOPPED VEGETABLES. THE BESAN FLOUR AND POMEGRANATE SEEDS MAKE A TANGY FLAVORFUL BATTER. MANGO CHUTNEY AND MINT CHUTNEY GO WELL WITH PAKORAS.

1¼ lb. shrimp
½ cup besan flour
1 large red onion, finely chopped
1 teaspoon dried pomegranate
    seeds
4 green chiles, seeded and
    finely chopped
2 tablespoons finely chopped
    cilantro leaves
pinch of baking soda
ghee or oil for deep-frying

MAKES 30

PEEL and devein the shrimp, then cut into small pieces. Put the besan flour in a bowl and add 2 tablespoons of water, or enough to make a thick batter, mixing with a fork to beat out any lumps. Add the remaining ingredients, except the oil, to the batter, season with salt and mix well.

FILL a karhai or heavy-bottomed saucepan a third full with ghee or oil and heat to 350°F (a cube of bread will brown in 15 seconds). Drop 1 heaping teaspoon of batter at a time into the ghee or oil and deep-fry in batches of six or eight pakoras until they are brown all over. Remove and drain on paper towels. Serve hot.

Deep-fry the pakoras in batches of six or eight so that the temperature of the oil remains constant. Cooking too many at once will cool the oil.

GOLL BHAJI

THESE ARE DEEP-FRIED NIBBLES ENJOYED AS TEA TIME SNACKS. THEY ARE KNOWN BY DIFFERENT NAMES IN DIFFERENT AREAS AND HAVE REGIONAL IDIOSYNCRASIES INCLUDING THEIR SHAPE AND THE TYPES OF FLOUR AND FLAVORINGS USED IN THE BATTER. SERVE WITH A CHUTNEY.

GOLL BHAJI

½ cup rice flour
⅓ cup cashew nuts
⅔ cup besan flour
pinch of baking soda
10 curry leaves, chopped
4 green chiles, seeded and
    finely chopped
¾ inch piece of ginger, finely
    chopped
1 red onion, finely chopped
1 tablespoon ghee
oil for deep-frying

MAKES 20

PLACE a small frying pan over low heat and dry-roast the rice flour until it turns light brown. Dry-roast the cashew nuts in the same pan until they brown, then finely chop them. Mix the rice flour with the besan flour, then add the baking soda and a pinch of salt. Add the cashew nuts, curry leaves, green chiles, ginger, onion and ghee. Mix together well, adding a few drops of water, if necessary, to make a stiff dough. Form into 20 small balls.

FILL a karhai or heavy-bottomed saucepan a third full with ghee or oil and heat to 350°F (a cube of bread will brown in 15 seconds). Fry five or six balls at a time until golden brown, then drain each batch on paper towels.

Chiles on display at the spice
market in Delhi.

KASHMIRI LAMB CUTLETS

THESE CUTLETS ARE SIMPLE TO MAKE AND LOOK VERY GOOD IN THIS BESAN COATING, WHICH PUFFS
AROUND THE CHOPS AND GIVES THEM A CRUNCHY, GOLDEN CRUST. THE PRE-COOKING MAKES THEM
VERY TENDER. THEY ARE AN IDEAL SNACK BECAUSE THE BONES MAKE THEM EASY TO PICK UP.

2 lb. lamb cutlets
3/4 teaspoon cumin seeds
1 teaspoon coriander seeds
3/4 teaspoon black peppercorns
2 cups milk
2 cinnamon sticks
10 cardamom seeds
10 cloves
3/4 inch piece of ginger, grated
2 onions, finely chopped
2/3 cup besan flour
2 teaspoons chili powder
1/2 cup plain yogurt (page 280)
oil for deep-frying
lime quarters

SERVES 6

TRIM the lamb of any fat and scrape the bone
ends clean. Place a small frying pan over low heat
and dry-roast the cumin seeds until aromatic.
Remove them and dry-roast the coriander seeds.
Crush the coriander and cumin seeds with the
peppercorns in a spice grinder or pestle and mortar.
Transfer to a large, heavy-bottomed saucepan
and add the milk, cinnamon, cardamom, cloves,
ginger and onions. Bring to a boil over medium heat,
then add the chops to the saucepan and return to
a boil. Reduce the heat and simmer for 30 minutes,
or until the meat is tender and very little liquid
remains. Remove the cutlets and drain them.

WHISK the besan flour and chili powder into the
yogurt with 1/4 cup water, to make a batter.

FILL a karhai or heavy-bottomed saucepan one-
third full of oil and heat to 350°F (a cube of bread
will brown in 15 seconds). Dip the cutlets in the
batter, shake off any excess, then fry them in
batches in the hot oil until they are crisp. Drain on
paper towels and keep them warm. Serve
sprinkled with a little lime juice and salt to taste.

CHILI LAMB CUTLETS

8 lamb cutlets
1/4 teaspoon chili powder
1/2 teaspoon ground turmeric
1 teaspoon garam masala
  (page 284)
3/4 inch piece of ginger, grated
1 garlic clove, crushed
1 tablespoon plain yogurt
  (page 280)
3 tablespoons lemon juice

MAKES 8

TRIM the lamb of any fat and scrape the bone
ends clean. Mix together the remaining ingredients
to form a paste, adding a little of the lemon juice
if necessary. Rub the paste over the chops, then
cover and refrigerate for 2 hours or overnight.

PREHEAT the broiler. Sprinkle the chops with
salt on both sides and broil them on each side
for 2–3 minutes, or until they are browned and
sizzling. Squeeze the remaining lemon juice over
them before serving.

CHILI LAMB CUTLETS

VEGETABLE BHAJI

THESE DEEP-FRIED VEGETABLES MAKE AN EXCELLENT SNACK OR APPETIZER. IN INDIA, STREET VENDORS LINE THE STREETS ALL DAY, DUCKING BETWEEN BICYCLES, CARS AND PEDESTRIANS WHILE SETTING UP STANDS SELLING SUCH ITEMS. USUALLY THE BUSIER THE STAND, THE TASTIER THE SNACK.

2$^1/_4$ cups besan flour
1 teaspoon chili powder
1 teaspoon ground turmeric
$^1/_4$ teaspoon asafoetida
$^1/_4$ lb. carrots, cut into thin sticks
$^1/_4$ lb. snow peas, cut into
   thin sticks
1 thin eggplant, cut into thin sticks
6 curry leaves
oil for deep-frying

MAKES 20

MIX together the besan flour, chili powder, turmeric, asafoetida and a pinch of salt. Add enough water to make a thick batter which will hold the vegetables together. Mix the vegetables and curry leaves into the batter.

FILL a karhai or heavy-bottomed saucepan a third full with oil and heat to 350°F (a cube of bread will brown in 15 seconds). Lift clumps of vegetables out of the batter and lower carefully into the oil. Fry until golden all over and cooked through, then drain on paper towels. Sprinkle with salt and serve hot with chutney or raita.

Fry the vegetable sticks in clumps. The batter will help them stick to each other and will set around them as they cook.

MASALA VADA

$^1/_2$ cup urad dal
$^2/_3$ cup chana dal
2 green chiles, seeded and
   finely chopped
8 curry leaves, roughly chopped
$^1/_2$ teaspoon fennel seeds, crushed
1 red onion, finely chopped
$^1/_2$ teaspoon garam masala
   (page 284)
3 tablespoons grated coconut
   (page 283)
1 inch piece of ginger, grated
4 tablespoons chopped cilantro
   leaves
3 tablespoons rice flour or
   urad dal flour
pinch of baking powder (optional)
oil for deep-frying

MAKES 18

SOAK the dal in cold water for 4 hours, then drain. Reserve 2 tablespoons of the soaked dal and coarsely grind the remainder in a food processor or pestle and mortar. Add the reserved dal to the ground dal for texture. Add the chopped chiles, curry leaves, fennel, onion, garam masala, coconut, ginger and cilantro leaves. Mix well and season with salt. Add the flour and baking powder, if using (it gives a crisper texture), then mix until the texture is soft but the dough can be shaped (you may need to add a little water). Divide the mixture into 18 portions and form each into a ball. Slightly flatten each ball to form a patty.

FILL a karhai or heavy-bottomed saucepan a third full with oil and heat to 350°F (a cube of bread will brown in 15 seconds). Fry the patties in the hot oil, in batches of four or five, until golden brown and crisp. Drain well on paper towels and serve hot with a chutney.

MASALA VADA

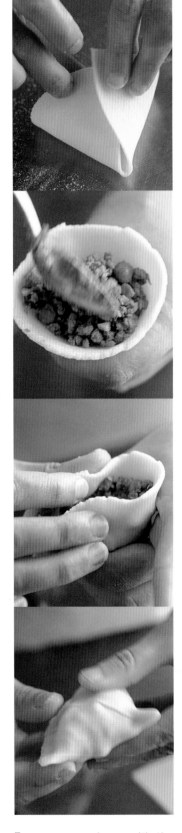

Form a cone shape with the pastry and use it to hold the filling. Fold in the top and seal so the singhara does not leak.

SINGHARAS

SINGHARAS, THE BENGALI VERSION OF SAMOSAS, ARE LITTLE PACKAGES SERVED AT EVERY INDIAN WEDDING OR FESTIVAL AS WELL AS BEING A POPULAR TIFFIN DISH. SAMOSAS ARE SEMI-CIRCULAR IN SHAPE, WHILE SINGHARAS ARE TRIANGULAR. THE VEGETABLE FILLING FROM PAGE 20 CAN BE USED.

PASTRY
2 cups maida or all-purpose flour
2 tablespoons ghee

MEAT FILLING
4 ripe tomatoes
2 tablespoons ghee or oil
2 cinnamon sticks
6 cloves
1 cardamom pod
3 green chiles, chopped
1 large onion, finely chopped
3–4 curry leaves
4 garlic cloves, crushed
1 teaspoon ground turmeric
2 inch piece of ginger, grated
1 lb. ground lamb
1 cup peas
1 teaspoon garam masala
   (page 284)

oil for deep-frying

MAKES 24

TO MAKE the pastry, sift the maida and a pinch of salt into a bowl. Rub in the ghee until the mixture resembles bread crumbs. Add about 1/2 cup warm water, a little at a time, to make a pliable dough. Turn out onto a floured surface and knead for 5 minutes on a floured surface, or until the dough is smooth. Cover and set aside for 30 minutes. Don't refrigerate or the ghee will harden.

TO MAKE the meat filling, score a cross in the top of each tomato. Plunge into boiling water for 20 seconds, drain and peel the skin away from the cross, then roughly chop, discarding the cores and seeds and reserving any juices. Heat the ghee or oil in a karhai or large saucepan over low heat and fry the cinnamon, cloves, cardamom and chiles. Add the onion, curry leaves, garlic, turmeric and ginger and fry for 5 minutes, or until the onion is brown. Add the lamb, fry until brown, then add the tomatoes and cover with a tight lid. Cook gently, stirring occasionally until the lamb is tender. Add the peas, cover and cook for 5 minutes. If there is any liquid left, turn up the heat and let it evaporate. Remove the whole spices. Season with salt to taste, and sprinkle with garam masala.

DIVIDE the dough into 12 portions, roll out each to a 5 inch circle, then cut each circle in half. Take one piece and form a hollow cone by folding the dough in half and sealing the two edges of the cut side together. You will probably find it easiest to wet one edge and make a small overlap. Fill three-quarters full with filling. Don't overfill. Seal the top edges, then pinch to give a fluted finish. Repeat with the remaining dough and filling.

FILL a karhai or heavy-bottomed saucepan a third full with oil and heat to 350°F (a cube of bread will brown in 15 seconds). Deep-fry the singharas in batches until well browned. Drain on a wire rack and keep them warm in a low oven.

Kolkata (Calcutta)

BANANA CHIPS

THESE CHIPS, ALONG WITH ROASTED FRIED PEANUTS, ARE SOLD BY INDIAN VENDORS WHO STROLL THE STREETS WITH LARGE BASKETS BALANCED ON THEIR HEADS. THEY WEAR BROADCLOTH TURBANS TO PROVIDE A FOOTHOLD FOR THE BASKET AND A PLACE TO KEEP THEIR MONEY.

10 small green bananas
oil for deep-frying
1 tablespoon salt
ground turmeric (optional)

SERVES 8

BEFORE you start, oil your hands or put on disposable gloves as a thick, sticky sap will be given off by the unripe bananas. Using a knife or mandolin, cut the bananas into 1/4 inch thick slices, oiling the blade if it gets sticky.

FILL a karhai or heavy-bottomed saucepan a third full with oil and heat to 350°F (a cube of bread will brown in 15 seconds). Put the sliced bananas directly into the hot oil in batches and stir while the chips cook. After 1 or 2 minutes, put in a teaspoon of salt (the oil will not splutter). You will need to do this for the first batch, then for every second batch.

REMOVE the banana chips when golden brown, drain on paper towels and toss them in some ground turmeric.

STORE the banana chips in an airtight container when they are completely cold. If the chips are not cooled completely, they will go soggy. The chips will keep for 2 weeks but may need refreshing after 10 days. Do this by heating them in a hot oven, or under a broiler, until they are crisp.

Green bananas give off a sticky substance so wear gloves when preparing them. Use a mandolin to give neat even slices.

RASAM

THIS SOUP-LIKE DISH WAS ORIGINALLY KNOWN AS "MULLIGA THANNI", LITERALLY TRANSLATED AS "PEPPER WATER". IN AN INDIAN SETTING, IT IS SERVED SPOONED OVER RICE AS PART OF THE MAIN MEAL. THE BRITISH VERSION IS CALLED MULLIGATAWNY.

Pepper, shown here in its fresh form, is indigenous to India.

3 tablespoons tamarind paste
  (page 280)
1½ tablespoons coriander seeds
2 tablespoons cumin seeds
1 tablespoon black peppercorns
1 tablespoon oil
5 garlic cloves, skins on,
  roughly pounded
1 red onion, thinly sliced
2–3 dried chiles, torn into pieces
2 stems curry leaves
½ lb. skinned, boneless chicken
  thighs, cut into small pieces

SERVES 4

MIX the tamarind paste with 3 cups water. Place a small frying pan over low heat and dry-roast the coriander seeds until aromatic. Remove, then dry-roast the cumin seeds, followed by the black peppercorns. Grind them together using a spice grinder or a pestle and mortar.

HEAT the oil in a large, heavy-bottomed saucepan over low heat, add the garlic and onion and fry until golden. Add the chiles and the curry leaves and fry for 2 minutes, or until they are aromatic. Add the tamarind water, the ground spices and season with salt. Bring to a boil, reduce the heat and simmer for 10 minutes.

ADD the chicken to the saucepan with 1 cup water and simmer for 20 minutes, gradually adding another cup of water as the soup reduces. Remove any garlic skin which has floated to the top. Season with salt to taste. Serve with rice (page 276).

TAMATAR SHORBA

TAMATAR SHORBA

2 tablespoons oil
1 onion, finely chopped
3 Indian bay leaves (cassia leaves)
2 inch piece of cinnamon stick
12 peppercorns
2 teaspoons ground cumin
2 teaspoons garam masala
  (page 284)
2 x 14 oz. cans diced tomatoes
1 teaspoon sugar
1 cup chicken or vegetable stock
cilantro leaves

SERVES 2

HEAT the oil over low heat in a heavy-bottomed saucepan and fry the onion, bay leaves, cinnamon and peppercorns until the onion is soft. Add the cumin, garam masala and the tomatoes, mashing the tomatoes with a fork to break them up into smaller pieces. Add the sugar and stock and slowly bring to a boil. Simmer over low heat for 30 minutes.

STRAIN the soup by pushing it through a strainer, using the back of a metal spoon to push against the solids and extract as much of the liquid as possible. Discard what's left in the strainer. Reheat, then season with salt to taste, and garnish with the cilantro leaves before serving.

SAMBHAR

SAMBHAR IS OFTEN SERVED WITH DOSAS OR RICE FOR BREAKFAST OR LUNCH. DRUMSTICKS ARE A LONG, POD-LIKE VEGETABLE AND COME FRESH OR CANNED. CANNED ONES SHOULD BE ADDED AT THE END OF COOKING. TO EAT DRUMSTICKS, SCRAPE OUT THE FLESH AND DISCARD THE OUTER SHELL.

1¹/₄ cups toor dal (yellow lentils)
2 tablespoons coriander seeds
10 black peppercorns
¹/₂ teaspoon fenugreek seeds
2 tablespoons grated coconut
  (page 283)
1 tablespoon roasted chana dal
6 dried chiles
2 drumsticks, cut into 2 inch pieces
2 carrots, cubed
1 onion, roughly chopped
¹/₄ lb. eggplant, cubed
6 small okra, ends trimmed
1 tablespoon tamarind paste
  (page 280)
2 tablespoons oil
1 teaspoon black mustard seeds
10 curry leaves
¹/₂ teaspoon ground turmeric
¹/₂ teaspoon asafoetida

SERVES 6

SOAK the dal in 2 cups of water for 2 hours. Drain the dal and put them in a saucepan with 4 cups of water. Bring to a boil, then skim off any impurities from the surface. Cover and simmer for 2 hours, or until the dal is cooked and tender.

PLACE a small frying pan over low heat and dry-roast the coriander, peppercorns, fenugreek, coconut, chana dal and chiles, stirring constantly until the coconut is golden brown. Grind the roasted mixture to a fine powder using a pestle and mortar or a spice grinder.

BRING 3 cups of water to a boil in a saucepan. Add the pieces of drumstick and the cubed carrot and bring back to a boil. Simmer for 10 minutes, then add the onion, eggplant and okra and more water if necessary. Simmer until the vegetables are almost cooked.

PUT the boiled dal and their liquid, the ground spices, the vegetables (with any vegetable water) and tamarind in a large saucepan and bring slowly to a boil. Reduce the heat and simmer for 30 minutes. Season with salt to taste.

HEAT the oil in a small saucepan over medium heat, add the mustard seeds, cover and shake the saucepan until they start to pop. Add the curry leaves, turmeric, asafoetida and a little salt. Pour onto the simmering dal and stir until well mixed.

Eggplant and drumsticks are a common sight in most south Indian markets.

FISH & SEAFOOD

PATRA NI MACCHI

THIS IS A DISH FROM THE PARSI PEOPLE, DESCENDANTS OF PERSIANS WHO MIGRATED TO THE WEST COAST OF INDIA, WHICH IS TYPICALLY SERVED AT WEDDINGS. THE LITTLE PACKAGES ARE QUITE AROMATIC WHEN OPENED AND LOOK VERY APPEALING. YOU CAN USE ANY FIRM, WHITE FISH.

1 lb. pomfret, sole or leatherjacket
   fillets, skin removed
young banana leaves
1 teaspoon ground cumin
1/2 teaspoon sugar
3 cups grated coconut (page 283)
4 green chiles, seeded and
   chopped
4 tablespoons chopped cilantro
   leaves
a few mint leaves
6 garlic cloves, chopped
1 green unripe mango, diced
3 tablespoons oil or ghee
3 tablespoons lime or lemon juice
mint leaves
whole green chiles

SERVES 4

WASH the fish fillets, pat dry and cut into 3 inch pieces. Cut the banana leaves into as many 9–10 inch squares as there are pieces of fish (you should have about six to eight) and soften the banana leaves by dipping them into a saucepan of very hot water. Wipe the pieces dry as they become pliant. If you can't find banana leaves, use aluminium foil.

GRIND the cumin, sugar, coconut, chiles, cilantro, mint, garlic and green mango to a paste in a food processor, blender or pestle and mortar. Heat 1 tablespoon of the oil or ghee in a frying pan and cook the paste over low heat until aromatic. Season with salt.

PLACE the banana leaf squares on a work surface. Apply the paste liberally to both sides of each piece of fish. Sprinkle some lime or lemon juice on the fish. Place a piece of fish on each banana leaf and wrap up like a package, tying firmly with kitchen string.

USING a large, heavy-bottomed frying pan which has a lid, heat the remaining oil or ghee and shallow-fry the fish parcels together on one side. After 5 minutes, turn the packages over and fry for another 5 minutes. The leaves will darken and shrink. Cover the pan and cook the fish for a few more minutes.

OPEN out each fish package on its plate. Garnish with mint leaves and green chile "flowers" (do this by making slits down into the chile from the top towards the stem so you form strips which fan out).

Wrap each piece of fish in banana leaf and then use pieces of string to tie up the packages so they don't spring open.

MOLEE

A MOLEE IS A RICH CREAMY DISH POPULAR IN KERALA ON INDIA'S WEST COAST WHERE IT IS MADE WITH LOCAL FISH. THERE ARE MANY VERSIONS, SOME VERY HOT. THIS ONE IS FAIRLY MILD AND THEREFORE PERFECT FOR THOSE WHO DON'T LIKE FIERY FOOD. YOU CAN ADAPT IT TO YOUR TASTE.

1 tablespoon oil
1 large onion, thinly sliced
3 garlic cloves, crushed
2 small green chiles, finely chopped
2 teaspoons ground turmeric
1 teaspoon ground coriander
1 teaspoon ground cumin
4 cloves
6 curry leaves
1²/₃ cups coconut milk (page 283)
¹/₂ teaspoon salt
1¹/₄ lb. pomfret, sole or leatherjacket fillets, skin removed
1 tablespoon chopped cilantro leaves
curry leaves

SERVES 6

HEAT the oil in a karhai or deep, heavy-bottomed frying pan, add the onion and cook for 5 minutes. Add the garlic and chiles and cook for another 5 minutes, or until the onion has softened and looks translucent. Add the turmeric, coriander, cumin and cloves and stir-fry with the onion for 2 minutes. Stir in the curry leaves, coconut milk and salt and bring to just below boiling point. Reduce the heat and simmer for 20 minutes.

CUT each fish fillet into two or three large pieces and add them to the sauce. Bring the sauce back to a simmer and cook for 5 minutes, or until the fish is cooked through and flakes easily. Check the seasoning, add more salt if necessary, then stir in the cilantro leaves. Garnish with the curry leaves.

A truck waiting to be loaded with fresh fish at Sassoon Docks in Mumbai (Bombay).

BOMBAY-STYLE FISH

2 garlic cloves, crushed
3 small green chiles, seeded and finely chopped
¹/₂ teaspoon ground turmeric
¹/₂ teaspoon ground cloves
¹/₂ teaspoon ground cinnamon
¹/₂ teaspoon ground cayenne pepper
1 tablespoon tamarind paste (page 280)
²/₃ cup oil
1³/₄ lb. pomfret, sole or leatherjacket fillets, skin removed
1¹/₄ cups coconut cream (page 283)
2 tablespoons chopped cilantro leaves

SERVES 4

MIX together the garlic, chiles, spices, tamarind and ¹/₂ cup of the oil. Place the fish fillets in a shallow dish and spoon the marinade over them. Turn the fish over, cover and refrigerate for 30 minutes.

HEAT the remaining oil in a large, heavy-bottomed frying pan and add the fish in batches. Cook for 1 minute on each side. Return all the fish to the pan, then reduce the heat to low and add any remaining marinade and the coconut cream. Season with salt and gently cook for 3–5 minutes, or until the fish is cooked through and flakes easily. If the sauce is too runny, remove the fish, simmer the sauce for a few minutes, then pour it over the fish. Garnish with the cilantro leaves.

BOMBAY-STYLE FISH

SHRIMP WITH GREEN MANGO

1/2 lb. large shrimp
1 1/2 teaspoons chili powder
1 teaspoon ground turmeric
1/2 teaspoon cumin seeds
1/2 teaspoon yellow mustard seeds
4 garlic cloves, roughly chopped
1 1/2 inch piece of ginger, roughly
　chopped
1 red onion, roughly chopped
4 tablespoons oil
1 red onion, thinly sliced
1 green unripe mango, finely
　chopped

SERVES 4

PEEL and devein the shrimp, leaving the tails intact. Put the chili powder, turmeric, cumin, mustard, garlic, ginger and chopped red onion in a blender, food processor or pestle and mortar and process to form a paste. If necessary, add a little water.

HEAT the oil in a karhai or heavy-bottomed frying pan and fry the sliced onion. When it starts to brown, add the curry paste and fry until aromatic.

ADD the shrimp and 3/4 cup water to the pan, then cover and simmer for 3–4 minutes, until the shrimp are cooked and start to curl up. Add the mango and cook for another minute or two to thicken the curry. Season with salt to taste.

Green unripe mangoes, often used in Indian cookery, have a firm flesh and are used to give a tart flavor to recipes.

CREAMY SHRIMP CURRY

THIS COCONUT-FLAVORED SHRIMP CURRY IS A SPECIALTY OF BENGAL. TRADITIONALLY, THE SHRIMP ARE COOKED INSIDE A PARTIALLY MATURED COCONUT. CARE SHOULD BE TAKEN NOT TO OVERCOOK THE SHRIMP OR THEY WILL BECOME RUBBERY.

1 lb. large shrimp
1 1/2 tablespoons lemon juice
3 tablespoons oil
1/2 onion, finely chopped
1/2 teaspoon ground turmeric
2 inch piece of cinnamon stick
4 cloves
7 cardamom pods
5 Indian bay leaves (cassia leaves)
3/4 inch piece of ginger, grated
3 garlic cloves, chopped
1 teaspoon chili powder
1/4 cup creamed coconut mixed
　with 1/2 cup water, or 1/2 cup
　coconut milk (page 283)

SERVES 4

PEEL and devein the shrimp, leaving the tails intact. Put them in a bowl, add the lemon juice, then toss together and leave them for 5 minutes. Rinse the shrimp under running cold water and pat dry with paper towels.

HEAT the oil in a karhai or heavy-bottomed frying pan and fry the onion until lightly browned. Add the turmeric, cinnamon, cloves, cardamom, bay leaves, ginger and garlic, and fry for 1 minute. Add the chili powder, creamed coconut or coconut milk, and salt to taste, and slowly bring to a boil. Reduce the heat and simmer for 2 minutes. Add the shrimp, return to a boil, then reduce the heat and simmer for 5 minutes, or until the shrimp are cooked through and the sauce is thick.

CREAMY SHRIMP CURRY

ROHU KALIA

THIS FISH DISH, IN WHICH THE FISH IS FRIED BEFORE BEING PUT INTO A SPICY YOGURT SAUCE, IS A BENGALI SPECIALTY. FROZEN PIECES OF ROHU (A TYPE OF CARP) ARE AVAILABLE IN INDIAN MARKETS. HOWEVER, AS ROHU HAS MANY BONES, YOU MAY PREFER SALMON, HALIBUT OR COD.

4–6 tablespoons mustard oil

1¾ lb. rohu, salmon, halibut or cod fillets or cutlets, skin removed, cut into fairly big chunks (approximately 12 pieces)

2 inch piece of cinnamon stick

5 cardamom pods

4 cloves

4 Indian bay leaves (cassia leaves)

1 onion, finely chopped

4 garlic cloves, crushed

3 inch piece of ginger, grated

½ teaspoon ground turmeric

1 teaspoon ground cumin

1 teaspoon chili powder (optional)

2 cups plain yogurt (page 280)

3 green chiles, shredded

SERVES 4

HEAT the oil in a karhai or heavy-bottomed frying pan over medium heat and fry the fish a few pieces at a time until golden brown on each side. Drain on paper towels. Add more oil, if necessary, and fry the cinnamon, cardamom, cloves and bay leaves over low heat for 1 minute. Add the onion and fry for 5 minutes, or until golden. Add the garlic, ginger, turmeric, cumin and chili powder, if using, and fry for 30 seconds.

REMOVE from the heat and stir in the yogurt a little at a time to prevent it curdling. Return to low heat, add the chiles and bring to a boil. Season with salt. Add the fish and bring to a boil. Simmer for 10 minutes or until the fish flakes easily and is cooked through. Serve immediately as if you let the dish rest, the fish may give off liquid and make the sauce thinner.

Draining the browned pieces of fish on paper towels will make the final dish less oily.

FISH IN YOGURT SAUCE

2 lb. firm white fish fillets such as cod, halibut or blue-eye, skin removed

3 tablespoons oil

1 onion, chopped

1½ inch piece of ginger, finely chopped

6 garlic cloves, chopped

1 teaspoon ground cumin

2 teaspoons ground coriander

¼ teaspoon ground turmeric

1 teaspoon garam masala (page 284)

¾ cup plain yogurt (page 280)

4 green chiles, finely chopped

cilantro leaves

SERVES 4

CUT each fish fillet into two pieces and very thoroughly pat them dry.

HEAT the oil in a heavy-bottomed frying pan over low heat and fry the onion until softened and lightly browned. Add the ginger, garlic and spices and stir for 2 minutes. Add the yogurt and green chiles and bring to a boil. Season with salt, then cover and simmer for 10 minutes. Gently add the pieces of fish and continue to simmer for 10–12 minutes, until the fish flakes easily and is cooked through. Don't overcook or the fish will give off liquid and the sauce will split.

GARNISH with cilantro leaves and serve immediately. If you let the dish rest, the fish may give off liquid and make the sauce thinner.

FISH IN YOGURT SAUCE

Pre-cut banana leaves on sale in Chennai (Madras) market.

CURRIED SQUID

FISH IN BANANA LEAF

THIS TRADITIONAL WAY OF PREPARING FISH IN BENGAL OFTEN USES HILSA (ELISH), A FAVOURITE FISH OF THE AREA. MUSTARD OIL IS AN IMPORTANT INGREDIENT IN BENGALI COOKING AND GIVES A UNIQUE FLAVOUR TO DISHES, THOUGH IF UNAVAILABLE YOU CAN USE SUNFLOWER OIL INSTEAD.

4 x $\frac{1}{4}$ lb. pieces hilsa (elish) or
  blue-eye fillet, skin removed
1$\frac{1}{2}$ tablespoons lemon juice
$\frac{1}{2}$ teaspoon salt
3 tablespoons brown mustard
  seeds
2 inch piece of ginger, chopped
4 green chiles, chopped
3 teaspoons mustard oil
$\frac{1}{4}$ teaspoon ground turmeric
1 teaspoon chili powder
4 pieces young banana leaf, or
  aluminium foil, cut into neat
  pieces big enough to wrap
  the fish

SERVES 4

WASH the fish and pat dry with paper towels. Mix the lemon juice and salt and rub into the fish.

GRIND the mustard seeds to a fine powder in a spice grinder or pestle and mortar. Put the mustard, ginger, chiles, mustard oil, turmeric and chili powder in a food processor or pestle and mortar and grind to a smooth paste. Soften the banana leaves by dipping them in very hot water. Wipe dry the pieces as they become pliant.

SMEAR the fish with the paste to thoroughly coat. Grease the leaves, or foil, with oil. Place a piece of fish and some marinade in the center of each and loosely fold into a package. Tie with kitchen string and put in a steamer over a saucepan of simmering water. Cover and steam for 10–12 minutes. Open a package to check that the fish flakes easily and is cooked. Serve in the banana leaves.

CURRIED SQUID

2 lb. fresh squid
1 teaspoon cumin seeds
1 teaspoon coriander seeds
1 teaspoon chili powder
$\frac{1}{2}$ teaspoon ground turmeric
2 tablespoons oil
1 onion, finely chopped
10 curry leaves
$\frac{1}{2}$ teaspoon fenugreek seeds
4 garlic cloves, crushed
3 inch piece of ginger, grated
4 tablespoons coconut milk powder
  mixed with $\frac{1}{2}$ cup water, or
  $\frac{1}{3}$ cup coconut cream (page 283)
3 tablespoons lime juice

SERVES 4

PULL the squid heads and tentacles out of the bodies, along with any innards, and discard. Peel off the skins. Rinse the bodies, pulling out the clear quills, then cut the bodies into 1 inch rings.

PLACE a small frying pan over low heat and dry-roast the cumin until aromatic. Remove, then dry-roast the coriander. Grind both to a fine powder with the chili and turmeric, using a spice grinder or pestle and mortar. Mix the spices with the squid.

IN a karhai or heavy-bottomed frying pan, heat the oil and fry the onion until lightly browned. Add the curry leaves, fenugreek, garlic, ginger and coconut. Bring slowly to a boil. Add the squid, then stir well. Simmer for 2–3 minutes, or until cooked and tender. Stir in the lime juice, season and serve.

The fish markets at Sassoon Dock, Mumbai (Bombay).

CHILI CRAB

THIS RECIPE COMBINES SWEET-TASTING CRAB MEAT WITH AROMATIC SPICES AND THE HEAT FROM CHILES. PROVIDE YOUR GUESTS WITH A CRAB CRACKER, PICKS, FINGER BOWLS AND PIECES OF ROTI TO MOP UP THE WONDERFUL JUICES. YOU CAN USE ANY KIND OF CRAB FOR THIS RECIPE.

4 x $^1/_2$ lb. small live crabs
  or 2 x 1 lb. live crabs
$^1/_2$ cup oil
2 garlic cloves, crushed
1$^1/_2$ inch piece of ginger, grated
$^1/_2$ teaspoon ground cumin
$^1/_2$ teaspoon ground coriander
$^1/_4$ teaspoon ground turmeric
$^1/_4$ teaspoon cayenne pepper
1 tablespoon tamarind paste
  (page 280)
1 teaspoon sugar
2 small red chiles, finely chopped
2 tablespoons chopped cilantro
  leaves

SERVES 4

PUT the crabs in the freezer for 2 hours to immobilize them. Using a large, heavy-bladed knife or cleaver, cut off the large front claws from each crab, then twist off the remaining claws. Turn each body over and pull off each apron piece, then pull out the spongy grey gills and discard them. Cut each crab body in half (quarters if you are using the large crabs). Crack the large front claws with the handle of a cleaver or a rolling pin. Rinse off any pieces of shell under cold running water and pat dry with paper towels.

MIX half the oil with the garlic, ginger, cumin, coriander, turmeric, cayenne pepper, tamarind, sugar, chiles and a generous pinch of salt until they form a paste. Heat the remaining oil in a karhai or large, heavy-bottomed, deep frying pan over medium heat. Add the spice paste and stir for 30 seconds, or until aromatic.

ADD the crab portions to the pan and cook, stirring for 2 minutes, making sure the spice mix gets rubbed into the cut edges of the crab. Add $^1/_4$ cup water, cover and steam the crabs, tossing them a couple of times during cooking, for another 5–6 minutes, or until cooked through. The crabs will turn pink or red when they are ready and the flesh will go opaque (make sure the large front claws are well cooked). Drizzle a little of the liquid from the pan over the crabs, scatter with the cilantro leaves and serve.

Pull the large front claws off the crab, pull the body open and remove the gills. Crack the larger claws with the handle of a cleaver.

Use the sharp edge of a spoon to scrape out the seeds and membrane of the bitter melon in one piece.

SHRIMP CURRY WITH TAMARIND

SHRIMP WITH BITTER MELON

MOST ASIANS EAT BITTER MELON BECAUSE ITS BITTER TASTE IS ONE OF THE FIVE SOUGHT-AFTER FLAVOURS: BITTER, SWEET, SOUR, SALTY AND AROMATIC. WHEN BITTER MELON IS DEGORGED, THE BITTERNESS IS LESSENED. PALER OR YELLOWER ONES ARE LESS BITTER BUT MORE FIBROUS.

2 lb. bitter melon
3/4 lb. large shrimp
1 tablespoon oil
1/2 tablespoon ground turmeric
1 tablespoon ground coriander
1 tablespoon ground cumin
1 teaspoon chili powder
4–5 green chiles
pinch of sugar
1 tablespoon ghee
4 curry leaves
1/4 teaspoon cumin seeds
chopped cilantro leaves (optional)

SERVES 4

SLICE the peeled bitter melon in half and scoop out any seeds and membrane. Slice into half-moon shapes 1/4 inch thick. Sprinkle with salt and drain in a colander for 30 minutes. Rinse and drain, then dry in a kitchen towel. Peel and devein the shrimp.

HEAT the oil in a heavy-bottomed frying pan, add the bitter melon, stir once or twice, then cover and cook for 3–4 minutes. The bitter melon will continue to sweat out liquid. Mix the turmeric, coriander, cumin and chili powder to a paste with a small amount of water. Add to the pan and cook over high heat until liquid is reduced to almost dry. Add the shrimp and green chiles and cook, tossing until dry. Season with the sugar and a little salt.

FOR the final seasoning (tarka), heat the ghee in a small pan, fry the curry leaves and cumin for 1 minute, then pour onto the bitter melon and stir in the cilantro, if using.

SHRIMP CURRY WITH TAMARIND

1 lb. large shrimp
1/2 teaspoon fennel seeds
1 tablespoon oil
2 cinnamon sticks
3 cardamom pods
1 large onion, finely chopped
5 garlic cloves, crushed
3/4 inch piece of ginger, grated
1 stalk of curry leaves
1 teaspoon turmeric
1 teaspoon chili powder
1 1/2 tablespoons tamarind paste (page 280)

SERVES 4

PEEL and devein the shrimp, leaving the tails intact. Place a small frying pan over low heat and dry-roast the fennel seeds until aromatic.

HEAT the oil in a karhai or heavy-bottomed frying pan and fry the fennel seeds, cinnamon, cardamom and onion until the onion is brown. Stir in the garlic, ginger and curry leaves, then add the shrimp, turmeric, chili powder and tamarind. Toss over high heat until the shrimp tails turn pink and the shrimp are cooked through. Remove from the heat and season with salt to taste.

SWORDFISH are huge fish that are usually cut into cutlets before being sold. The flesh is very meaty and dense and stands up well to all types of cooking as well as heavy spicing.

ANCHOVIES these hairtail anchovies are caught off the west coast of India. They are often left whole, dipped in flour and spices, then deep-fried and eaten as a snack.

ASIAN SPINY LOBSTERS are a type of lobster which, unlike North Atlantic lobsters, don't have large front claws. They are found in an array of colors and are often cooked in their shells.

CLAMS are not eaten all over India but are a specialty of Kerala, Goa and Karnataka where they are dug from the beaches. They are often served in coconut-flavored sauces.

CRABS have a sweet flesh that marries particularly well with spices. Crabs are often cut into halves or quarters before being cooked so that any marinade will penetrate the flesh.

CUTTLEFISH have the same texture as squid and can be used in a similar way. The flesh is very tender when cooked slowly. The inner shell must be removed before cooking.

GREY MULLET have a firm, white flesh which has an excellent flavor. They are often cut into fillets or cutlets, or cut into cubes to make tikka. They are sometimes used whole.

POMFRET are one of the most popular fish in India. They have firm, white flesh which carries flavors well. Pomfret can be used in most fish recipes that call for white fish.

SHRIMP both seawater and freshwater shrimp are often used in Indian cuisine. Larger shrimp can be cooked on skewers in a tandoor and smaller ones can be used in pakoras or pulaos.

INDIAN GOAT FISH similar to red mullet, these fish have a delicate white flesh and a pretty red coloring. They are used both whole, for their color, and also cut into cutlets and fillets.

SARDINES there are hundreds of types of sardines found all over the world. In India, the sardines are eaten whole in curries, or deep-fried, rather than being canned or salted.

BANDED PEARLSPOT caught off the coast of south India, these attractive fish have a sweet, white flesh. In India, they are often used to make the popular Keralan dish "molee."

MUMBAI'S (BOMBAY) Sassoon Docks are a scene of frenetic activity in the early mornings. Fishing boats moor at the jetty and unload their catch by throwing it upwards in baskets onto the quay with amazing accuracy. The seafood is then sold in the noisy, crowded market. Shoppers include restaurateurs and individuals, all with an eye for a bargain and discerning in their choices.

SEAFOOD

INDIA HAS ABOUT 4400 MILES OF COASTLINE SPLIT BETWEEN ITS EAST AND WEST COASTS. IT ALSO HAS A LARGE NETWORK OF BACKWATERS, RIVERS, TANKS (RESERVOIRS) AND PONDS, ALL OF WHICH TEEM WITH FISH AND CRUSTACEANS.

Fish dishes abound in the cuisines of Bengal, Maharashtra, Kerala and Goa and, although seawater fish are popular in Maharashtra, Goa and Kerala on the western coast, freshwater fish are more highly prized in Bengal in the East. Everything caught is utilized. Tiny fish are eaten whole and large fish such as shark, swordfish or king mackerel are cut into fillets or cutlets. Shrimp, both seawater and freshwater, are used all over India. Crabs and lobsters are eaten on the coast or in restaurants. Bivalves, including oysters, mussels and clams, are eaten on the west coast but elsewhere are largely ignored. In areas where fresh fish are not available, dried fish such as the renowned Bombay duck are used.

Fishing itself takes place in many forms. Most fish are caught from small boats, or by individual fishermen, rather than from large commercial vessels. The Koli fishermen in Mumbai (Bombay) are known for their deep-sea fishing. They put out to sea in colorful fishing boats. In Kerala, fish are caught in Chinese fishing nets or from snake boats rowed out to sea. There are also individuals with rods and nets stationed by virtually every pond, river and tank at some stage during the day, catching fish for that day's meals.

SALMON CURRY

THERE ARE SEVERAL STAGES TO THE MAKING OF THIS GOAN-STYLE DISH AND IT TAKES A LITTLE TIME

TO PREPARE THE SPICES AND THE SAUCE. THE END RESULT IS A DRY TYPE OF CURRY WITH A FAIRLY

THICK SAUCE THAT WORKS WELL WITH THE RICH FLESH OF THE SALMON CUTLETS.

SPICE MIX
6 dried chiles
1 tablespoon cumin seeds
1 teaspoon coriander seeds
1 teaspoon mustard seeds
1/4 teaspoon garam masala
   (page 284)
1/2 teaspoon ground turmeric

3 tablespoons oil
1 onion, finely sliced
1 ripe tomato, chopped
2 onions, finely chopped
8 garlic cloves, chopped
6 green chiles, chopped
2 inch piece of ginger, grated
1/2 cup tamarind paste (page 280)
3 tablespoons coconut milk powder
   or coconut cream (page 283)
2 lb. salmon cutlets

SERVES 6

PREPARE the spice mix by grinding the chiles, cumin, coriander and mustard seeds to a fine powder using a spice grinder or pestle and mortar, then mixing with the garam masala and turmeric.

HEAT the oil over low heat in a heavy-bottomed frying pan large enough to hold the pieces of fish in a single layer. Add the sliced onion and fry until golden. Add the tomato, chopped onions, garlic, green chiles and ginger and fry, stirring occasionally, for 20 minutes, or until the oil separates from the sauce.

ADD the spice mix and the tamarind to the pan and bring to a boil. Add the coconut milk powder or coconut cream and stir until well mixed. Season with salt to taste. Add the fish and bring slowly to a boil. The sauce is not very thin but it needs to be made very hot in order to cook the fish. Simmer for 5 minutes, then turn the pieces of fish over and simmer for another 5 minutes, or until the fish is cooked through and the sauce is thick.

Flesh being extracted from semi-dried coconuts in Kerala. The dried flesh is called copra.

SALMON CURRY

Cut the lobster in half down the center and pull the two halves apart. Scrape the flesh away from the shell using a small knife.

TANDOORI LOBSTER

THERE ARE AS MANY TANDOORI RECIPES AS THERE ARE TANDOORS, BUT THIS LOBSTER RECIPE IS PARTICULARLY INTERESTING AS IT DOESN'T TAKE LONG TO COOK AND THE COLORS OF THE SPICES AND THE LOBSTER SHELLS ARE EVOCATIVE OF CELEBRATION. YOU CAN ALSO USE LARGE SHRIMP.

2 large or 4 small live lobsters
1 egg
1 1/2 inch piece of ginger, grated
1/2 teaspoon paprika
2 teaspoons light brown sugar
1/2 cup whipping cream
pinch of ajowan
4 garlic cloves, crushed
2 tablespoons lemon juice
2 tablespoons besan flour
2 teaspoons garam masala
   (page 284)
1/2 teaspoon ground white pepper
1 tablespoon unsalted butter,
   melted, for basting
cilantro leaves

SERVES 4

PLACE the lobsters in the freezer for 2 hours to immobilize them. Using a large, heavy-bladed knife or cleaver, cut the lobsters in half. Remove the flesh from the tail shells in one piece, then cut the flesh into large chunks. Clean out the head ends of the shells and wash the shells all over, scrubbing out any membrane.

BREAK the egg into a bowl, add the ginger, paprika, sugar, cream, ajowan, garlic, lemon juice, besan flour, garam masala, white pepper and a pinch of salt and whisk together. Brush the lobster pieces with the mixture, then cover and marinate in the fridge for 2 hours.

PREHEAT the oven to its highest setting. Skewer the lobster pieces on long metal skewers, keeping the pieces 3/4 inch apart. Put the skewers on a wire rack set over a baking sheet.

ROAST the lobster for 6 minutes, turning once. Baste with the butter and roast again for 2–4 minutes, until the lobster is cooked through. Roast the shells on a separate sheet until they turn red. Take the lobster pieces off the skewers and put them back in the shells, garnish with cilantro leaves and serve hot.

THE BACKWATERS and seas off the coast of Kerala are a rich source of fish and seafood, not only for the local community but also for the national and international market. Despite the calm, idyllic scenes on the coast and waterways, the seafood industry is booming and when the fishermen are not out fishing, they are busy selling their catch, mending their nets or tending to their boats.

Fish is bought from wet fish stands at markets, or direct from the dock or beach as it is unloaded. In Kochi (Cochin) in Kerala, fish is sold by a fast-talking auctioneer from a large rectangle of blue plastic mat laid out on the shore or beach. Each batch of fish or shrimp is tipped onto the plastic and haggled over before being scooped up and spirited away to be cleaned and cooked. At the Sassoon Docks in Mumbai (Bombay), huge quantities of seafood are unloaded onto the quay, then sold out of baskets. The scene is a colorful melee of women, fishermen, commercial buyers and private shoppers.

Fish caught locally are not only eaten in India but are also sold, fresh and frozen, to the international market. Prized fish particular to Indian cuisine, such as hilsa, rohu and pomfret, are airfreighted to be sold to Indian communities worldwide. Other seafood such as tuna and shrimp, suitable for the markets in Japan and Europe, are flown there daily.

FRESH shrimp, such as these tiny ones, are sold in Mumbai (Bombay) at the fish markets, either with their shells still on, or peeled (as they are here) and ready for use.

MAKING FISH MOLEE

FISH MOLEE is one of Kerala's best-known dishes and uses a combination of the region's ingredients. The fish (here pearlspot) is trimmed *(above left)* and the flesh slashed to allow the flavors to soak in. Garlic, chiles, ginger, onions and curry leaves *(center left)* are fried and then turmeric, mango and coconut milk are added along with the fish *(center right)*. Everything is cooked together to form a sauce around the fish.

CHINESE FISHING NETS

CHINESE FISHING NETS line the harbor of Fort Kochi (Cochin) in Kerala, a throwback to a time long before the arrival of the Portuguese or British when China traded spices with India via the ports on the Malabar coast. The nets operate using a series of counterweights and pulleys operated by a fisherman. The nets are lowered into the water and left for a while before being raised, catching any passing fish in the process.

DRIED FISH AND SHRIMP

DRIED FISH AND SHRIMP of various types are used all over India, especially where fresh fish is not readily available. Bombay duck *(center right)*, is India's most famous dried fish. Rather than being used as a main ingredient, the fish is often fried, then crumbled over dishes for added flavor, or left in pieces and eaten as a snack. Smaller fish *(left and center left)* and shrimp *(right)* are used as a flavorful addition to curries.

FISH WITH KOKUM

3 x 2 inch pieces kokum or
  2 tablespoons tamarind paste
  (page 280)
4 ripe tomatoes
2 tablespoons oil
1 teaspoon black mustard seeds
1/2 teaspoon fenugreek seeds
1 inch piece of ginger, grated
4 green chiles, slit in half
1 garlic clove, crushed
2 onions, sliced
1 teaspoon ground turmeric
1 tablespoon ground coriander
1 cup coconut milk (page 283)
1 3/4 lb. pomfret, sole or
  leatherjacket fillets, skin removed,
  cut into large chunks
1 stalk of curry leaves

SERVES 6

RINSE the kokum, remove any pits and put the kokum in a bowl with cold water for a few minutes to soften. Meanwhile, score a cross in the top of each tomato. Plunge them into boiling water for 20 seconds, then drain and peel away the skin from the cross. Roughly chop the tomatoes, discarding the cores and seeds and reserving any juices.

REMOVE the kokum from the water and slice it into pieces.

HEAT the oil over low heat in a karhai or deep, heavy-bottomed frying pan, add the mustard seeds and cook until they start to pop. Add the fenugreek, ginger, chiles, garlic and onions and fry until the onions are soft. Add the turmeric and coriander and fry for 2 minutes. Add the coconut milk, tomatoes and kokum, bring to a boil and simmer for 5 minutes. Add the fish to the liquid and simmer for 2–3 minutes or until the fish flakes easily and is cooked through. Season with salt to taste, and add the curry leaves.

BENGALI FRIED FISH

1 1/4 lb. rainbow trout or salmon
  cutlets
1 1/2 tablespoons lemon juice
1/2 teaspoon ground turmeric
1/2 teaspoon salt
3 green chiles, chopped
3 ripe tomatoes, chopped
2 inch piece of ginger, chopped
4 tablespoons mustard oil or oil
2 teaspoons panch phoron
  (page 284)
1/2 teaspoon garam masala
  (page 284)

SERVES 4

BENGALI FRIED FISH

SPRINKLE the fish with the lemon juice and leave for 10 minutes. Wash in cold water and pat dry. Rub the fish with the combined turmeric and salt.

PUT the chiles, tomatoes and ginger in a food processor and chop until smooth, or finely chop together with a knife.

HEAT the oil in a heavy-bottomed frying pan over low heat and fry the fish a few pieces at a time until brown on both sides. Drain on paper towels. Add more oil if necessary, add the panch phoron and fry for 1 minute until aromatic. Add the tomato mixture and fry for another 2 minutes. Add 3/4 cup of water and bring slowly to a boil. Simmer for 3 minutes, add the fish, slowly return to a boil, then simmer for another 3 minutes. Sprinkle with the garam masala and season with salt to taste.

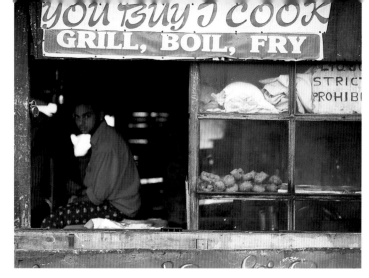

A fish stall at Fort Kochi (Cochin), Kerala.

Fish is sold fresh off the boats in the early hours of the morning all along India's coast.

FISH TIKKA

TIKKA IS THE HINDI WORD FOR CHUNK. HERE, FISH CHUNKS ARE MARINATED IN A BLEND OF SPICES AND YOGURT AND COOKED. IN INDIA, A TANDOOR, A CHARCOAL-FIRED CLAY OVEN, WOULD BE USED. HOWEVER, BARBECUING IS A GOOD SUBSTITUTE AS IT ALSO IMPARTS A SMOKY FLAVOR.

MARINADE
2 cups plain yogurt (page 280)
1/2 onion, finely chopped
3/4 inch piece of ginger, grated
4 garlic cloves, crushed
1 teaspoon ground coriander
2 tablespoons lemon juice
1 1/2 tablespoons garam masala (page 284)
1 teaspoon paprika
1 teaspoon chili powder
2 tablespoons tomato paste
1 teaspoon salt

1 lb. firm white fish such as halibut, monkfish or blue-eye, skin removed
2 onions, each cut into 8 chunks
2 small green or red peppers, each cut into 8 chunks

1/4 cup cucumber, peeled and diced
1 tablespoon chopped cilantro
lemon wedges

SERVES 8

TO MAKE the marinade, mix half the yogurt with all the other marinade ingredients in a shallow dish that is long enough and deep enough to take the prepared skewers. You will need eight metal skewers.

CUT the fish into 24–32 bite-sized chunks. On each metal skewer, thread three or four pieces of fish and chunks of onion and pepper, alternating them as you go. Put the skewers in the marinade and turn them so that all the fish and vegetables are well coated. Cover and marinate in the fridge for at least 1 hour, or until you are ready to cook.

PREHEAT the barbecue or broiler. Lift the skewers out of the marinade. Cook on the barbecue, or under a broiler on a wire rack set above a baking sheet, for 5–6 minutes, turning once, or until the fish is cooked and firm and both the fish and the vegetables are slightly charred.

MEANWHILE, stir the cucumber and cilantro into the other half of the yogurt. Serve the fish with the yogurt and lemon wedges.

POULTRY & MEAT

CHICKEN TIKKA

LOOSELY TRANSLATED TO MEAN CHUNKS OF CHICKEN, THIS DISH CONTAINS CHICKEN MARINATED IN
A SPICY YOGURT SAUCE, THEN COOKED IN A TANDOOR. YOU CAN USE AN OVEN OR BROILER.

MARINADE
1/2 tablespoon paprika
1 teaspoon chili powder
2 tablespoons garam masala
   (page 284)
1/4 teaspoon tandoori food coloring
11/2 tablespoons lemon juice
4 garlic cloves, roughly chopped
2 inch piece of ginger, roughly
   chopped
1/2 cup cilantro leaves, chopped
1/2 cup plain yogurt (page 280)

1 lb. skinned boneless chicken
   breast fillets, cut into 1 inch cubes
lemon wedges

SERVES 4

FOR the marinade, blend all the ingredients together in a food processor until smooth, or chop the garlic, ginger and cilantro leaves more finely and mix with the rest of the marinade ingredients. Season with salt to taste.

PUT the chicken cubes in a bowl with the marinade and mix thoroughly. Cover and marinate overnight in the fridge.

HEAT the oven to 400°F. Thread the chicken pieces onto four metal skewers and put them n a metal rack above a baking sheet. Roast, uncovered, for 15–20 minutes, or until the chicken is cooked through and browned around the edges. Serve with lemon wedges to squeeze over the chicken.

CHICKEN TIKKA MASALA

CHICKEN TIKKA MASALA

1 tablespoon oil
1 onion, finely chopped
2 cardamom pods
2 garlic cloves, crushed
14 oz. can diced tomatoes
1/4 teaspoon ground cinnamon
1 tablespoon garam masala
   (page 284)
1/2 teaspoon chili powder
1 teaspoon jaggery or
   light brown sugar
11/4 cups whipping cream
1 tablespoon ground almonds
1 quantity chicken tikka (above)
1 tablespoon chopped cilantro
   leaves

SERVES 6

HEAT the oil in a karhai or heavy-bottomed saucepan over low heat. Add the onion and cardamom pods and fry until the onion is soft and starting to brown. Add the garlic to the saucepan, cook for 1 minute, then add the tomatoes and cook until the paste is thick.

ADD the cinnamon, garam masala, chili powder and sugar to the saucepan and cook for 1 minute. Stir in the cream and almonds, then add the cooked chicken tikka pieces and gently simmer for 5 minutes, or until the chicken is heated through. Garnish with the chopped cilantro.

The Naya Bazaar in Delhi.

MURGH MASALA

THIS IS A MILD DISH WHICH ORIGINATED IN NORTHERN INDIA. BECAUSE OF ITS SUBTLE FLAVOR, IT IS SUITABLE FOR SERVING AT ANY MEAL. A COMBINATION OF TOMATOES, GINGER AND SPICES GIVES FLAVORING, AND THE YOGURT ENRICHES THE SAUCE.

3 lb. skinned chicken thighs or chicken cutlets
2 teaspoons ground cumin
2 teaspoons ground coriander
1 1/2 teaspoons garam masala (page 284)
1/4 teaspoon ground turmeric
2 onions, finely chopped
4 garlic cloves, roughly chopped
2 inch piece of ginger, roughly chopped
2 very ripe tomatoes, chopped
3 tablespoons oil or ghee
5 cloves
8 cardamom pods
2 inch piece of cinnamon stick
10 curry leaves
1/2 cup plain yogurt (page 280)

SERVES 4

TRIM off any excess fat or skin from the chicken. Mix the cumin, coriander, garam masala and turmeric together and rub it into the chicken.

PUT half the onions with the garlic, ginger and chopped tomatoes in a food processor and blend to a smooth paste. If you don't have a blender, finely chop the ingredients and mix them together.

HEAT the oil or ghee in a karhai or casserole over low heat, add the remaining onion, the cloves, cardamom, cinnamon and curry leaves and fry until the onion is golden brown. Add the tomatoes and onion paste and stir for 5 minutes. Season with salt to taste. Add the spiced chicken, stir in the yogurt and bring slowly to a boil.

REDUCE the heat, cover and simmer for 50 minutes or until the oil separates from the sauce. Stir the ingredients occasionally to prevent the chicken from sticking. If the sauce is too thin, simmer for a couple of minutes with the lid off. Season with salt to taste.

Butchers shops in Kerala advertise their wares through pictures. Lamb or goat and chicken are the most popular.

CARDAMOM CHICKEN

THIS DISH HAS A HIGHLY AROMATIC SAUCE FLAVORED WITH CARDAMOM. THE YOGURT MAKES THE SAUCE DELICIOUSLY CREAMY. IF YOU DON'T MAKE YOUR OWN YOGURT, DRAIN COMMERCIAL YOGURT OVERNIGHT. THIS MAKES THE SAUCE MUCH RICHER BY GETTING RID OF ANY EXCESS LIQUID.

3 lb. chicken or chicken cutlets
25 cardamom pods
4 garlic cloves, crushed
1 inch piece of ginger, grated
1$\frac{1}{4}$ cups plain yogurt (page 280)
1$\frac{1}{2}$ teaspoons ground black pepper
grated zest of 1 lemon
2 tablespoons ghee or oil
1$\frac{2}{3}$ cups coconut milk (page 283)
6 green chiles, pricked all over
2 tablespoons chopped cilantro leaves
3 tablespoons lemon juice

SERVES 4

IF USING a whole chicken, cut it into eight cutlets by removing both legs and cutting between the joint of the drumstick and thigh. Cut down either side of the backbone and remove the backbone. Turn the chicken over and cut through the cartilage down the center of the breastbone. Cut each breast in half, leaving the wing attached to the top half. Trim off the wing tips. Remove the skin if you prefer.

REMOVE the seeds from the cardamom pods and crush them in a spice grinder or pestle and mortar. In a blender, mix the garlic and ginger with enough of the yogurt ($\frac{1}{4}$ cup) to make a paste, or, if you prefer, mix them with a spoon. Add the cardamom, pepper and grated lemon rind. Spread this over the chicken cutlets, cover, and leave in the fridge overnight.

HEAT the ghee or oil in a karhai or heavy-bottomed frying pan over low heat and brown the chicken cutlets all over. Add the remaining yogurt and coconut milk to the pan, bring to a boil, then add the whole chiles and the cilantro leaves. Simmer for 20–30 minutes or until the chicken is cooked through. Season with salt to taste, and stir in the lemon juice.

QUAIL MASALA

QUAIL IS AN EXOTIC DISH, EVEN IN INDIA. MANY OF THE ROYAL HOUSEHOLDS TRADITIONALLY USED QUAIL IN MANY DIFFERENT WAYS. HERE IT IS INCORPORATED INTO A DRY-STYLE, STEAMED RECIPE. TENDER YOUNG CHICKEN OR POUSSIN CAN BE SUCCESSFULLY USED INSTEAD.

6 x 1/4 lb. quails

MARINADE
2/3 cup blanched almonds
3 garlic cloves, crushed
1 inch piece of ginger, grated
1/2 onion, finely chopped
1/2 teaspoon chili powder
1/2 teaspoon ground cloves
1/2 teaspoon ground cinnamon
1 teaspoon ground cumin
1 teaspoon garam masala
   (page 284)
2 tablespoons mint leaves,
   finely chopped
3/4 cup plain yogurt (page 280)
1 teaspoon jaggery or
   light brown sugar

RICE STUFFING
1/3 cup rice
1 teaspoon amchoor powder
1/3 cup chopped pine nuts
1 1/2 tablespoons lemon juice

2 young banana leaves
3 tablespoons lemon juice
cucumber slices
mango or green mango slices
mint leaves

SERVES 6

CLEAN the quails by rinsing them well and wiping them dry. Prick the flesh all over so that the marinade will penetrate the meat.

TO MAKE the marinade, grind the almonds in a food processor or finely chop them with a knife, then mix them with the remaining marinade ingredients. Coat the quails evenly with the marinade, then cover and marinate for 4 hours, or overnight, in the fridge.

TO MAKE the rice stuffing, preheat the oven to 400°F. Cook the rice in boiling water for 15 minutes or until just tender. Drain well and allow to cool. Combine the rice, amchoor powder, pine nuts and lemon juice and season with salt. Just before cooking, fill the quails with the rice stuffing and brush some marinade on the quails. If you are making the stuffing in advance, make sure you refrigerate it until you are ready to use it.

CUT the banana leaves into neat pieces big enough to wrap a quail. Soften the leaves by dipping them into a saucepan of very hot water. Wipe them dry as they become pliant. If you can't buy banana leaves, use aluminium foil. Brush with oil.

WRAP each quail individually in a piece of banana leaf, drizzling with any excess marinade. Tie firmly with a piece of kitchen string. Place the packages, with the seam side up, on a rack above a baking sheet and bake for 25–30 minutes. Check to see if the quails are cooked by opening one—the flesh should be slightly pink but the juices should run clear when the flesh is pierced. If necessary, cook the quails for another 5 minutes. Open the packages completely for 3 minutes at the end of cooking, to brown the quail slightly. Sprinkle a dash of lemon juice over each quail. Serve in the packages with some sliced cucumber, sliced mango and mint leaves.

To make sure none of the flavor or juices escape while the quails cook, wrap them in banana leaves as if they are little packages.

KASHMIRI CHICKEN

THIS CHICKEN DISH, COMBINING NUTS AND SAFFRON, IS DELICATELY FLAVORED WITH A CREAMY SAUCE. TO MAKE THE SPICES MORE AROMATIC, IT IS BEST TO DRY-ROAST THEM AS SUGGESTED IN THE RECIPE, RATHER THAN USE PRE-GROUND ONES.

Saffron from Kashmir is considered to be of a very high quality and is sold in small boxes.

3 lb. chicken or chicken cutlets
6 cardamom pods
1/2 teaspoon coriander seeds
1/2 teaspoon cumin seeds
1 inch piece of cinnamon stick
8 peppercorns
6 cloves
2/3 cup blanched almonds
1/2 cup shelled pistachios
2 tablespoons ghee or oil
1 onion, finely chopped
4 garlic cloves, finely chopped
2 inch piece of ginger, finely
  chopped
1/2 cup chicken stock
1 cup plain yogurt (page 280)
1/2 teaspoon saffron threads

SERVES 4

IF USING a whole chicken, cut it into eight pieces by removing both legs and cutting between the joint of the drumstick and thigh. Cut down either side of the backbone and remove the backbone. Turn the chicken over and cut through the cartilage down the center of the breastbone. Remove the skin from the chicken and cut the flesh off the bones. Cut the chicken into bite-sized pieces. (You can reserve the carcass for making stock if you wish.)

REMOVE the seeds from the cardamom pods. Place a small frying pan over low heat and dry-roast the coriander seeds until aromatic. Remove and dry-roast the cumin seeds, then the piece of cinnamon stick. Grind the cardamom seeds, roasted spices, peppercorns and cloves to a fine powder using a spice grinder or pestle and mortar. Finely chop the almonds and pistachios in a food processor or spice grinder, or with a knife.

HEAT the ghee or oil in a karhai or casserole over low heat and fry the onion until golden brown. Add the garlic, ginger and chicken and fry rapidly for 5 minutes. Add the ground spices and the chicken stock and simmer, covered tightly for 30 minutes.

STIR the ground nuts into the yogurt. Mix the saffron with 1 teaspoon of hot water. Add the yogurt and the saffron to the pan and bring to a boil. Simmer, uncovered, for 10 minutes. Season with salt to taste.

SPICY GRILLED CHICKEN

THIS IS IDEAL TO COOK ON A BARBECUE AND SERVE WITH SALADS, OR MAKE IN ADVANCE AND
EAT COLD AT PICNICS. IT ALSO MAKES A GOOD APPETIZER OR SNACK FOOD WHEN SERVED WITH A
CHUTNEY OR RAITA. THE AROMATIC FRESHLY ROASTED SPICES ADD SPICINESS TO THE FLAVOR.

MARINADE
3 teaspoons coriander seeds
2 teaspoons cumin seeds
1 1/2 inch piece of cinnamon stick
1 teaspoon cardamom seeds
1 onion, roughly chopped
6–8 garlic cloves, roughly chopped
1 inch piece of ginger,
  roughly chopped
1/2 teaspoon ground cloves
1/2 teaspoon cayenne pepper
3 tablespoons oil
1 tablespoon tomato paste
3 tablespoons clear vinegar
1 teaspoon salt

1 1/4 lb. skinned, boneless chicken
  breast fillets, cut into 1/2 inch
  strips

SERVES 6

TO MAKE the marinade, place a small frying pan
over low heat and dry-roast the coriander seeds
until aromatic. Remove the coriander seeds and
dry-roast the cumin, then the cinnamon. Grind the
roasted spices and the cardamom to a fine powder
using a spice grinder or pestle and mortar.

BLEND all the marinade ingredients in a blender
or food processor until smooth. If you don't have
a blender, finely chop the onion, garlic and ginger
and pound together in a pestle and mortar, or
very finely chop all the large pieces with a knife
and mix with the remaining marinade ingredients.
Mix the paste thoroughly with the chicken strips.
Cover and marinate in the fridge overnight.

PREHEAT a griddle or barbecue until it is very hot,
or preheat the broiler. Cook the chicken pieces for
4 minutes on each side on the griddle or
barbecue, or spread the pieces on a baking
sheet and broil for 8–10 minutes on each side,
until almost black in patches.

Domestic stoves in India are
usually wood-fired. Cooking pots
are placed over the opening at
the top and fuel is lit from below.

KASHMIRI CHICKEN LIVERS

1/2 lb. chicken livers, trimmed
  of all sinew
3 tablespoons oil
2 onions, finely chopped
3 garlic cloves, chopped
1 teaspoon cumin seeds
1 teaspoon chili powder
3/4 inch piece of ginger, grated
1/2 teaspoon ground turmeric

SERVES 4

CUT the chicken livers into bite-sized pieces.

HEAT the oil in a karhai or heavy-bottomed
saucepan. Add the onions and cook until
transparent but not browned. Add the garlic
and cumin seeds and fry for 1 minute. Add
the chili powder, ginger and turmeric.

TURN up the heat slightly and fry the liver for
2–3 minutes. Add 1 cup of water, bring to a boil
and simmer for 10–15 minutes, or until the livers
are just cooked and the sauce has thickened.
Season with salt to taste.

KASHMIRI CHICKEN LIVERS

Bicycles are a common form of transport all over India.

BUTTER CHICKEN

BUTTER CHICKEN, OR MURGH MAKHNI, IS A MOGHUL DISH THAT HAS MANY VERSIONS. THE BUTTER IN THE TITLE REFERS TO GHEE, A TYPE OF CLARIFIED BUTTER. RICE IS AN IDEAL ACCOMPANIMENT AND PIECES OF ROTI OR NAAN CAN BE USED TO MOP UP THE DELICIOUS JUICES.

1 inch piece of ginger, roughly chopped
3 garlic cloves, roughly chopped
1/2 cup blanched almonds
1/2 cup plain yogurt (page 280)
1/2 teaspoon chili powder
1/4 teaspoon ground cloves
1/4 teaspoon ground cinnamon
1 teaspoon garam masala (page 284)
4 cardamom pods, lightly crushed
14 oz. can diced tomatoes
1 1/4 teaspoons salt
2 lb. skinned, boneless chicken skinless, thigh fillets, cut into fairly large pieces
5 tablespoons ghee or clarified butter
1 large onion, thinly sliced
6 tablespoons finely chopped cilantro leaves
4 tablespoons whipping cream

SERVES 6

BLEND the ginger and garlic together to a paste in a food processor or pestle and mortar, or crush the garlic and finely grate the ginger and mix them together. Grind the almonds in a food processor or finely chop with a knife. Put the paste and almonds in a bowl with the yogurt, chili powder, cloves, cinnamon, garam masala, cardamom pods, tomatoes and salt, and blend together with a fork. Add the chicken pieces and stir to coat thoroughly. Cover and marinate for 2 hours, or overnight, in the fridge.

PREHEAT the oven to 350°F. Heat the ghee or clarified butter in a karhai or deep, heavy-bottomed frying pan, add the onion and fry until softened and brown. Add the chicken mixture and fry for 2 minutes. Mix in the cilantro. Put the mixture into a shallow baking dish, pour in the cream and stir with a fork.

BAKE for 1 hour. If the top is browning too quickly during cooking, cover with a piece of aluminium foil. Allow to rest for 10 minutes before serving. The oil will rise to the surface. Just before serving, place the dish under a broiler for 2 minutes to brown the top. Before serving, slightly tip the dish and remove any extra oil with a spoon.

PARSI CHICKEN WITH APRICOTS

IN THIS DELICIOUS PARSI DISH FROM MUMBAI (BOMBAY), THE USE OF DRIED APRICOTS, JAGGERY AND VINEGAR GIVE A SWEET SOUR FLAVOR. THE POTATO STRAWS MAKE AN UNUSUAL GARNISH AND ADD A CONTRASTING CRUNCHY TEXTURE TO ENHANCE THE RECIPE.

3 lb. chicken or chicken pieces
3 tablespoons oil
2 large onions, finely sliced
1 clove garlic, finely chopped
2 inch piece of ginger, finely
  chopped
3 dried chiles
1 1/2 teaspoons garam masala
  (page 284)
2 tablespoons tomato paste
1 teaspoon salt
2 tablespoons clear vinegar
1 1/2 tablespoons jaggery
  or soft brown sugar
12 dried apricots

POTATO STRAWS
1 large waxy potato
1 tablespoon salt
oil for deep-frying

SERVES 4

IF USING a whole chicken, cut it into eight pieces by removing both legs and cutting between the joint of the drumstick and thigh. Cut down either side of the backbone and remove the backbone. Turn the chicken over and cut through the cartilage down the center of the breastbone. Cut each breast in half, leaving the wing attached to the top half. Trim off the wing tips.

HEAT the oil in a karhai or casserole. Add the onions and stir over medium heat until softened and starting to brown. Stir in the garlic, ginger, dried chiles and garam masala, then add all the chicken pieces. Stir and brown the chicken for 5 minutes, taking care not to burn the onions. Add the tomato paste, salt and 1 cup of water. Bring to a boil, then reduce the heat, cover and simmer gently for 20 minutes.

ADD the vinegar, jaggery and dried apricots to the pan, cover and simmer for another 15 minutes.

TO MAKE the potato straws, grate the potato on the largest holes of a grater, then put in a large bowl with 6 cups water and the salt. Stir and remove some of the potato a handful at a time, squeezing and patting it dry on a kitchen towel. Fill a karhai or deep, heavy-bottomed saucepan a third full with oil. Heat the oil slowly to 315°F (a cube of bread will brown in 30 seconds), then add a small handful of the potato. Be careful not to add too much as it will make the oil bubble and rise at first. When the potato is golden and crisp, remove it and drain on paper towels. Cook all the potato in the same way.

SERVE the chicken pieces garnished with the potato straws.

Street decorations on a busy street in Mumbai (Bombay) during the festival of Divali.

CHICKEN WITH CILANTRO AND ALMONDS

ALMONDS ARE PLENTIFUL IN NORTHERN INDIA AND ARE OFTEN COMBINED WITH CREAM IN SAVOURY DISHES AND DESSERTS. THIS DISH IS OFTEN SERVED ON SPECIAL OCCASIONS WITH PUNJABI BREADS SUCH AS CHAPATIS OR NAAN. ALOO GOBI OR INDIAN-STYLE CABBAGE ARE IDEAL ACCOMPANIMENTS.

3 lb. chicken or chicken pieces
1/3 cup blanched almonds
2 onions, roughly chopped
4 garlic cloves, roughly chopped
2 green chiles, roughly chopped
2 inch piece of ginger, roughly chopped
7 tablespoons oil or ghee
2 Indian bay leaves (cassia leaves)
1 1/2 tablespoons ground coriander
1 tablespoon ground cumin
1/4 teaspoon chili powder
1/4 teaspoon ground turmeric
1/4 teaspoon paprika
2 teaspoons salt
1 teaspoon ground black pepper
4 tablespoons finely chopped cilantro leaves
2/3 cup cream (or double cream for thicker sauce)

SERVES 4

IF USING a whole chicken, cut it into eight pieces by removing both legs and cutting between the joint of the drumstick and thigh. Cut down either side of the backbone and remove the backbone. Turn the chicken over and cut through the cartilage down the center of the breastbone. Cut each breast in half, leaving the wing attached to the top half. Trim off the wing tips.

GRIND the almonds in a food processor or finely chop with a knife.

BLEND the onions, garlic, chiles and ginger together in a food processor until finely chopped, but not puréed. If you don't have a food processor, finely chop them together with a knife.

HEAT the oil or ghee in a karhai or casserole over medium heat, add the onion mixture and bay leaves and stir until lightly browned. Add the chicken to the pan and fry, turning constantly for 10 minutes, or until golden on all sides.

ADD the coriander, cumin, chili powder, turmeric, paprika, salt and pepper to the pan and stir with the chicken for 3 minutes until well absorbed into the meat. Add 1/3 cup of water, stirring the chicken for another 5 minutes over medium heat. The water will have reduced to a rich, thick sauce. Add another 2/3 cup of water and bring to a boil. Reduce the heat, cover and simmer for 20 minutes. Add three-quarters of the cilantro to the chicken and stir.

BLEND the almonds with 1/2 cup of the cream in a blender to form a smooth paste. If you don't have a blender, just mix the cream with the ground nuts. Add to the chicken, stir well and cook until heated through. Stir in the remaining cream before serving, to create a creamy, even sauce. Sprinkle with the remaining cilantro.

TANDOORI CHICKEN

TRADITIONALLY COOKED IN A TANDOOR (CLAY OVEN), THIS IS PERHAPS THE MOST POPULAR CHICKEN DISH FROM NORTHERN INDIA, WHERE IT IS SERVED WITH NAAN AND LACCHA. YOU CAN NEVER GET EXACTLY THE SAME RESULTS AT HOME BUT THIS IS A VERY GOOD APPROXIMATION.

3 lb. chicken or skinned chicken
  thighs and drumsticks

MARINADE
2 teaspoons coriander seeds
1 teaspoon cumin seeds
1 onion, roughly chopped
3 garlic cloves, roughly chopped
2 inch piece of ginger, roughly
  chopped
1 cup plain yogurt (page 280)
grated zest of 1 lemon
3 tablespoons lemon juice
2 tablespoons clear vinegar
1 teaspoon paprika
2 teaspoons garam masala
  (page 284)
1/2 teaspoon tandoori food coloring
  (optional)

2 tablespoons ghee
onion rings
lemon wedges

SERVES 4

Newly made yogurt is left to set in porous earthenware bowls, which help to drain and thicken it.

REMOVE the skin from the chicken and cut the chicken in half. Using a sharp knife, make 1 inch long diagonal incisions on each limb and breast, taking care not to cut through to the bone. If using thighs and drumsticks, trim away any excess fat and make an incision in each piece.

TO MAKE the marinade, place a frying pan over low heat and dry-roast the coriander seeds until aromatic. Remove and dry-roast the cumin seeds. Grind the roasted seeds to a fine powder using a spice grinder or pestle and mortar. In a food processor, blend all the marinade ingredients to form a smooth paste. Season with salt to taste. If you don't have a food processor, chop the onion, garlic and ginger more finely and mix with the rest of the ingredients in a bowl.

MARINATE the chicken in the spicy yogurt marinade for at least 8 hours, or overnight. Turn the chicken occasionally in the marinade to ensure that all sides are soaked.

HEAT the oven to 400°F. Place the chicken on a wire rack on a baking sheet. Cover with aluminium foil and roast on the top shelf for 45–50 minutes or until cooked through (test by inserting a skewer into a thigh—the juices should run clear). Baste the chicken with the marinade once during cooking. Remove the foil 15 minutes before the end of cooking, to brown the tandoori mixture. Preheat the broiler.

PRIOR to serving, while the chicken is still on the rack, heat the ghee, pour it over the chicken halves and cook under the broiler for 5 minutes to blacken the edges of the chicken like a tandoor.

SERVE the chicken garnished with onion rings and lemon wedges. The chicken pieces can also be broiled, barbecued or spit-roasted.

SPICY ROAST CHICKEN IN BANANA LEAVES

IN THIS RECIPE, THE CHICKEN IS WRAPPED IN BANANA LEAVES BEFORE IT IS ROASTED. THIS CREATES A DISTINCTIVE AROMA AND FLAVOR. ENCLOSING IT IN BANANA LEAVES ALSO KEEPS THE CHICKEN MOIST AND SUCCULENT WHILE IT COOKS. FOR A SPECIAL OCCASION, SERVE IT WITH PLAIN PULAO.

4 lb. chicken
3 tablespoons lemon juice
1 tablespoon oil
2 large onions, roughly chopped
4 garlic cloves, crushed
1¹/₂ inch piece of ginger, roughly
  chopped
3 tablespoons ground almonds
¹/₂ teaspoon chili powder
1 teaspoon ground turmeric
2 teaspoons garam masala
  (page 284)
3 cilantro roots, chopped
4 tablespoons chopped cilantro
  leaves
3–4 young banana leaves

SERVES 6

TRIM any excess fat from the chicken. Pat the chicken completely dry with paper towels and prick all over with a skewer so the marinade can penetrate the flesh. Rub the lemon juice and 1 teaspoon of salt all over the skin and inside the cavity of the chicken.

HEAT the oil in a heavy-bottomed frying pan over low heat, add the onion and cook until the onions start to brown. Add the garlic and ginger and cook for 2 minutes, or until soft. Add the almonds, chili powder, turmeric and garam masala and cook for 1 minute. Allow the onion mixture to cool completely.

PLACE the cooled mixture in a food processor or a pestle and mortar, along with the cilantro roots and leaves. Grind to a smooth paste and rub the paste thoroughly all over the chicken and inside the cavity. Cover and refrigerate for 6 hours or overnight.

PREHEAT the oven to 400°F. Soften the banana leaves by dipping them into a saucepan of very hot water. Wipe the pieces dry as they become pliant. Tie the legs of the chicken together to keep them in place.

WRAP the chicken in the banana leaves, making sure that it is well covered. Tie a piece of kitchen string around the chicken like a package. If you can't buy banana leaves, wrap the chicken in a large sheet of aluminium foil instead. Place the chicken in a roasting pan and bake for 1¹/₂ hours. Unwrap the banana leaves or the foil from around the top of the chicken, baste the chicken with some of the juices and return it to the oven for 10 minutes, or until well browned. Check that the chicken is cooked by pulling away one leg—the juices should run clear. Allow the the chicken to rest for 10 minutes before carving.

Banana leaves on sale in Kolkata's (Calcutta) New Market.

AMCHOOR or amchur powder is made from finely ground, dried green mangoes. It is used as a souring agent in northern dishes and is one of the main flavorings in chaat masala.

TAMARIND adds a sour flavor to dishes and is particularly popular in the South. The shells and seeds are removed and the surrounding pulp is compressed into a cake.

CLOVES are one of the spices brought to India from the Moluccas. Cloves are dried flower buds. They are widely used in Indian cooking and have a distinctive aroma and flavor.

BLACK PEPPER is native to Kerala on India's spice coast. Black pepper is made by fermenting and drying ripe peppercorns. It is very aromatic and is the original "hot" flavor.

GINGER the rhizomes of a plant which are used both fresh and dried. Ginger has a pungent, hot flavor which is sweeter in younger "roots." Ginger is used fresh in many Indian dishes.

FENUGREEK known as methi, this spice has a curry aroma and slightly bitter flavor. Fenugreek is often dry-roasted to intensify its flavor and is used in many masala mixes.

KALONJI also called nigella, these tiny black seeds have an onion flavor. They add a distinctive taste to breads, raitas and vegetable dishes and are used in Bengali panch phoron.

POMEGRANATE SEEDS are actually dried seeds and flesh which are used whole or ground as a souring agent. They are popular in the Punjab and are often used in chickpea dishes.

SAFFRON made from the stigmas of a type of crocus, this is the world's most expensive spice. Saffron was introduced into Indian food by the Moghuls and it is grown in Kashmir.

KOKUM is the dried fruit of the gamboge tree. This adds a tart flavor and is often used in Kerala to flavor fish dishes. It also balances sweetness in coconut-based dishes.

CURRY LEAVES are aromatic leaves with a strong curry-like fragrance and flavor. They are used liberally in the South, either added to dishes during cooking or fried to use as a garnish.

TURMERIC dried turmeric is one of the main ingredients of curry powders. It has both flavor and color and is widely used. It is available as a fresh root, dried whole root, or a ground powder.

NAYA BAZAAR is Delhi's spice market. Here in a labyrinth of alleyways and staircases, chiles, turmeric, ginger and seed spices are sold in bulk. Porters stagger backwards and forwards, weighed down by huge sacks that are heaved on and off large scales. The covered buildings around the edges of the bazaar hold the godowns and offices of the traders and all available space is used to display wares.

SPICES

SPICES BECAME IMPORTANT ITEMS OF COMMERCE EARLY IN THE EVOLUTION OF TRADE. THEY WERE SMALL, EASILY TRANSPORTED AND OFTEN WORTH THEIR WEIGHT IN GOLD.

India was essentially "discovered" by Vasco da Gama in May 1498 as he searched for the "Indies," the origin of the spices that were arriving in Europe via Arab traders. It is said that he came ashore and shouted "for Christ and for spices." The discovery of the spice coast of India had a profound effect on the European spice trade as it broke the stranglehold of the Arab traders and cut out the middlemen.

Cloves and nutmeg from the East Indies were taken by Muslim traders from Malacca to southern India where black pepper and cinnamon (from Kerala and Sri Lanka) were added to the cargo. The whole lot was then sold onwards to Europe from the spice ports on the west coast of India. The use of maritime trading routes meant that war, religious differences and other disruptions to the overland routes did not upset the flow of spices to Europe. This kept their prices relatively constant and affordable. The next logical step was to grow spices like cloves and nutmeg in southern India which had only previously been available from the Moluccas.

Kochi (Cochin) in Kerala became a bustling spice port in 1341 after a flood in the area created a natural harbor. The area around Mattancherry is still busy with major trading and carts of spices trundle back and forth between the wholesale dealers and their godowns (warehouses) all day.

CARDAMOMS are the world's third most expensive spice. They are native to south India and here are shown growing in the hills around Kumily in Kerala. The seed pods are picked by hand just before they ripen and split. They are dried for 24 hours before being polished to remove the flower husks. Cardamoms are graded by size. They are sorted by passing them through strainers and then picked over by hand.

Amongst the spices of India, pepper, cardamom, nutmeg, mace, ginger, vanilla and turmeric are grown in Kerala and Tamil Nadu, seed spices such as coriander, cumin, dill and fennel are found in Gujarat and Rajasthan, and chiles grow in every state and union territory in India. Saffron is cultivated in Kashmir, mustard in Andhra Pradesh and fenugreek in Uttar Pradesh.

Spices have a strong association with Indian food of all types and Indian cuisine is probably the most highly spiced in the world. In the North, spices are often dry-roasted and ground before use, warming mixtures such as garam masala are used as a seasoning and chiles are not always important. In the South, spices are ground with coconut or fresh herbs to make a wet paste and a seasoning (tarka) of mustard seeds, curry leaves and dried chiles, all fried in oil, may be stirred into the dish at the end of cooking.

JEW TOWN, the centre of India's spice trade, is built on a plot of land given to the Jewish community by the Raja of Kochi (Cochin) in the 16th century.

NUTMEG

NUTMEG grows on a tropical evergreen tree indigenous to the Moluccas. The inner nut is surrounded by a red lacy aril and a yellow nutmeg fruit. When the fruit is ripe, it splits to show the aril and nut. The nut and aril are separated and dried. As the aril dries, it loses its color and becomes the spice known as mace. The nut inside is cracked open and the kernel, the nutmeg, is removed.

CHILES

CHILES give Indian food heat, color and flavor. The heat factor depends on the variety and there is no rule as to what the hottest or mildest chiles look like. The most common Indian chiles are red or green finger-like ones *(left and center left)*. They are used fresh or dried and usually have a medium heat. Mundu chiles *(center right)* are quite hot but the hottest are the tiny dhani (bird's-eye) chiles *(right)*.

SUPARI MIXES

SUPARI mixes are another way in which spices are used. Eaten after a meal to aid digestion and freshen the breath they range from fennel seeds and cardamom pods coated in silver to colorful mixes of split, roasted coriander seeds, sugar balls, sesame seeds, sugar-coated fennel seeds, coconut shreds, bits of betel nut and aniseed. Look for plates of these beside the cash register and take a pinch as you leave.

ROGAN JOSH

THERE ARE MANY CURRY PASTES AVAILABLE FOR MAKING THIS CLASSIC. HOWEVER, NOTHING COMPARES WITH A VERSION MADE WITH FRESHLY GROUND SPICES. THE COLOR COMES FROM THE CHILI POWDER AND PAPRIKA. IN KASHMIR, RED COCKSCOMB FLOWERS ARE TRADITIONALLY USED FOR COLOR.

8 garlic cloves, crushed

2 inch piece of ginger, grated

2 teaspoons ground cumin

1 teaspoon Kashmiri chili powder

2 teaspoons paprika

2 teaspoons ground coriander

2 lb. boneless leg or shoulder of lamb, cut into 1 inch cubes

5 tablespoons ghee or oil

1 onion, finely chopped

6 cardamom pods

4 cloves

2 Indian bay leaves (cassia leaves)

3 inch piece of cinnamon stick

3/4 cup plain yogurt (page 280)

4 strands saffron, mixed with 2 tablespoons milk

1/4 teaspoon garam masala (page 284)

SERVES 6

MIX the garlic, ginger, cumin, chili powder, paprika and coriander in a large bowl. Add the meat and stir thoroughly to coat the meat cubes well. Cover and marinate for at least 2 hours, or overnight, in the fridge.

HEAT the ghee or oil in a karhai or casserole over low heat. Add the onion and cook for about 10 minutes, or until the onion is lightly browned. Remove from the pan.

ADD the cardamom pods, cloves, bay leaves and cinnamon to the pan and fry for 1 minute. Increase the heat to high, add the meat and onion, then mix well and fry for 2 minutes. Stir well, then reduce the heat to low, cover and cook for 15 minutes. Uncover and fry for another 3 minutes, or until the meat is quite dry. Add 1/2 cup of water, cover and cook for 5–7 minutes, until the water has evaporated and the oil separates out and floats on the surface. Fry the meat for another 1–2 minutes, then add 1 cup of water. Cover and cook for 40–50 minutes, gently simmering until the meat is tender. The liquid will reduce quite a bit.

STIR in the yogurt when the meat is almost tender, taking care not to allow the meat to catch on the bottom of the pan. Add the saffron and milk. Stir the mixture a few times to mix in the saffron. Season with salt to taste. Remove from the heat and sprinkle with the garam masala.

The poppy seeds used in Indian cuisine are white rather than black. They are used to thicken kormas and are usually ground, then mixed into a wet paste.

A shop selling freshly made yogurt in Hyderabad.

LAMB KORMA

THIS MILD DISH, WHICH COMES IN MANY GUISES, NEEDS TO BE COOKED VERY SLOWLY TO LET THE SUBTLE FLAVORS EMERGE. THIS VERSION USES WHITE POPPY SEEDS AND CASHEW NUTS TO THICKEN THE SAUCE AND YOGURT TO MAKE IT CREAMY.

2 lb. boneless leg or shoulder
of lamb, cut into 1 inch cubes
2 tablespoons plain yogurt
(page 280)
1 tablespoon coriander seeds
2 teaspoons cumin seeds
5 cardamom pods
2 onions
2 tablespoons grated coconut
(page 283)
1 tablespoon white poppy seeds
(khus khus)
3 green chiles, roughly chopped
4 garlic cloves, crushed
2 inch piece of ginger, grated
1 tablespoon cashew nuts
6 cloves
1/4 teaspoon ground cinnamon
2 tablespoons oil

SERVES 4

PUT the meat in a bowl, add the yogurt and mix to coat thoroughly.

PLACE a small frying pan over low heat and dry-roast the coriander seeds until aromatic. Remove and dry-roast the cumin seeds. Grind the roasted mixture to a fine powder using a spice grinder or pestle and mortar. Remove the seeds from the cardamom pods and grind them.

ROUGHLY chop one onion and finely slice the other. Put just the roughly chopped onion with the ground spices, coconut, poppy seeds, chiles, garlic, ginger, cashew nuts, cloves and cinnamon in a blender, add 1/2 cup of water and process to a smooth paste. If you don't have a blender, crush everything together in a pestle and mortar, or finely chop with a knife, before adding the water.

HEAT the oil in a karhai or casserole over medium heat. Add the finely sliced onion and fry until lightly browned. Pour the blended mixture into the pan, season with salt and cook over low heat for 1 minute, or until the liquid evaporates and the sauce thickens. Add the lamb with the yogurt and slowly bring to a boil. Cover tightly and simmer for 1 1/2 hours, or until the meat is very tender. Stir the meat occasionally to prevent it from sticking to the pan. If the water has evaporated during the cooking time, add another 1/2 cup of water to make a sauce. The sauce should be quite thick.

MOGHUL-STYLE LAMB

FOR THIS DISH, THE LAMB IS MARINATED, PREFERABLY OVERNIGHT, BEFORE IT IS COOKED. THIS ENSURES THAT THE MEAT IS TENDER AND FULL OF FLAVOR. THE CREAM IS ADDED TO TEMPER THE STRONG COMBINATION OF SPICES.

6 garlic cloves, roughly chopped
2 inch piece of ginger, roughly
  chopped
1/4 cup blanched almonds
2 onions, thinly sliced
1 1/2 lb. boneless leg or shoulder
  of lamb, cut into 1 inch cubes
2 teaspoons coriander seeds
2 tablespoons ghee
7 cardamom pods
5 cloves
1 cinnamon stick
1 teaspoon salt
1 1/4 cups cream
1/2 teaspoon cayenne pepper
1/2 teaspoon garam masala
  (page 284)
sliced toasted almonds

SERVES 4

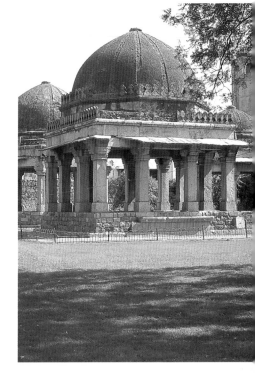

BLEND the garlic, ginger, almonds and 1/3 cup of the onions in a blender or food processor. If you don't have a blender, finely chop them with a knife or grind together in a pestle and mortar. Add a little water if necessary to make a smooth paste, then put in a bowl with the lamb and mix thoroughly to coat the meat. Cover and marinate in the fridge for 2 hours, or overnight.

PLACE a small frying pan over low heat, dry-roast the coriander seeds until aromatic, then grind to a fine powder using a spice grinder or pestle and mortar.

The remains of an ancient college built in 1354 in Haus Khas village, Delhi.

HEAT the ghee in a karhai or casserole. Add the cardamom pods, cloves and cinnamon stick and, after a few seconds, add the remaining onions and fry until they are soft and starting to brown. Transfer the onions to a plate.

FRY the meat and marinade in the pan until the mixture is quite dry and has started to brown a little. Add 1/2 cup of hot water to the pan, cover tightly and cook over low heat for 30 minutes, stirring occasionally.

ADD the ground coriander, salt, cream, cayenne pepper and cooked onions to the pan, cover and simmer for another 30 minutes, or until the lamb is tender. Stir occasionally to prevent the lamb from sticking to the pan. Remove the cardamom pods, cloves and cinnamon stick, then stir in the garam masala. Sprinkle with sliced almonds.

In Hyderabad, kheema matar is served for breakfast with poppadoms and chutney.

KHEEMA MATAR

DURING THE WINTER MONTHS, WHEN PEAS ARE IN SEASON IN NORTHERN INDIA, THIS DRY-STYLE GROUND LAMB CURRY IS OFTEN SERVED WITH UBIQUITOUS VEGETABLE DISHES SUCH AS ALOO GOBI AND ALOO METHI. LEAVE OUT THE CHILES FOR A MILD VERSION.

2 onions, roughly chopped
4 garlic cloves, roughly chopped
2 inch piece of ginger, roughly
   chopped
4 green chiles
2/3 cup oil
2 Indian bay leaves (cassia leaves)
1 lb. ground lamb
pinch of asafoetida
2 tablespoons tomato paste
1/4 teaspoon ground turmeric
1/2 teaspoon chili powder
2 tablespoons ground coriander
2 tablespoons ground cumin
2 tablespoons plain yogurt
   (page 280)
3 teaspoons salt
1 teaspoon ground black pepper
1/2 lb. fresh or frozen peas
1/4 teaspoon garam masala
   (page 284)
5 tablespoons finely chopped
   cilantro

SERVES 4

PUT the onions, garlic, ginger and two of the chiles in a food processor and process until very finely chopped. If you don't have a food processor, finely chop the ingredients or grind them together in a mortar and pestle.

HEAT the oil in a karhai or heavy-bottomed frying pan over medium heat, add the onion mixture and bay leaves and fry for 3–4 minutes, or until golden brown. Add the ground lamb and fry for 15 minutes, stirring occasionally to prevent the meat from sticking. Break up any lumps of ground lamb with the back of a fork. During this time, the flavors of the onions, garlic, ginger and chiles will infuse into the meat. Add the asafoetida and tomato paste, stir and lower the heat to a simmer.

ADD the turmeric, chili powder, coriander and cumin and stir for 1 minute. Add the yogurt, salt and pepper and continue frying for 5 minutes. Add 3/4 cup of water, a little at a time, stirring after each addition until it is well absorbed. Add the peas and the two remaining whole chiles, stir well, then cover and simmer for 20 minutes, or until the peas are cooked through. If using frozen peas, cook the ground lamb and chiles for 20 minutes and add the peas 5 minutes before the end of cooking. Add the garam masala and chopped cilantro and stir for 1 minute before serving.

A hand-painted film poster in Chennai (Madras).

Fresh, aromatic curry leaves are bought from market vendors on a daily basis.

LAMB MADRAS

TRADITIONALLY IN INDIA, HOGGET (SHEEP) OR GOAT MEAT IS OFTEN THE ONLY MEAT AVAILABLE. AS GOAT CAN BE TOUGH WHEN COOKED THIS WAY, WE HAVE USED LAMB. IT IS COOKED SLOWLY SO THE SAUCES ARE ABSORBED AND THE CURRY MATURES TO A FULL FLAVOR. BEEF CAN ALSO BE USED.

2 lb. boneless leg or shoulder of lamb, cut into 1 inch cubes
1 1/2 teaspoons ground turmeric
2 tablespoons coriander seeds
2 teaspoons cumin seeds
10 dried chiles
12 curry leaves
10 garlic cloves, roughly chopped
2 inch piece of ginger, roughly chopped
1 teaspoon fennel seeds
1 tablespoon tamarind paste (page 280)
4 tablespoons oil or ghee
3 large onions, sliced
2 1/2 cups coconut milk (page 283)
3 inch piece of cinnamon stick
6 cardamom pods
curry leaves

SERVES 6

RUB the cubed lamb with the ground turmeric. Place a small frying pan over low heat and dry-roast the coriander seeds until aromatic. Remove and dry-roast the cumin seeds, then repeat with the chiles. Grind them all to a powder in a pestle and mortar or spice grinder. Add six curry leaves, the garlic and ginger and grind to a paste.

DRY-ROAST the fennel seeds in the pan until they brown and start to pop. Dissolve the tamarind in 1/2 cup of hot water.

HEAT the oil or ghee in a karhai or casserole over low heat and fry the onions for 5–10 minutes until soft. Add the chile paste and cook for a few minutes or until aromatic. Add the meat and toss well to mix with the paste. Add 2 cups of the coconut milk and 1/4 cup of water. Bring to a boil and simmer over medium heat for 10 minutes, or until the liquid has reduced.

WHEN the liquid has reduced, add the remaining coconut milk, the cinnamon stick, cardamom pods and whole fennel seeds. Season with salt and pepper. Cover and cook, partially covered over medium heat, for 1 hour or until the meat is tender, stirring occasionally. When the meat is tender, add the tamarind and check the seasoning. Stir until the oil separates out from the meat, then remove with a spoon or blot with paper towels before removing the pan from the heat.

STIR well and add the remaining six curry leaves. Garnish with more curry leaves.

Enclose the egg completely by shaping the meat around it with your hands. Gently smooth over the seam and neaten the shape.

An egg stall at Kolkata's (Calcutta) New Market, formerly known as Hogg Market.

NARGISI KOFTA

NARGISI KOFTA ARE SO NAMED BECAUSE, WHEN SLICED OPEN, THEY LOOK LIKE THE ALMOND-SHAPED FLOWER OF THE NARCISSUS. THEY ARE SHAPED BY HAND, THEN FRIED AND DIPPED INTO A SPICY SAUCE TO BE SERVED AS A MAIN MEAL. MAKE THEM WITHOUT THE SAUCE AS A SNACK.

KOFTAS
10 small eggs
1 onion, finely chopped
4 garlic cloves, crushed
1 teaspoon salt
1/2 teaspoon ground turmeric
1 teaspoon garam masala
  (page 284)
1 teaspoon chili powder
1 lb. ground lamb
3 tablespoons rice flour
oil for deep-frying

SAUCE
2 large ripe tomatoes
1 tablespoon oil
1 onion, finely sliced
2 garlic cloves, chopped
3/4 inch piece of ginger, grated
1 teaspoon ground turmeric
1 teaspoon salt
1/2 teaspoon chili powder (optional)
1/2 teaspoon sugar
1 teaspoon garam masala
  (page 284)
1/2 cup plain yogurt (page 280)

SERVES 4

TO MAKE the koftas, cook eight of the eggs in boiling water for 10 minutes to hard-boil, then cool them immediately in cold water to prevent grey rings around the yolks. When cold, peel them.

MIX the onion, garlic, salt, turmeric, garam masala and chili powder in a large bowl. Add the ground lamb and knead the mixture well. Beat one of the remaining eggs in a bowl and knead it into the ground lamb until completely amalgamated.

DIVIDE the meat mixture into eight portions and shape each portion into a ball. Flatten a ball into a pancake on the palm of your hand and place a hard-boiled egg in the center. Wrap the mixture around the egg, smoothing the outside of the kofta and distributing the meat evenly to make a smooth shape. Make the rest in the same way, then dust with rice flour.

FILL a karhai or deep, heavy-bottomed saucepan a third full with oil and heat to 350°F (a cube of bread will brown in 15 seconds). Beat the remaining egg with a little water. Dip each kofta in the beaten egg, shake off any excess, then deep-fry one at a time until golden. Drain on paper towels. Discard the oil.

TO MAKE the sauce, score a cross in the top of each tomato, then plunge into boiling water for 20 seconds. Drain, peel away from the cross, then finely chop the tomatoes, discarding the cores and seeds and reserving any juices. Heat the oil in the karhai and fry the onion, garlic and ginger for 5 minutes. Stir in the turmeric, salt, chili powder, sugar and garam masala, then add the tomatoes. Simmer for a few minutes, then stir in the yogurt and 1/2 cup of hot water. Simmer for 3 minutes, season, then add the koftas and simmer gently for 5 minutes on each side, or until warmed through. Cut the koftas in half and serve with the sauce.

SAAG GOSHT

THIS IS A RICHLY FLAVORED, TRADITIONAL DISH FROM THE NORTHERN PART OF INDIA. IT IS COOKED UNTIL THE SAUCE IS VERY THICK. IT CAN BE SERVED WITH EITHER RICE OR BREADS. IF YOU CAN'T BUY FRESH SPINACH, YOU CAN USE DEFROSTED, DRAINED, FROZEN SPINACH INSTEAD.

2 teaspoons coriander seeds
1¹/₂ teaspoons cumin seeds
3 tablespoons oil
2 lb. boneless leg or shoulder
of lamb, cut into 1 inch cubes
4 onions, finely chopped
6 cloves
6 cardamom pods
4 inch piece of cinnamon stick
10 black peppercorns
4 Indian bay leaves (cassia leaves)
3 teaspoons garam masala
(page 284)
¹/₄ teaspoon ground turmeric
1 teaspoon paprika
3 inch piece of ginger, grated
4 garlic cloves, crushed
³/₄ cup plain yogurt (page 280)
1 lb. spinach or amaranth leaves,
roughly chopped

SERVES 6

Amaranth is a green or red leafy vegetable used in India instead of spinach. It is interchangeable with spinach in all saag recipes.

PLACE a small frying pan over low heat and dry-roast the coriander seeds until aromatic. Remove them and dry-roast the cumin seeds. Grind the roasted seeds to a fine powder using a spice grinder or pestle and mortar.

HEAT the oil in a karhai or casserole over low heat and fry a few pieces of meat at a time until browned. Remove from the pan. Add more oil to the pan, if necessary, and fry the onions, cloves, cardamom pods, cinnamon stick, black peppercorns and bay leaves until the onions are lightly browned. Add the cumin and coriander, garam masala, turmeric and paprika and fry for 30 seconds. Add the meat, ginger, garlic, yogurt and 1³/₄ cups of water and bring to a boil. Reduce the heat to a simmer, cover and cook for 1¹/₂–2 hours, or until the meat is very tender. At this stage, most of the water should have evaporated. If it hasn't, remove the lid, increase the heat and fry until the moisture has evaporated. Season with salt to taste.

COOK the spinach briefly in a little simmering water until it is just wilted, then refresh in cold water. Drain thoroughly, then finely chop. Squeeze out any extra water by putting the spinach between two plates and pushing them together.

ADD the spinach to the lamb and cook for 3 minutes, or until the spinach and lamb are well mixed and any extra liquid has evaporated.

LAMB KEBAB

5 garlic cloves, roughly chopped
2 inch piece of ginger, roughly chopped
3 green chiles, roughly chopped
1 onion, roughly chopped
3 tablespoons plain yogurt (page 280)
3 tablespoons cilantro leaves
1/2 teaspoon ground black pepper
1 lb. ground lamb
red onion rings
lemon wedges

SERVES 4

COMBINE the garlic, ginger, chiles, onion, yogurt and cilantro leaves in a food processor to form a thick smooth paste. If you don't have a processor, chop the vegetables more finely and use a pestle and mortar. Add the pepper, season with salt, then mix in the ground lamb. If you are using a pestle and mortar, mix the lamb with the paste in a bowl. Divide the meat into 16 portions, approximately 2 tablespoons each. Shape each portion into an oval patty, cover and chill for 20 minutes.

HEAT the broiler to high. Using four metal skewers, thread four meatballs onto each. Broil for 7 minutes, or until brown on top. Turn over and brown the other side. Check that the meatballs are cooked. Serve with onion rings and lemon wedges.

DO PIAZA

DO PIAZA LITERALLY MEANS "ONIONS TWICE." THIS CAN BE INTERPRETED AS DOUBLE THE QUANTITY OF ONIONS AS FOR MEAT, OR ONIONS USED IN TWO DIFFERENT FORMS AS IN THIS VERSION.

DO PIAZA

1 1/2 teaspoons cumin seeds
2 1/2 teaspoons coriander seeds
4 garlic cloves, roughly chopped
3 inch piece of ginger, roughly chopped
1 lb. onions, finely chopped
3 tablespoons oil
2 lb. boneless leg of lamb, cut into 1 inch cubes
2 teaspoons garam masala (page 284)
1 teaspoon ground turmeric

SERVES 4

PLACE a small frying pan over low heat and dry-roast the cumin seeds until aromatic. Remove, then dry-roast the coriander seeds. Grind the roasted mixture to a fine powder using a spice grinder or pestle and mortar. In a food processor or with a knife, finely chop together the garlic, ginger and two-thirds of the onions.

HEAT the oil in a karhai or casserole and fry the remaining onions until golden brown. Add the lamb and cook until the meat is brown all over. Stir in the cumin and coriander, garam masala and turmeric. Add the onions, ginger and garlic mixture and 1 cup of water and bring slowly to a boil. Cover tightly, reduce the heat to a simmer and cook for 1 hour, or until the meat is very tender. If the liquid evaporates quickly, add 1/2 cup of hot water. When the meat is cooked, it should have a thick coating sauce. If the sauce is too thin, simmer for a few minutes with the lid off. Season with salt to taste.

DHANSAK

A FLAVORFUL PARSI DISH THAT IS SERVED AT SPECIAL OCCASIONS, THIS VERSION HAS EVOLVED FROM A LAVISH RECIPE THAT USED EVEN MORE TYPES OF DAL. THE COMBINATION OF VARIOUS TYPES OF DAL GIVES A VARIED TEXTURE BUT YOU CAN USE JUST MASOOR OR TOOR.

$1/2$ cup toor dal (yellow lentils)
1 tablespoon moong dal
1 tablespoon chickpeas
$1/4$ cup masoor dal
1 eggplant, unpeeled
1 cup pumpkin, unpeeled
3 cups amaranth or spinach leaves
2 tomatoes
2 green chiles
2 tablespoons ghee or oil
1 onion, finely chopped
3 garlic cloves, crushed
1 inch piece of ginger, grated
2 lb. boneless leg or shoulder
  of lamb, cut into 1 inch cubes
1 inch piece of cinnamon stick
5 cardamom pods, smashed
3 cloves
1 tablesoon ground coriander
1 teaspoon ground turmeric
1 teaspoon chili powder,
  or to taste
3 tablespoons lime juice

SERVES 6

SOAK the toor dal, moong dal and chickpeas in plenty of water for 2 hours. Drain well.

PUT the legumes in a saucepan, along with the masoor dal, add 4 cups of water, cover and bring to a boil. Uncover and simmer for 15 minutes, skimming off any impurities that form on the surface, and stirring occasionally to make sure all the lentils and the chickpeas are cooking at the same rate and are soft. Lightly mash all the soft legumes to the same texture.

COOK the eggplant and pumpkin in boiling water for 10–15 minutes, or until soft. Scoop out the pumpkin flesh and cut it into pieces. Peel the eggplant carefully (it may be very pulpy) and cut it into small pieces. Cut the amaranth or spinach into 2 inch pieces, halve the tomatoes and split the chiles lengthwise, removing any seeds.

HEAT the ghee or oil in a karhai or casserole and fry the onion, garlic and ginger for 5 minutes, or until lightly brown and softened. Add the lamb and brown for about 10 minutes, or until aromatic. Add the cinnamon, cardamom pods, cloves, coriander, turmeric and chili powder and fry for 5 minutes to allow the flavors to develop. Add $3/4$ cup of water, cover and simmer for 40 minutes, or until the lamb is tender.

ADD the mashed lentils and all the cooked and raw vegetables to the pan. Season with the lime juice and salt and pepper. Simmer for 15 minutes (if the sauce is too thick, add a little water). Stir well, then check the seasoning. The dhansak should be flavorful, aromatic, tart and spicy.

ALOO GOSHT

THIS MILD, SUBTLY FLAVORED NORTH INDIAN DISH COMBINES TENDER LAMB WITH CHUNKS OF POTATO. ADDING THE BONES, WITH THE MARROW STILL IN THEM, RESULTS IN A MUCH TASTIER GRAVY, WHILE STARCH FROM THE POTATOES HELPS TO THICKEN THE SAUCE.

3 lb. bone-in leg of lamb
3/4 lb. waxy potatoes
1 1/2 teaspoons coriander seeds
1 1/2 teaspoons cumin seeds
2 tablespoons oil
1 onion, chopped
2 Indian bay leaves (cassia leaves)
1/4 teaspoon ground turmeric
2 teaspoons garam masala
  (page 284)
14 oz. can diced tomatoes
3 green chiles, chopped
4 garlic cloves, crushed
1 inch piece of ginger, grated
1 tablespoon tomato paste

SERVES 6

TRIM away any excess fat from the lamb, remove the bone and cut the lamb into 1 inch cubes. Reserve the bones with their marrow.

CUT each potato into large chunks and put in a bowl of cold water.

PLACE a small frying pan over low heat and dry-roast the coriander seeds until aromatic. Remove them, then dry-roast the cumin seeds. Grind the roasted spices to a fine powder using a spice grinder or pestle and mortar.

HEAT the oil in a karhai or casserole over low heat. Add the onion and bay leaves and fry over low heat until lightly browned. Stir in the coriander and cumin mixture, turmeric and 1 teaspoon of garam masala. Add the tomatoes, chiles, garlic and ginger and fry until the oil separates out of the sauce. Stir in the tomato paste, then 1 cup of water. Add the lamb and bone and mix well. Bring to a boil, cover tightly, reduce the heat and simmer for 1 hour.

ADD the potato chunks to the pan and cook for another hour, occasionally shaking the pan to prevent the meat from sticking. If all the liquid has evaporated, add 1/2 cup of hot water. When the meat is cooked, the sauce should be fairly thick. Season with salt to taste.

REMOVE the bone before serving. Serve sprinkled with the remaining garam masala.

KOFTA IN TOMATO AND YOGURT SAUCE

EVERY NATION SEEMS TO HAVE A VERSION OF KOFTA, RANGING FROM MEATBALLS AND CROQUETTES TO RISSOLES AND DUMPLINGS. THIS RECIPE IS THE NORTH INDIAN WAY OF PREPARING THEM. THE RICH TOMATO AND YOGURT SAUCE IS PERFECT WHEN SERVED WITH NAAN BREAD.

KOFTA
1 onion
1 lb. ground lamb
1 inch piece of ginger, grated
3 garlic cloves, finely chopped
2 green chiles, seeded and
   finely chopped
1/2 teaspoon salt
1 egg

TOMATO AND YOGURT SAUCE
2 teaspoons coriander seeds
2 teaspoons cumin seeds
3 tablespoons oil
4 inch piece of cinnamon stick
6 cloves
6 cardamom pods
1 onion, finely chopped
1/2 teaspoon ground turmeric
1 teaspoon paprika
1 teaspoon garam masala
   (page 284)
1/2 teaspoon salt
7 oz. can diced tomatoes
1/2 cup plain yogurt (page 280)

cilantro leaves

SERVES 4

TO MAKE the kofta, grate the onion, put it in a strainer and use a spoon to press out as much of the liquid as possible. Put it in a bowl and combine with the lamb, ginger, garlic, green chiles, salt and the egg. Mix thoroughly, then divide into 20 equal portions and shape each into a ball. Cover with plastic wrap and refrigerate for 2 hours. Alternatively, the meatballs can be put in the freezer while the sauce is being prepared, making them sufficiently firm enough to stay in shape when they are added to the sauce.

TO MAKE the sauce, place a small frying pan over low heat and dry-roast the coriander seeds until aromatic. Remove, then dry-roast the cumin seeds. Grind the roasted mixture to a fine powder using a spice grinder or pestle and mortar.

HEAT the oil in a karhai or heavy-bottomed frying pan over low heat. Add the cinnamon stick, cloves, cardamom pods and onion and fry until the onion is golden. Add all the ground spices and the salt and fry for 30 seconds. Stir in the tomatoes, then remove from the heat and slowly stir in the yogurt. Return the pan to the heat, carefully add the chilled meatballs and bring to a boil. Simmer, uncovered, for 1 hour, over very low heat. It may be necessary to shake the pan from time to time to prevent the meatballs from sticking. If during cooking the sauce dries out, add 1/2 cup of water as required and continue to cook for the full hour. Remove any whole spices before serving and serve garnished with cilantro leaves.

Cardamom pods are harvested by hand. They grow on small stalks at the base of the plant.

Store whole spices in a special, lidded spice container so they are easily accessible.

Methi is sold in small bundles in Indian markets.

METHI GOSHT

IN INDIA, METHI IS THE NAME FOR FENUGREEK. IN NORTHERN INDIA, METHI LEAVES ARE OFTEN COMBINED WITH LAMB (GOSHT) AND SERVED AS A DELICACY. METHI PRODUCES A DISTINCTIVE AROMATIC FLAVOR IN THIS DISH. SERVE WITH INDIAN BREADS OR RICE.

2 onions, roughly chopped
4 garlic cloves, roughly chopped
3 inch piece of ginger, roughly
  chopped
3 green chiles (seed them for
  less heat)
1/2 cup oil
2 Indian bay leaves (cassia leaves)
2 lb. boneless lamb leg or shoulder,
  cut into 1 inch cubes
1 tablespoon ground cumin
2 tablespoons ground coriander
1/2 teaspoon garam masala
  (page 284)
1/2 teaspoon chili powder
2 teaspoons salt
1/2 teaspoon ground black pepper
4 bunches of fresh methi leaves,
  finely chopped (about 1/2 lb.)

SERVES 4

BLEND the onions, garlic, ginger and chiles together in a blender or food processor until finely chopped. If you don't have a blender, finely chop them together with a knife or crush them in a pestle and mortar.

HEAT the oil in a karhai or large casserole over medium heat and add the chopped mixture and the bay leaves. Cook for 3 minutes, or until golden and just starting to catch on the bottom of the pan. Add the cubed lamb in batches, stirring for 20 minutes, until it is all browned. The juices of the meat will start to run clear and the oil will separate out. You need to keep stirring or the meat will catch on the bottom of the pan.

ADD all the spices, and the salt and pepper, and fry for 3 minutes, or until all pieces of the lamb are thoroughly coated. Add 3/4 cup of water, bring to a boil, then reduce the heat, cover and simmer for 45 minutes, adding a little more water if necessary. The sauce should tend towards dry rather than runny. Gently stir in the methi and cook for another 15 minutes, or until the oil separates from the lamb and the sauce has turned a rich olive green.

MEMSAHIB'S LAMB RAAN

THIS DISH LOOKS VERY IMPRESSIVE EVEN THOUGH IT CAN BE MADE WITHOUT MUCH FUSS. IT IS EXCELLENT FOR DINNER OR A SPECIAL LUNCH, BUT IT DOES NEED TO BE MARINATED OVERNIGHT SO THE FLAVORS CAN PERMEATE THE LAMB. SERVE IT WITH A COUPLE OF VEGETABLE DISHES AND SOME RICE.

3¹/₂ lb. leg of lamb

MARINADE
1 teaspoon cardamom seeds
1 onion, roughly chopped
4 garlic cloves, roughly chopped
1 inch piece of ginger, roughly
    chopped
3 green chiles, seeded
2 teaspoons ground cumin
¹/₂ teaspoon ground cloves
1¹/₂ tablespoons lemon juice
1 cup plain yogurt (page 280)

ALMOND COATING
3 tablespoons blanched almonds
1 tablespoon jaggery or
    light brown sugar
¹/₂ cup plain yogurt (page 280)
¹/₂ teaspoon red food coloring
    (optional)

cilantro leaves (optional)

SERVES 6

TRIM the excess fat from the lamb and pierce the meat all over with a sharp skewer so that the marinade will penetrate.

TO MAKE the marinade, grind the cardamom seeds to a fine powder using a spice grinder or pestle and mortar. Chop the onion, garlic and ginger to a paste with the green chiles in a blender or food processor. If you don't have a processor, finely chop them with a knife, then grind to a paste in a pestle and mortar. Mix in the ground cardamom seeds, cumin and cloves. Add the lemon juice and yogurt and mix well.

COAT the lamb thickly all over, using half the marinade. Cover with plastic wrap and marinate in the fridge overnight. Cover the remaining marinade and refrigerate it.

TO MAKE the almond coating, preheat the oven to 375°F. Finely chop the almonds in a food processor or with a knife. Mix the reserved marinade with the ground almonds, jaggery, yogurt and food coloring, if using. Uncover the lamb and coat it all over with the mixture, especially on the top and sides. Transfer the lamb to a shallow roasting pan and cover loosely with oiled aluminium foil. Bake for 1 hour, then remove the foil and bake for another 30 minutes, or until the lamb is cooked and the coating set and browned. Test the meat nearest to the bone to see whether it is cooked—a skewer should emerge very hot.

CAREFULLY press on any yogurt and almond coating that has dropped off during cooking, so that the finished product looks neat.

CARVE the meat at the table for full effect. Garnish with cilantro if you like. On top of each serving place a little of the almond coating.

The High Court in Kolkata (Calcutta), built in 1872 and copied from the Staadhaus in Ypres, Belgium.

MOGHUL LAMB WITH TURNIPS

THIS DISH FROM THE PUNJAB REGION WOULD HAVE BEEN SERVED IN THE ROYAL PALACES OF THE MOGHULS WHEN THEY WERE THE RULERS OF INDIA. EVEN TODAY, THIS RECIPE IS USUALLY RESERVED FOR SPECIAL OCCASIONS AND SERVED WITH PUNJABI BREADS SUCH AS CHAPATIS OR NAAN.

2 onions, roughly chopped
4 garlic cloves, roughly chopped
2 inch piece of ginger, roughly
  chopped
2 green chiles
2/3 cup oil
2 Indian bay leaves (cassia leaves)
2 lb. boneless lamb leg or shoulder,
  cut into 1 inch cubes
pinch of asafoetida
1 teaspoon chili powder
2 tablespoons ground coriander
2 tablespoons ground cumin
1/4 teaspoon ground turmeric
1/2 teaspoon garam masala
  (page 284)
1 tablespoon tomato paste
2 tablespoons plain yogurt
  (page 280)
1 tablespoon salt
1 teaspoon ground black pepper
1 lb. baby turnips, large
  ones halved

SERVES 4

PUT the onions, garlic, ginger and chiles in a food processor and chop them to form a paste. If you don't have a food processor, chop everything finely or grind them in a pestle and mortar.

HEAT the oil in a karhai or casserole and add the onion mixture with the bay leaves. Fry over high heat for 5 minutes, then reduce the heat to medium and fry for another 2 minutes. Don't let the onions turn more than golden brown. Add the meat and stir until all the pieces are thoroughly coated with the onion mixture. Fry for 15 minutes, stirring constantly. This is a very important part of the cooking process as the longer you fry the meat, the more flavor it will absorb. It is ready when the oil starts to separate out from the meat.

ADD the asafoetida, chili powder, cilantro, cumin, turmeric and garam masala and stir in well. Cook for 1–2 minutes, then add the tomato paste and yogurt. Fry for another minute and add the salt and pepper. Pour in 2 cups of water a little at a time, stirring into the mixture after each addition. This will ensure that the dish retains the heat throughout and will be constantly bubbling until you have a rich, thick sauce. Cover the pan and simmer for 30 minutes.

ADD the turnips to the pan and continue simmering for another 45 minutes, or until both the lamb and turnips have completely softened and the oil has separated from the sauce and turned bright orange.

Columns at Delhi's Jama Masjid, built in the 17th century.

LAMB KALIA

IN INDIA, MUTTON IS USED MORE OFTEN THAN LAMB AND BECAUSE IT CAN BE TOUGH IT REQUIRES LONG HOURS OF TENDERIZING. IN THIS RECIPE, LAMB HAS BEEN USED INSTEAD, SO THE MARINATING TIME IS NOT AS LONG. THE GINGER AND THE YOGURT BOTH ACT AS TENDERIZERS.

2 1/2 teaspoons cumin seeds
1/2 cup plain yogurt (page 280)
2 teaspoons clear vinegar
1 teaspoon salt
1 tablespoon ginger juice
  (page 280)
3 teaspoons chili powder
1 teaspoon ground turmeric
2 lb. lamb leg, cut into 1 inch cubes
2 potatoes, cut into 1 inch cubes
oil for deep-frying
1 inch piece of cinnamon stick
2 cardamom pods, crushed
4 garlic cloves, crushed
1/2 teaspoon sugar
4 onions, sliced
2 Indian bay leaves (cassia leaves)
1 tablespoon tomato paste

SERVES 6

PLACE a small frying pan over low heat and dry-roast 2 teaspoons of the cumin seeds until aromatic. Grind the roasted cumin seeds to a fine powder using a spice grinder or pestle and mortar.

COMBINE the ground cumin with the yogurt, vinegar, salt, ginger juice, chili powder and 1/2 teaspoon of the turmeric in a large bowl. Add the lamb and coat well. Cover and marinate for at least 2 hours in the fridge.

COAT the potatoes with the remaining 1/2 teaspoon of turmeric. Fill a karhai or casserole a third full with oil and heat to 350°F (a cube of bread will brown in 15 seconds). Fry the potato cubes until they are golden brown, then remove and drain on paper towels. Let the oil cool a little, then pour out all but 2 tablespoons.

PLACE the pan back over medium heat and fry the remaining cumin seeds until they start to pop. Add the cinnamon stick, cardamom pods, garlic, sugar and onions and fry until golden.

ADD the meat to the pan and fry until the meat is browned (you may need to add a bit more of the oil). Add the bay leaves, tomato paste and 1 cup of water and reduce the heat. Cover and simmer for 1 hour, or until the lamb is tender. If the sauce is still a little thin when the lamb is cooked, simmer with the lid off until it thickens. Toss the potatoes through the meat before serving.

Removing the seeds from the chiles will make the dish slightly milder. Gently stir the spices to evenly roast them.

MANGALOREAN PORK BAFATH

MANGALOREAN FOOD IS SOUTH INDIAN WITH MANY OTHER INFLUENCES, INCLUDING PORTUGUESE. THIS RECIPE IS MILDLY SWEET BECAUSE OF THE KASHMIRI CHILES. THE PORK HAS OILS THAT ALMOST ROAST THE SPICES WITHIN THE MEAT WITH A BEAUTIFUL, AROMATIC RESULT.

20 red Kashmiri chiles, seeded
2 teaspoons coriander seeds
1 teaspoon cumin seeds
1/2 teaspoon ground turmeric
10 black peppercorns
2 tablespoons tamarind paste
  (page 280)
3 lb. boneless pork leg or shoulder,
  cut into 1 inch cubes
1 tablespoon oil
2 onions, cut into 1 inch pieces
3/4 inch piece of ginger, finely
  chopped
6 green chiles, slit lengthwise
  into halves
8 cloves
3/4 inch piece of cinnamon stick,
  pounded roughly
1 tablespoon dark vinegar
3 garlic cloves, finely chopped
1 green chile, extra, seeded, finely
  sliced lengthwise

SERVES 6

PLACE a small frying pan over low heat and dry-roast the red chiles, coriander seeds, cumin seeds, ground turmeric and peppercorns until aromatic. Grind the roasted mixture to a fine powder using a spice grinder or pestle and mortar.

MIX all the roasted, ground ingredients with the tamarind and meat. Cover and marinate in the fridge for 2 hours.

HEAT the oil in a karhai or casserole over high heat, add the meat mixture in batches and brown all over. Return all the meat to the pan, then add the onions, ginger, chiles, cloves and cinnamon. Stir thoroughly to mix with the pork. Reduce the heat to low and cook for about 20 minutes, until the meat juices appear and mix with the spice, creating a thick sauce.

ADD the vinegar, garlic and 3/4 cup of water and cook for 1–1 1/4 hours, until the pork is very tender. Season with salt to taste. Cook until the oil separates from the spice mixture, which indicates the meat is ready. You can skim off the oil or blot it from the surface with paper towels if you prefer. Garnish with the extra green chile before serving.

The Indian version of the pestle and mortar. The base is the *sil* and the crushing stone the *nora*.

PORK WITH PEPPERS AND POTATOES

THIS IS A FAVORITE IN SIMLA IN THE NORTH OF INDIA. THE "POTATO OF THE MOUNTAIN" AND THE

GREEN PEPPER ARE COOKED WITH PORK. THIS DISH IS IDEAL SERVED WITH ANY INDIAN BREADS SUCH

AS PARATHAS, PURIS OR CHAPATIS.

The spice market in Delhi houses offices and dwellings on its upper floors.

$^1/_2$ cup oil

1 large onion, chopped

4 garlic cloves, crushed

3 inch piece of ginger, chopped

2 Indian bay leaves (cassia leaves)

1$^1/_4$ lb. pork sparerib chops,
  bones removed, meat cut
  into 1 inch cubes

pinch of asafoetida

1 teaspoon chili powder

$^1/_2$ teaspoon ground turmeric

1$^1/_2$ tablespoons ground cumin

1$^1/_2$ tablespoons ground coriander

$^1/_2$ teaspoon garam masala
  (page 284)

1$^1/_2$ tablespoons lemon juice

4 dried chiles

1 teaspoon kalonji (nigella seeds)

1 teaspoon yellow mustard seeds

2 tomatoes, finely chopped

4 green chiles

2 teaspoons paprika

2 red peppers, cut into
  1 inch pieces

2 green peppers, cut into
  1 inch pieces

1 tablespoon salt

1 teaspoon ground black pepper

1 lb. potatoes, cut into
  1 inch cubes

10 curry leaves

1 teaspoon garam masala
  (page 284)

SERVES 6

HEAT $^1/_2$ cup of the oil in a karhai or casserole over medium heat. Add half of each of the onion, garlic and ginger, along with the bay leaves and fry for 2 minutes, until the onion is soft. Increase the heat to high, add the meat and asafoetida and fry for 2 minutes, stirring until all the meat is brown. Reduce the heat to medium and cook for 10 minutes. Remove from the heat, lift out the meat with a spatula and place in a large bowl.

ADD the chili powder, turmeric, 1$^1/_4$ tablespoons cumin, 2 teaspoons coriander and the garam masala to the meat, stirring in while the meat is still warm. Stir in the lemon juice.

HEAT the remaining oil in the same pan over medium heat and fry the remaining onion, garlic and ginger for a few minutes until the onion is soft. Add the dried chiles, kalonji, yellow mustard seeds and the remaining coriander and cumin. Fry for 2 minutes, or until the seeds start to pop. Add the chopped tomatoes and fry for 1 minute. Reduce the heat to simmering and cook for 5 minutes, or until the liquid from the tomatoes has reduced.

STIR in the green chiles and the paprika. Add the meat and stir over medium heat for 2 minutes, or until all the sauce has been absorbed by the meat. Add the red and green peppers, then reduce the heat to simmering and cover the pan. The peppers will release their own water so no extra water is necessary. Cook for 10 minutes, then add the salt, pepper and cubed potatoes. Add $^1/_2$ cup of water, cover and simmer for 1 hour, stirring occasionally. Add the curry leaves and cook for another 15 minutes. The meat and potatoes should be very tender, but if not, cook for another 15 minutes. Add the garam masala and season with salt to taste.

Fenugreek is a spice used to impart a 'curry' flavor.

PORK VINDALOO

VINDALOO IS NOTORIOUS FOR BEING HOT AND SPICY. THE NAME IS PORTUGUESE FOR "VINEGAR AND GARLIC." VINDALOO WAS INVENTED BY THE PORTUGUESE IN GOA. THE VINEGAR IS MADE FROM COCONUT (CLEAR) AND MOLASSES (DARK) BUT WHITE AND BALSAMIC CAN BE USED INSTEAD.

2 lb. bone-in leg of pork
6 cardamom pods
1 teaspoon black peppercorns
4 dried chiles
1 teaspoon cloves
4 inch piece of cinnamon stick, roughly broken
1 teaspoon cumin seeds
1/2 teaspoon ground turmeric
1/2 teaspoon coriander seeds
1/4 teaspoon fenugreek seeds
4 tablespoons clear vinegar
1 tablespoon dark vinegar
4 tablespoons oil
2 onions, finely sliced
10 garlic cloves, finely sliced
2 inch piece of ginger, cut into matchsticks
3 ripe tomatoes, roughly chopped
4 green chiles, chopped
1 teaspoon jaggery or light brown sugar

SERVES 4

TRIM any excess fat from the pork, remove the bone and cut the pork into 1 inch cubes. Reserve the bone.

SPLIT open the cardamom pods and remove the seeds. Finely grind the cardamom seeds, peppercorns, dried chiles, cloves, cinnamon stick, cumin seeds, turmeric, coriander seeds and fenugreek seeds in a spice grinder or pestle and mortar.

IN a large bowl, mix the ground spices together with the vinegars. Add the pork and mix thoroughly to coat well. Cover and marinate in the fridge for 3 hours.

HEAT the oil in a karhai or casserole over low heat and fry the onions until lightly browned. Add the garlic, ginger, tomatoes and chiles and stir well. Add the pork, increase the heat to high and fry for 3–5 minutes, or until browned. Add 1 cup of water and any of the marinade liquid left in the bowl, reduce the heat and bring slowly back to the boil. Add the jaggery and the pork bone. Cover tightly and simmer for 1 1/2 hours, stirring occasionally until the meat is very tender. Discard the bone. Season with salt to taste.

FRIED BEEF KERALA

oil for deep-frying
1 potato, cut into small cubes
1 lb. beef rump steak, thinly sliced
3 garlic cloves, crushed
1 teaspoon ground black pepper
1 tablespoon ginger juice (page 280)
2 tablespoons oil, extra
2 onions, sliced in rings
1/4 cup beef stock
2 tablespoons tomato paste
1/2 tablespoon soy sauce
1 teaspoon chili powder
3 tablespoons lemon juice
3 tomatoes, chopped
1/3 cup fresh or frozen peas
cilantro leaves (optional)

SERVES 4

FILL a deep, heavy-bottomed saucepan a third full with oil and heat to 350°F (a cube of bread will brown in 15 seconds). Deep-fry the potato cubes until golden brown. Drain on paper towels.

PUT the steak in a bowl, add the garlic, pepper and ginger juice and toss well. Heat the oil and fry the beef quickly in batches over high heat. Keep each batch warm as you remove it. Reduce the heat, fry the onions until golden, then remove.

PUT the stock, tomato paste, soy sauce, chili powder and lemon juice in the saucepan and cook over medium heat until reduced. Add the fried onions, cook for 3 minutes, add the chopped tomatoes and the peas, then stir well and cook for 1 minute. Add the beef and potato and toss well until heated through. Garnish with cilantro leaves if you like.

Rice growing in paddy fields near Kochi (Cochin), Kerala.

GOAN BEEF CURRY

8 cardamom pods
1 teaspoon fennel seeds
8 cloves
4 inch piece of cinnamon stick
1/2 teaspoon fenugreek seeds
1/2 teaspoon ground black pepper
3 teaspoons coriander seeds
3 teaspoons cumin seeds
1/2 cup oil
2 onions, finely chopped
6 garlic cloves, finely chopped
4 inch piece of ginger, grated
2 lb. braising or stewing steak,
    cut into 1 inch cubes
1/2 teaspoon ground turmeric
2 teaspoons chili powder
1/2 cup creamed coconut, dissolved
    in 1 1/4 cups water, or 1 1/4 cups
    coconut milk (page 283)

SERVES 6

REMOVE the seeds from the cardamom pods and grind them in a spice grinder or pestle and mortar with the fennel seeds, cloves, cinnamon stick, fenugreek seeds, black pepper and the coriander and cumin seeds, until they form a fine powder.

HEAT the oil in a karhai, heavy-bottomed frying pan or casserole over medium heat and fry the onions, garlic and ginger until lightly browned. Add the meat and fry until brown all over. Add all the spices and fry for 1 minute. Add the creamed coconut and bring slowly to a boil. Cover, reduce the heat and simmer for 1 hour, or until the meat is tender.

IF the liquid evaporates during cooking, add about 3/4 cup of boiling water and stir to make a thick sauce. If the sauce is still too thin at the end of the cooking time, simmer with the lid off until it evaporates. Season with salt to taste.

GOAN BEEF CURRY

VEGETABLES

Snake gourds are exceptionally long vegetables which grow hanging down from raised vines.

SNAKE GOURDS
WITH YOGURT

ALOO GOBI

3 tablespoons oil
1/2 teaspoon black mustard seeds
1/2 onion, finely chopped
1/2 lb. potatoes, cut into cubes
1/4 teaspoon ground turmeric
1 teaspoon ground cumin
1 teaspoon ground coriander
1 1/2 teaspoons garam masala
   (page 284)
4 ripe tomatoes, chopped
1 large cauliflower, cut into florets
3/4 inch piece of ginger
1 teaspoon sugar

SERVES 4

HEAT the oil in a karhai or deep, heavy-bottomed frying pan over low heat. Add the mustard seeds, cover the pan and wait for the seeds to pop. Add the onion and potatoes and fry until lightly browned.

ADD the turmeric, cumin, coriander and garam masala to the pan and fry for a couple of seconds. Add the tomatoes and stir until the spices are well mixed. Add the cauliflower florets and stir until well mixed. Stir in the ginger, sugar and 1/2 cup of water, increase the heat to medium and bring to a boil. Reduce the heat, cover and simmer for 15 minutes, or until the vegetables are tender. Season with salt to taste.

UNCOVER the pan and if the sauce is too runny, simmer it for another 1–2 minutes before serving.

SNAKE GOURDS WITH YOGURT

THIS IS A VERSATILE RECIPE THAT CAN BE MADE USING SNAKE GOURD, BITTER MELON OR EGGPLANT. SNAKE GOURDS ARE LONG AND THIN, SOMETIMES CURLY, VEGETABLES THAT GROW ON VINES. GROWERS SOMETIMES TIE A WEIGHT TO THE VEGETABLE TO STRAIGHTEN IT AS IT GROWS.

1/2 lb. snake gourds
1 teaspoon ground turmeric
1 tablespoon oil
1/2 teaspoon black mustard seeds
1/2 teaspoon whole urad dal
2 dried chiles, cut in half
4 stalks of curry leaves
1 1/2 red onions, finely chopped
1 cup plain yogurt (page 280)

SERVES 4

PEEL the snake gourds, slice in half horizontally and then slice diagonally into pieces about 1/2 inch thick. Add the turmeric and a pinch of salt and rub into the pieces of gourd. Put the gourd in a strainer to allow any liquid to drain off.

HEAT the oil in a karhai or heavy-based frying pan over low heat. Add the mustard and urad dal and when the mustard seeds pop, add the chiles and curry leaves and a third of the onion. Cook until the onions are browned and softened. Add the snake gourds and toss over medium heat for 10 minutes, or until the mixture looks dry and the gourds are tender. Remove from the heat.

COMBINE the yogurt and the remaining onions in a bowl and stir well. Fold the fried snake gourds into the yogurt just before serving and season with salt to taste.

SPICY EGGPLANT

THIS IS A WONDERFUL DISH IN WHICH EGGPLANT IS COOKED WITH PICKLING STYLE SPICES. THE
EGGPLANT CAN BE SERVED AS PART OF AN INDIAN FEAST OR AS A SPICY ACCOMPANIMENT. IT IS ALSO
GOOD AS A VEGETARIAN MAIN DISH WITH RICE AND SOME YOGURT.

Drain the fried eggplant to get rid
of any excess oil.

1³/₄ lb. eggplant, cut into wedges
   1¹/₂–2 inches long
³/₄ lb. ripe tomatoes or 13 oz. can
   diced tomatoes
1 inch piece of ginger, grated
6 garlic cloves, crushed
1¹/₄ cups oil
1 teaspoon fennel seeds
¹/₂ teaspoon kalonji (nigella seeds)
1 tablespoon ground coriander
¹/₄ teaspoon ground turmeric
¹/₂ teaspoon cayenne pepper
1 teaspoon salt

SERVES 6

PUT the eggplant pieces in a colander, sprinkle
them with salt and leave them for 30 minutes to
allow any bitter juices to run out. Rinse, squeeze
out any excess water, then pat dry with paper
towels. If using fresh tomatoes, score a cross in
the top of each and plunge into boiling water for
20 seconds. Drain and peel away from the cross.
Roughly chop the tomatoes, discarding the cores
and seeds and reserving any juices.

PUREE the ginger and garlic with a third of the
tomatoes in a blender or food processor. If you
don't have a blender, finely chop the tomatoes
and mix with the ginger and garlic.

HEAT ¹/₂ cup of the oil in a large, deep, heavy-
bottomed frying pan and when hot, add as many
eggplant pieces as you can fit in a single layer.
Cook over medium heat until brown on both
sides, then transfer to a strainer over a bowl so
that the excess oil can drain off. Add the
remaining oil to the pan as needed and cook the
rest of the eggplant in batches.

REHEAT the oil that's left in the pan and add the
fennel seeds and kalonji. Cover and allow to pop
for a few seconds. Add the tomato and ginger
mixture and the remaining ingredients, except the
eggplant. Cook, stirring regularly for 5–6 minutes,
until the mixture becomes thick and fairly smooth
(be careful as it may spit at you). Carefully add the
cooked eggplant so the pieces stay whole, cover
the pan and cook gently for 10 minutes.

STORE the eggplant in the sauce in the fridge.
Pour off any excess oil before serving. The
eggplant can either be served cold or gently
warmed through.

BHINDI MASALA

BHINDI, WHICH IS MORE COMMONLY KNOWN AS OKRA OR LADIES' FINGERS, IS FOUND IN ABUNDANCE THROUGHOUT INDIA. WHEN BUYING BHINDI, BE CAREFUL TO ENSURE THAT THEY ARE A BRIGHT GREEN COLOR, LOOK CRISP AND FIRM, AND THAT THEY YIELD SLIGHTLY AT THE NARROW END.

1 lb. okra, about 2 inches long
3 green chiles
3 tablespoons oil
1 teaspoon black mustard seeds
1 red onion, finely chopped
1 teaspoon ground cumin
1 teaspoon ground coriander
2 teaspoons garam masala
  (page 284)
1 teaspoon ground turmeric
4 garlic cloves, finely chopped

SERVES 4

WASH the okra and pat dry with paper towels. Trim the ends. Ignore any sticky, glutinous liquid that appears because this will disappear as the okra cooks.

CUT the chiles in half lengthwise, leaving them attached at the stems, and scrape out any seeds. Heat the oil in a karhai or deep, heavy-bottomed frying pan, add the mustard seeds and onion and cook until the seeds pop and the onion is light brown. Add the cumin, coriander, garam masala and turmeric and cook until the popping stops.

ADD the garlic, okra and chiles to the pan, fry for 5 minutes, stir and cook for 2 minutes. Add 1/4 cup of water, 1 tablespoon at a time, and stir to make a sauce. Season with salt to taste. Simmer for 15 minutes, until the okra is cooked through and the sauce is thick and dry.

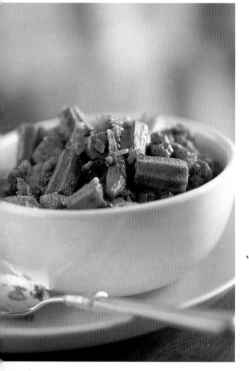

BHINDI BHAJI

BHINDI BHAJI

1 lb. okra
2 tablespoons oil
1 small onion, finely chopped
1/2 teaspoon ground cumin
1/2 teaspoon ground coriander
1/2 teaspoon chili powder (optional)
1/4 teaspoon ground turmeric
5 oz. canned, diced tomatoes

SERVES 4

WASH the okra and pat dry with paper towels. Trim the ends and cut into 1 inch pieces. Ignore any sticky, glutinous liquid that appears because this will disappear as the okra cooks.

HEAT the oil in a karhai or deep, heavy-bottomed frying pan over medium heat and fry the onion until lightly browned. Add the spices and tomatoes and fry for 1 minute until well mixed, squashing the tomatoes to break them up.

ADD the okra and stir until well coated. Bring to a boil, cover and simmer for 5–8 minutes, until the okra is cooked through and no longer slimy. If there is any excess liquid, simmer, uncovered, until the liquid evaporates. Season with salt to taste.

STUFFED PEPPERS

STUFFING VEGETABLES IS A COOKING METHOD USED FOR SPECIAL OCCASIONS. THESE STUFFED PEPPERS ARE SIMMERED IN A COCONUT-FLAVORED SAUCE. THE PEPPERS SHOULD BE THE SMALL VARIETY USUALLY USED IN INDIA, RATHER THAN LARGE ONES. RED OR YELLOW ONES CAN BE USED.

Make sure that the stuffing fills the peppers adequately, but don't pack it in too firmly or it may spill out as it bakes.

1 lb. potatoes, quartered
6 small green peppers
2 tablespoons oil
2 onions, finely chopped
2 teaspoons ground cumin
2 teaspoons ground coriander
1/2 teaspoon ground turmeric
1/2 teaspoon chili powder

SAUCE
1/2 onion, finely chopped
6 cloves
6 cardamom pods
2 garlic cloves, finely chopped
3/4 inch piece of ginger, finely chopped
1 cinnamon stick
1 teaspoon ground coriander
1 teaspoon ground cumin
1/4 teaspoon ground turmeric
1/2 teaspoon chili powder
1/4 cup creamed coconut, mixed with 1 cup water, or
1 cup coconut cream (page 283)

SERVES 6

COOK the potatoes in a saucepan of simmering water for 15 minutes, or until tender, then drain and cut into small cubes. Bring a large saucepan of water to a boil, add the peppers and blanch for 5 minutes. Refresh the peppers in cold water, cut round the stems and remove both stems and seeds. Drain well upside down.

HEAT the oil in a small frying pan and cook the onions over medium heat until soft but not browned. Add the cumin, coriander, turmeric and chili powder and mix thoroughly. Mix in the potatoes and season with salt to taste. Remove from the heat and leave until cool. Divide into six portions and fill each pepper.

TO MAKE the sauce, combine all the sauce ingredients in a deep, heavy-bottomed frying pan and bring slowly to a boil. Reduce the heat to low, cover and simmer for 20 minutes. Season with salt to taste. Add the stuffed peppers to the pan, arranging them so that they stand upright in a single layer, and cook for another 5 minutes, or until the sauce is thick. Serve the peppers with a little sauce spooned over the top.

SHEBU BHAJI

DILL IS A HERB THAT CAN BE USED IN ABUNDANCE, AS IT IS IN THIS DISH, WITHOUT BEING OVERPOWERING. IT HAS A MILD BUT VERY DISTINCTIVE FLAVOR. INDIAN DILL IS SIMILAR TO EUROPEAN DILL AND THEY ARE INTERCHANGEABLE IN THIS RECIPE.

1/2 lb. potatoes
3 cups dill
2 tablespoons oil
2 garlic cloves, chopped
1/4 teaspoon ground turmeric
1 teaspoon black mustard seeds
pinch of asafoetida
1 dried chile

SERVES 2

CUT the potatoes into 1 inch cubes and cook in a saucepan of simmering water for 15 minutes or until just tender. Drain well.

WASH the dill in several changes of water and trim off the tough stems. Roughly chop the dill.

HEAT the oil in a heavy-bottomed saucepan, add the garlic and fry for 30 seconds over low heat. Add the turmeric, mustard seeds, asafoetida and the whole chile, cover and briefly allow the seeds to pop. Stir in the potatoes until well mixed. Add the dill, cover and cook over low heat for 5 minutes. The dill contains sufficient moisture to cook without the addition of any water. Season with salt to taste.

MOOLI BHAJI

THE ASIAN RADISH, OR MOOLI AS IT IS ALSO KNOWN, IS MUCH MILDER IN FLAVOR THAN ITS WESTERN COUNTERPART. IT LOOKS LIKE A HUGE, WHITE CARROT AND HAS A CRISP, JUICY FLESH. BHAJI IS THE NAME GIVEN TO MANY VEGETABLE DISHES AND LOOSELY IT MEANS FRIED VEGETABLES.

1 lb. mooli
1/3 cup grated coconut (page 283)
2 tablespoons oil
1/4 teaspoon black mustard seeds
1 onion, chopped
1/4 teaspoon ground turmeric
pinch of asafoetida
1 green chile, finely chopped

SERVES 4

CUT the mooli into batons. Heat a frying pan over low heat and dry-roast the coconut, stirring constantly until it browns lightly.

HEAT the oil in a karhai or heavy-bottomed saucepan over low heat. Add the mustard seeds, cover and allow to pop briefly. Add the onion and cook until lightly browned. Stir in the turmeric, asafoetida, chile and the mooli until well mixed. Add 1/2 cup of water and simmer for 5–7 minutes, until the mooli is cooked through and tender. Season with salt to taste. Garnish with coconut.

MOOLI BHAJI

SPICED BANANA FLOWER

ALL PARTS OF THE BANANA PLANT ARE USED IN DIFFERENT WAYS: THE LEAVES SERVE AS AN AROMATIC FOOD WRAPPER AND AS A "PLATE" FOR INDIAN MEALS; THE FRUIT, FLOWER, AND TENDER INNER RINGS OF THE STEM ARE EATEN. WEAR PLASTIC GLOVES TO STOP THE SAP STAINING YOUR HANDS.

1 banana flower
1/2 lemon
1/2 lb. shrimp
1/3 cup grated coconut (page 283)
1 tablespoon oil
1/2 cup lime juice
1 red chile, finely chopped
2 tablespoons jaggery or
 light brown sugar
1 tablespoon grated lime zest,
 or lime leaves
mint leaves

SERVES 4

PEEL off one leaf at a time from the banana flower. Remove the yellow, stick-like immature bananas and discard both them and the leaves until you reach the white inner core. Chop off the top end and discard it. Chop what is left into quarters and soak it in a bowl of water with 1 teaspoon salt for 1 hour. Drain the banana flower, transfer to a saucepan, cover with fresh water and add the juice from the half lemon. Bring to a boil and cook for 15–20 minutes, or until soft. The banana flower will darken in color as it cooks. Drain and slice into julienne strips. Peel and devein the shrimp and cut each in half.

PLACE a heavy-bottomed frying pan over low heat and dry-roast the coconut, stirring constantly until the coconut is golden brown. Finely grind in a pestle and mortar or in a spice grinder.

HEAT the oil in the frying pan and fry the shrimp until they are pink and cooked through. Mix the shrimp with the lime juice, chile, jaggery and lime zest. Season with salt to taste, then allow to cool.

JUST before serving, add the banana hearts and coconut to the shrimp and toss well. Serve cold, garnished with the mint leaves.

Peel off the leaves and immature bananas until you reach the core, then chop off the end. Soak the quarters of core in salted water.

CABBAGE WITH SPLIT PEAS

THE COMBINATION OF SPLIT PEAS AND CABBAGE GIVES THIS DISH AN UNUSUAL TEXTURE. THE MUSTARD SEEDS CRACKLE WHEN FRIED AND DEVELOP A NUTTY SWEETNESS IN THE PROCESS. THE SPLIT PEAS ARE SOAKED WELL IN ADVANCE TO SOFTEN THEM AND REDUCE THE COOKING TIME.

2/3 cup split peas
3 tablespoons oil
1/4 teaspoon black mustard seeds
2 teaspoons cumin seeds
8 curry leaves
2 dried chiles
pinch of asafoetida
1/4 teaspoon ground turmeric
1 lb. green cabbage, shredded
cilantro leaves (optional)

SERVES 4

SOAK the split peas in 3 cups of boiling water for 2 hours. Drain thoroughly.

HEAT the oil in a karhai or deep, heavy-bottomed frying pan over low heat. Add the mustard and cumin seeds, cover and allow to pop briefly. Add the curry leaves, dried chiles and split peas and fry for 5 minutes, stirring often. Add the asafoetida, turmeric and cabbage and fry over low heat until the cabbage is cooked through and tender. Season with salt to taste. Serve garnished with cilantro leaves if you wish.

PUNJABI CABBAGE

ONE OF NORTHERN INDIA'S FAVORITE VEGETABLE DISHES, SERVED WITH OTHER VEGETARIAN OR MAIN MEAT DISHES, AND OF COURSE BREADS SUCH AS PARATHAS, PHULKAS OR CHAPATIS. IT IS AN EXCELLENT DISH TO SERVE WITH CHICKEN OR A GROUND BEEF CURRY SUCH AS KHEEMA MATAR.

PUNJABI CABBAGE

1/2 onion, roughly chopped
1 garlic clove, roughly chopped
1 inch piece of ginger, chopped
2 green chiles, seeded and chopped
4 tablespoons oil
1 teaspoon cumin seeds
1 teaspoon ground turmeric
1 lb. green cabbage, finely
   shredded
1 teaspoon salt
1/2 teaspoon ground black pepper
2 teaspoons ground cumin
1 teaspoon ground coriander
1/4 teaspoon chili powder
1 tablespoon unsalted butter

SERVES 4

PUT the onion, garlic, ginger and chiles in a food processor and chop until finely chopped but not a paste, or chop together with a knife.

HEAT the oil in a karhai or heavy-bottomed frying pan over low heat and fry the onion mixture until softened but not browned. Add the cumin seeds and turmeric to the pan and stir for 1 minute. Mix in the cabbage, stirring thoroughly until all the leaves are coated in the yellow paste. Add the salt, pepper, ground cumin, coriander and chili powder. Stir to coat the cabbage, then cook for 10 minutes with the pan partially covered, stirring occasionally until the cabbage is soft. If the cabbage becomes too dry and starts sticking to the pan, add 1–2 tablespoons water. Stir in the butter and season with salt to taste.

MATAR PANEER

IN THE NORTH OF INDIA, DAIRY PRODUCTS SUCH AS PANEER ARE SERVED REGULARLY. THIS VERSION OF MATAR PANEER IS DRY BUT IT COMES IN VARIOUS GUISES. IF YOU DON'T WANT TO MAKE YOUR OWN PANEER, YOU CAN OFTEN BUY IT FROM INDIAN FOOD SHOPS OR SUPERMARKETS.

1/2 lb. or 1/2 quantity paneer
  (page 279)
2 tablespoons ghee
1/3 cup onion, chopped
1 1/3 cups fresh or frozen peas
1/2 teaspoon sugar
2 inch piece of ginger, grated
2–3 green chiles, finely chopped
1 scallion, finely chopped
1/2 teaspoon garam masala
  (page 284)
1 tablespoon chopped cilantro
  leaves

SERVES 4

CUT the paneer into 3/4 inch cubes. Heat the ghee in a karhai or heavy-bottomed frying pan over medium heat and carefully fry the paneer until golden on all sides. Remove from the pan.

FRY the onion lightly in the same ghee, until softened and lightly golden. Remove the onion from the pan. Add 5 tablespoons hot water and a pinch of salt to the ghee and simmer for 1 minute. Add the peas and sugar, cover and cook for 5–6 minutes, until the peas are nearly cooked.

ADD the onions, paneer, ginger, chiles and scallion to the pan and cook for 2–3 minutes. Add the garam masala and cilantro leaves. Season with salt to taste.

Fry the cubes of paneer until they are golden brown. Make sure the oil is hot enough, otherwise they may stick to the pan.

SAAG PANEER

LEAFY GREENS ARE USED IN MANY INNOVATIVE RECIPES FROM THE NORTH TO THE SOUTH OF INDIA. IN THIS RECIPE, SPINACH, TOMATOES AND PANEER ARE USED IN A MORE TEXTURED DISH THAN THE SMOOTH PUREED VERSIONS SERVED IN MANY NORTHERN INDIAN RESTAURANTS.

1 lb. spinach leaves
1/2 teaspoon ground cumin
1/2 teaspoon ground coriander
1/2 teaspoon fenugreek seeds
1 tablespoon oil
1 red onion, thinly sliced
5 garlic cloves, chopped
7 oz. can diced tomatoes
3/4 inch piece of ginger, grated
1 teaspoon garam masala
  (page 284)
1/2 lb. or 1/2 quantity paneer
  (page 279), cubed

SERVES 4

BLANCH the spinach leaves in boiling water for 2 minutes, then refresh in cold water, drain and very finely chop. Place a small frying pan over low heat and dry-roast the cumin until aromatic. Remove, dry-roast the coriander, then the fenugreek.

HEAT the oil in a karhai or heavy-bottomed frying pan over low heat and fry the onion, garlic, cumin, coriander and fenugreek until brown and aromatic. Stir in the tomatoes, ginger and garam masala and bring to a boil. Add the spinach and cook until the liquid has reduced. Fold in the paneer, trying to keep it in whole pieces. Stir gently until heated through. Season with salt, to taste.

SAAG PANEER

Using a pair of tongs, hold the eggplant in the gas flame until it is charred on all sides. You should be able to remove the skin easily.

SMOKY SPICED EGGPLANT

WHEN EGGPLANT ARE IN SEASON IN INDIA, THEY ARE OFTEN PLACED ON THE DYING EMBERS OF A CHARCOAL FIRE AND LEFT TO SMOKE OVERNIGHT, READY TO BE FRIED AND BLENDED WITH SPICES THE FOLLOWING MORNING. SERVE THIS DISH WITH BREADS OR AS A COLD RELISH WITH A MAIN MEAL.

2 large eggplant
1 red onion, chopped
1 garlic clove, chopped
1 inch piece of ginger, chopped
1 green chile, chopped
1/3 cup oil
1/4 teaspoon chili powder
1/2 teaspoon garam masala
  (page 284)
2 teaspoons ground cumin
2 teaspoons ground coriander
2 teaspoons salt
1/2 teaspoon ground black pepper
2 ripe tomatoes, chopped
3–4 tablespoons cilantro leaves,
  finely chopped

SERVES 4

SCORCH the eggplant by holding them over a medium gas flame, or heating them under a broiler or on an electric hotplate. Keep turning them until the skin is blackened on all sides. Set aside until cool, then peel off the charred skin. Roughly chop the flesh. Don't worry if black specks remain on the flesh because they add to the smoky flavor.

COMBINE the onion, garlic, ginger and chile in a blender and process until chopped together but not a paste. Alternatively, chop finely with a knife and mix in a bowl.

HEAT the oil in a deep, heavy-bottomed frying pan over medium heat, add the onion mixture and cook until slightly browned. Add all the spices, and the salt and pepper, and stir for 1 minute. Add the chopped tomatoes and simmer until the liquid has reduced. Put the eggplant in the pan and mash them with a wooden spoon, stirring around with the spices. Simmer for 10 minutes, or until the eggplant are soft.

STIR in the chopped cilantro leaves and season with salt to taste.

GAJAR MATAR

IN NORTHERN INDIA, PEAS (MATAR) FROM SIMLA, IN HIMACHAL PRADESH, ARE FAMOUS FOR THEIR SWEET FLAVOR. THEY ARE OFTEN SERVED WITH CARROTS IN WINTER WHEN BOTH VEGETABLES ARE IN SEASON. GAJAR MATAR IS A STAPLE VEGETABLE DISH THAT GOES WELL WITH ALL INDIAN MEALS.

1 small onion, roughly chopped
1 garlic clove, roughly chopped
1 inch piece of ginger, chopped
1/2 cup oil
1 teaspoon cumin seeds
1 1/2 teaspoons ground turmeric
2 cups diced carrots
1 teaspoon ground cumin
1 teaspoon ground coriander
2 cups fresh or frozen peas
3 teaspoons salt
1/4 teaspoon sugar
1/4 teaspoon chili powder
4 teaspoons pomegranate seeds
  (optional)
1/2 teaspoon garam masala
  (page 284)

SERVES 6

PUT the onion, garlic and ginger in a food processor and blend until finely chopped, or chop them with a knife and mix together.

HEAT the oil in a karhai or frying pan, then add the onion mixture and stir over high heat for 2 minutes, or until softened. Reduce the heat to medium and add the cumin seeds and turmeric. When the seeds are sizzling, add the carrots and stir for 2 minutes. Add the ground cumin and coriander and fry for 2 minutes. Stir in the peas and then the salt, sugar and chili powder. Add 2 tablespoons of water if using frozen peas, or 4 tablespoons if using fresh peas. Reduce the heat to a simmer, add the pomegranate seeds, if using, and stir before partially covering the pan. Simmer for 15 minutes, or until the carrots and peas are tender. Stir in the garam masala.

SAAG BHAJI

1/4 lb. small turnips, finely chopped
2 lb. mixed spinach and amaranth
  leaves, finely shredded
1/2 teaspoon chili powder
1 tablespoon ghee or oil
1 inch piece of ginger, grated
1 onion, finely chopped
1 1/2 tablespoons lemon juice

SERVES 4

BRING 1/2 cup of water to the boil in a large heavy-bottomed saucepan over medium heat. Add the turnip, cook for 1–2 minutes, then add the spinach and amaranth. Stir in the chili powder and a pinch of salt and cook for 2–3 minutes, or until almost all the water has evaporated. Mash the mixture well and remove from the heat.

HEAT the ghee or oil in a heavy-bottomed saucepan over low heat and fry the ginger and onion for 2–3 minutes. Add the mashed vegetables, mix well and keep tossing until everything is well mixed. Season with salt to taste. Serve warm with a dash of lemon juice.

SAAG BHAJI

Bangla Sahib Gurudwara, Delhi.

METHI ALOO

THE SCENTED AROMA AND DISTINCTIVE FLAVOR OF METHI (FRESH FENUGREEK), WHETHER COOKED WITH MEAT OR VEGETABLES, TRANSFORMS ANY DISH. METHI ALOO CAN BE SERVED WITH MOST INDIAN MAIN MEALS. METHI CAN BE BOUGHT FROM SHOPS THAT SPECIALIZE IN INDIAN FOODS.

Methi leaves add a distinctive flavor to dishes they are used in. Fresh ones can be found at Indian markets.

1 small onion, roughly chopped
2 garlic cloves, roughly chopped
1 inch piece of ginger, roughly chopped
4 tablespoons oil
1/4 teaspoon ground turmeric
1 1/4 lb. potatoes, cut into cubes
2 green chiles, seeded and finely chopped
1/4 teaspoon chili powder
1/2 teaspoon ground cumin
1/2 teaspoon ground coriander
3 teaspoons salt
1/2 teaspoon ground black pepper
2 bunches of methi (about 3 cups of methi leaves), roughly chopped
unsalted butter (optional)

SERVES 4

COMBINE the onion, garlic and ginger in a food processor and chop together, but not to a paste, or chop with a knife and mix together.

HEAT the oil in a karhai or heavy-bottomed frying pan over medium heat and fry the onion mixture until softened. Stir in the turmeric. Add the potatoes and chiles and fry for 5 minutes. Add the chili powder, cumin, coriander, salt and pepper and stir for another minute.

ADD 2 tablespoons water to the pan, cover, reduce the heat and simmer. As the potatoes cook, they might start to stick to the pan, so after 10 minutes, add 2 more tablespoons of water if necessary. At no stage during the cooking time should the potatoes be allowed to brown.

AFTER another 10 minutes, stir in the methi and cook over low heat for 15 minutes, or until the potatoes are soft (the type of potatoes you use will determine the length of cooking time). Season with salt to taste. Serve with a knob of unsalted butter melted on top if you like.

STUFFED OKRA

STUFFED OKRA IS SERVED AS A DELICACY IN NORTHERN INDIAN HOMES. ONE HAS TO PREPARE THIS DISH WITH A LITTLE LOVE AND A LOT OF PATIENCE BUT ALL EFFORTS ARE REWARDED WHEN THE FINAL DISH IS PRESENTED AT THE TABLE. IT IS DELICIOUS SERVED WITH INDIAN BREADS.

1 red onion, roughly chopped
4 garlic cloves, roughly chopped
4 inch piece of ginger, grated
5 teaspoons ground cumin
1 tablespoon ground coriander
2 teaspoons ground turmeric
1 teaspoon chili powder
2 teaspoons garam masala
   (page 284)
1 teaspoon ground black pepper
1 tablespoon salt
1^{1}/$_{4}$ lb. okra
^{1}/$_{2}$ cup oil
pinch of asafoetida

SERVES 6

COMBINE the onion, garlic and ginger in a food processor and blend them to form a paste, or chop them all finely and pound them together in a pestle and mortar. Transfer to a bowl and add 4 teaspoons of the cumin, the coriander, 1^{1}/$_{4}$ teaspoons of the turmeric, the chili powder and garam masala and mix well. Stir in the pepper and 3 teaspoons of the salt.

CUT off the bottoms of the okra, then use a knife to make a slit lengthwise in each of them, stopping just short of the tapered end. Using your hands or a small knife, put a little of the spice mixture into the insides of the okra. Some of it will fall out but that's fine. This process will take a little time but the end result is delicious. Carefully cut all the okra into ^{1}/$_{2}$ inch pieces, or if you prefer, you can leave them whole.

HEAT the oil in a karhai or large, wide, heavy-bottomed frying pan over low heat. Add the asafoetida and remaining turmeric to the pan and stir it around so that the oil absorbs the flavor. Add the okra and stir so it is coated in the flavored oil. Add 2 tablespoons water. Cover and cook for 10 minutes, shaking the pan occasionally to prevent the okra from sticking to the pan (add 2 more tablespoons of water if necessary).

ADD the remaining salt and remaining ground cumin to the pan. Shake the pan, then simmer the mixture for 5–10 minutes, until the okra is quite soft. The okra will retain a slight crunch on the outside because of its unique texture.

Stuffing the okra adds an extra dimension to the flavor. Use a small knife to help you insert the stuffing into each piece.

A vegetable shop in Kerala.

CAULIFLOWER WITH MUSTARD

THIS IS A LOVELY DISH USING CAULIFLOWER AND MANY SPICES. IN INDIA, THE VARIATIONS OF THIS DISH ALL PUT THE EMPHASIS ON QUITE DIFFERENT SPICE COMBINATIONS. THIS MUSTARD ONE GOES WELL WITH RICE AND PIECES OF ROTI BUT IS ALSO A GOOD ACCOMPANIMENT TO MEAT DISHES.

2 teaspoons yellow mustard seeds
2 teaspoons black mustard seeds
1 teaspoon ground turmeric
1 teaspoon tamarind paste
 (page 280)
2–3 tablespoons mustard oil or oil
2 garlic cloves, finely chopped
1/2 onion, finely chopped
11/4 lb. cauliflower, broken into
 small florets
3 mild green chiles, seeded
 and finely chopped
2 teaspoons kalonji (nigella seeds)

SERVES 4

GRIND the mustard seeds together to a fine powder in a spice grinder or pestle and mortar. Mix with the turmeric, tamarind paste and 1/3 cup of water to form a smooth, fairly thin paste.

HEAT 2 tablespoons oil in a karhai or large, heavy-bottomed saucepan over medium heat until almost smoking. Reduce the heat to low, add the garlic and onion and fry until golden. Cook the cauliflower in batches, adding more oil if necessary, and fry until lightly browned. Add the chiles and fry for 1 minute, or until brown around the edges.

RETURN all the cauliflower to the saucepan, sprinkle it with the mustard mixture and kalonji and stir well. Increase the heat to medium and bring to a boil, even though there's not much sauce. Reduce the heat to low, cover and cook until the cauliflower is nearly tender and the seasoning is dry. You may have to sprinkle a little more water on the cauliflower as it cooks to prevent it from sticking to the saucepan. If there is still excess liquid when the cauliflower is cooked, simmer with the lid off until it dries out. Season with salt to taste, and remove from the heat.

AVIAL

THIS MIXED VEGETABLE CURRY IS FROM SOUTHERN INDIA WHERE DISHES OFTEN HAVE MORE SAUCE
TO SERVE WITH RICE WHICH IS A STAPLE THERE. DESPITE THE CHILES, THIS IS QUITE A MILD DISH AS
THE COCONUT AND YOGURT SAUCE TONE DOWN THE HEAT.

A depiction of a Hindu deity painted on a door in Hyderabad.

$1/2$ teaspoon ground turmeric
$1/2$ lb. carrots, cut into batons
$1/2$ lb. sweet potato, cut into batons
$1/2$ lb. green beans, topped
    and tailed and cut in half
1 cup grated coconut (page 283)
2 inch piece of ginger, grated
3 green chiles, finely chopped
$1^1/2$ teaspoons ground cumin
$1^2/3$ cups plain yogurt (page 280)
1 tablespoon oil
10 curry leaves

SERVES 4

BRING 2 cups of water to a boil in a saucepan, add the turmeric and carrots, reduce the heat and simmer for 5 minutes. Add the sweet potatoes and the beans, return to a boil, then reduce the heat and simmer for another 5 minutes, or until the vegetables are almost cooked.

PUT the coconut, ginger and chiles in a blender or pestle and mortar, with a little water, and blend or grind to a paste. Add to the vegetables with the cumin and some salt and simmer for 2 minutes. Stir in the yogurt and heat through.

FOR the final seasoning (tarka), heat the oil over low heat in a small saucepan. Add the curry leaves and allow to crisp. Pour the hot oil and the leaves over the vegetables.

CAULIFLOWER BHAJI

CAULIFLOWER BHAJI

1 teaspoon cumin seeds
3–4 tablespoons oil
$1/4$ teaspoon black mustard seeds
$1/2$ lb. potatoes, cut into small
    cubes
$3/4$ lb. cauliflower, broken into florets
$1/2$ teaspoon ground cumin
$1/2$ teaspoon ground coriander
$1/4$ teaspoon ground turmeric
$1/2$ teaspoon garam masala
    (page 284)
2 garlic cloves, finely chopped
2 green chiles, seeded and
    finely chopped
5 curry leaves

SERVES 4

PLACE a small frying pan over low heat and dry-roast $1/4$ teaspoon of the cumin seeds until aromatic. Grind the roasted seeds to a fine powder using a pestle and mortar.

HEAT the oil over low heat in a karhai or heavy-bottomed saucepan. Add the mustard seeds and remaining cumin seeds, cover and allow to pop for a couple of seconds. Uncover, add the diced potatoes and fry for 1 minute, stirring occasionally to prevent the potato from sticking to the saucepan. Add the cauliflower, all the remaining spices, garlic, chiles and curry leaves and stir until well mixed. Add $1/4$ cup of water and bring to a boil. Cover and simmer for 5–7 minutes, or until the cauliflower is cooked and tender. Season with salt to taste.

SPINACH KOFTA IN YOGURT SAUCE

THIS IS A TYPICAL GUJARATI DISH AND IS MORE SUBSTANTIAL THAN SOME VEGETARIAN DISHES. YOU CAN EAT THE YOGURT SAUCE AND THE SPINACH KOFTA AS SEPARATE DISHES BUT THEY GO VERY WELL TOGETHER AS IN THIS RECIPE.

YOGURT SAUCE
1 1/2 cups plain yogurt (page 280)
4 tablespoons besan flour
1 tablespoon oil
2 teaspoons black mustard seeds
1 teaspoon fenugreek seeds
6 curry leaves
1 large onion, finely chopped
3 garlic cloves, crushed
1 teaspoon ground turmeric
1/2 teaspoon chili powder

SPINACH KOFTAS
1 bunch spinach (about 1 lb.),
  leaves picked off the stems, or
  1 1/4 lb. frozen spinach, thawed
  and drained
1 1/2 cups besan flour
1 red onion, finely chopped
1 ripe tomato, finely diced
2 garlic cloves, crushed
1 teaspoon ground cumin
2 tablespoons cilantro leaves

oil for deep-frying
cilantro leaves (optional)

SERVES 6

TO MAKE the yogurt sauce, in a large bowl, whisk the yogurt, besan flour and 3 cups of water to a smooth paste. Heat the oil in a heavy-bottomed saucepan or deep frying pan over low heat. Add the mustard and fenugreek seeds and the curry leaves, cover and allow the seeds to pop for 1 minute. Add the onion and cook for 5 minutes, or until soft and starting to brown. Add the garlic and stir for 1 minute, or until soft. Add the turmeric and chili powder and stir for 30 seconds. Add the yogurt mixture, bring to a boil and simmer over low heat for 10 minutes. Season with salt to taste.

TO MAKE the spinach koftas, blanch the spinach in boiling water for 1 minute and refresh in cold water. Drain, squeeze out any extra water by putting the spinach between two plates and pushing them together. Finely chop the spinach. Combine with the remaining kofta ingredients and up to 1/4 cup of water, a little at a time, adding enough to make the mixture soft but not runny. If it becomes too runny, add more besan flour. Season with salt to taste. (To test the seasoning, fry a small amount of the mixture and taste it.) Shape the mixture into balls by rolling it in dampened hands, using 1 tablespoon of mixture for each.

FILL a karhai or heavy-bottomed saucepan a third full with oil and heat to 350°F (a cube of bread will brown in 15 seconds). Lower the koftas into the oil in batches and fry until golden and crisp. Don't crowd the pan. Remove the koftas as they cook, shake off any excess oil and add them to the yogurt sauce.

GENTLY reheat the yogurt sauce and sprinkle with the cilantro leaves if using.

LEGUMES

Asafoetida is used as a pungent seasoning in many dishes. It is also used in dishes made with beans because it helps dissipate the gases they create. Powdered versions like this often contain rice flour and turmeric as well.

Pulses are on sale all over India, in their uncooked form and also fried as snacks.

CHANA MASALA

CHANA MASALA IS SERVED UP BY TRAVELING VENDORS, IN BAZAARS OR ON THE STREETS OF INDIA, AND EATEN WITH PURIS. IT IS ENJOYED BY EVERYBODY AT ALL TIMES OF THE DAY AS A SNACK OR A LIGHT MEAL AND MAKES A GOOD ACCOMPANIMENT TO ANY INDIAN MEAL.

1 cup chickpeas
1 large onion, roughly chopped
2 garlic cloves, roughly chopped
2 inch piece of ginger, roughly chopped
1 green chile, chopped
2/3 cup oil
1 tablespoon ground cumin
1 tablespoon ground coriander
1 teaspoon chili powder
pinch of asafoetida
2 tablespoons plain yogurt (page 280)
2 1/4 tablespoons garam masala (page 284)
2 teaspoons tamarind paste (page 280)
1/2 lemon
3 green chiles, extra
1/4 teaspoon ground black pepper
3 teaspoons salt
2 teaspoons chaat masala (page 284)
1/2 red onion, sliced into thin rings
1 inch piece of ginger, cut into thin strips
cilantro leaves, roughly chopped (optional)

SERVES 6

SOAK the chickpeas overnight in 8 cups of water. Drain, then put the chickpeas in a large saucepan with another 8 cups of water. Bring to a boil, spooning off any impurities from the surface, then simmer over low heat for 1–1 1/2 hours, until soft. It is important that the chickpeas are soft at this stage as they won't soften once the sauce has been added. Drain, reserving the cooking liquid.

BLEND the onion, garlic, ginger and chopped chile to a paste in a food processor or very finely chop them together with a knife.

HEAT the oil in a heavy-bottomed saucepan over medium heat and fry the onion mixture until golden brown. Add the cumin, coriander, chili powder and asafoetida, then stir for 1 minute. Add the yogurt and stir for another minute. Stir in 2 tablespoons of the garam masala and pour in 5 cups of the reserved cooking liquid, a little at a time, stirring after each addition. Bring to a boil, then reduce the heat to a simmer.

ADD the tamarind paste, lemon, whole chiles, chickpeas, pepper and the salt. Partially cover the saucepan, simmer for 30 minutes, then remove the lemon. Cook the sauce for another 30 minutes, or until all the liquid has reduced, leaving the softened chickpeas coated in a rich dark brown sauce.

ADD the chaat masala and remaining garam masala and stir in the raw onion rings, ginger and cilantro leaves if using.

A Hindu shrine.

Test to see if the toor dal are cooked by gently squeezing them between your thumb and index finger. They should be soft.

TOOR DAL

IN SOME PARTS OF INDIA IT IS COMMON TO COMBINE A SWEET AND SOUR TASTE, PARTICULARLY IN LENTIL CURRIES SUCH AS THIS ONE. PLAN IN ADVANCE WHEN YOU WANT TO MAKE THIS DISH AS THE DAL HAS TO BE SOAKED BEFORE YOU COOK IT.

$2^2/_3$ cups toor dal (yellow lentils)
5 x 2 inch pieces of kokum
2 teaspoons coriander seeds
2 teaspoons cumin seeds
2 tablespoons oil
2 teaspoons black mustard seeds
10 curry leaves
7 cloves
4 inch piece of cinnamon stick
5 green chiles, finely chopped
$1/_2$ teaspoon ground turmeric
13 oz. can diced tomatoes
1 heaping tablespoon jaggery or
  2 teaspoons molasses
cilantro leaves

SERVES 8

SOAK the lentils in cold water for 2 hours. Rinse the kokum, remove any stones and put the kokum in a bowl with cold water for a few minutes to soften. Drain the lentils and put them in a heavy-bottomed saucepan with 4 cups of water and the pieces of kokum. Bring slowly to a boil, then simmer for 40 minutes, or until the lentils feel soft when pressed between the thumb and index finger.

PLACE a small frying pan over low heat and dry-roast the coriander seeds until aromatic. Remove and dry-roast the cumin seeds. Grind the roasted seeds to a fine powder using a spice grinder or pestle and mortar.

FOR the final seasoning (tarka), heat the oil in a small saucepan over low heat. Add the mustard seeds and allow to pop. Add the curry leaves, cloves, cinnamon, chiles, turmeric and the roasted spice mix and cook for 1 minute. Add the tomatoes and cook for 2–3 minutes until the tomatoes are soft and can be broken up easily and incorporated into the sauce. Add the jaggery, then pour the spicy mixture into the simmering lentils and cook for another 10 minutes. Season with salt to taste. Garnish with cilantro leaves.

When the beans are soaked sufficiently, they will be creamy in color and plump.

BLACK-EYED BEANS WITH MUSHROOMS

BLACK-EYED BEANS OR LOBHIA ARE SOMETIMES CALLED BLACK-EYED PEAS. THE EARTHY FLAVOR OF THE LOBHIA COMBINED WITH MUSHROOMS AND TOMATOES MAKES THIS AN EXCELLENT VEGETARIAN MAIN COURSE. THE DISH IS ALSO SUITABLE FOR SERVING ON THE SIDE WITH MEAT OR VEGETABLES.

1 cup black-eyed beans
1 lb. ripe tomatoes or 13 oz. can
    diced tomatoes
$1/2$ cup oil
1 teaspoon cumin seeds
1 inch piece of cinnamon stick
1 cup chopped onion
4 garlic cloves, finely chopped
$1/2$ lb. mushrooms, sliced
2 teaspoons ground coriander
1 teaspoon ground cumin
$1/2$ teaspoon ground turmeric
$1/4$ teaspoon cayenne pepper
2 tablespoons chopped cilantro
    leaves

SERVES 6

PUT the black-eyed beans in a large saucepan with 4 cups of water and bring to a boil. Cover and simmer for 2 minutes. Remove from the heat and allow to rest for 1 hour. Alternatively, if you prefer, you can soak the black-eyed beans overnight in the cold water.

SCORE a cross in the top of each ripe tomato. Plunge into boiling water for 20 seconds, then drain and peel away from the cross. Roughly chop the tomatoes, discarding the cores and seeds and reserving any juices.

BRING the black-eyed beans back to a boil, then simmer for 20–30 minutes, until tender. Drain well.

MEANWHILE, heat the oil in a karhai or deep, heavy-bottomed frying pan or saucepan. Add the cumin seeds and cinnamon stick, let them sizzle for 10 seconds, then add the onions and garlic. Stir over medium heat until soft and starting to brown. Add the mushrooms and fry for 2–3 minutes. Add the tomatoes, ground coriander, cumin, turmeric and cayenne pepper. Cover and cook over low heat for 10 minutes.

COMBINE the black-eyed beans with the tomato and mushroom mixture and season with salt, to taste. Stir in the cilantro leaves and simmer, uncovered, for 30 minutes.

SWEET AND SOUR CHICKPEAS

2¹/₄ cups chickpeas
2 tablespoons oil or ghee
2 large red onions, thinly sliced
1 inch piece of ginger, finely chopped
2 teaspoons sugar
2 teaspoons ground coriander
2 teaspoons ground cumin
pinch of chili powder (optional)
1 teaspoon garam masala
   (page 284)
3 tablespoons tamarind paste
   (page 280)
4 ripe tomatoes, chopped
4 tablespoons cilantro or mint
   leaves, finely chopped

SERVES 6

SOAK the chickpeas overnight in 8 cups of water. Drain, then put the chickpeas in a large saucepan with 8 cups of water. Bring to a boil, removing any impurities from the surface with a large spoon. Cover and simmer over low heat for 1–1¹/₂ hours, until soft. It is important they are soft at this stage as they won't soften any more once the sauce has been added. Drain.

HEAT the oil in a karhai or heavy-bottomed frying pan. Fry the onions until soft and brown, then stir in the ginger. Add the chickpeas, sugar, coriander, cumin, chili powder, garam masala and a pinch of salt. Stir, then add the tamarind and tomatoes and simmer for 2–3 minutes. Add 2 cups of water, bring to a boil and cook until the sauce has thickened. Stir in the cilantro leaves. Serve with roti (page 220).

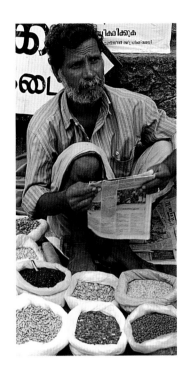

CHOLE CHAAT

THIS IS A NORTH INDIAN WAY OF COOKING CHICKPEAS. IT IS USUALLY EATEN AT THE START OF A MEAL, OR SERVED AS A SIDE DISH. YOU CAN USE TWO 13 OZ. CANS OF CHICKPEAS IF YOU PREFER. DRAIN THEM, MASH A CUPFUL AND ADD THEM TO THE ONION AND SPICES WITH 1²/₃ CUPS OF WATER.

1 cup chickpeas
2 tablespoons oil
¹/₂ onion, chopped
1 teaspoon ground coriander
1 teaspoon ground cumin
¹/₄ teaspoon ground turmeric
1 teaspoon garam masala
   (page 284)
1 inch piece of ginger, grated
2 red chiles, finely chopped
7 oz. can diced tomatoes, drained

SERVES 4

SOAK the chickpeas overnight in 8 cups of water. Drain, then put the chickpeas in a large saucepan with another 8 cups of water. Bring to a boil, removing any impurities from the surface with a spoon, then simmer over low heat for 1–1¹/₂ hours, until soft. It is important that the chickpeas are soft at this stage as they won't soften any more once the sauce has been added. Drain, reserving the cooking liquid. Remove ¹/₂ cup of the chickpeas and thoroughly mash them with a fork.

HEAT the oil in a heavy-bottomed saucepan over low heat and cook the onion until golden brown. Add the coriander, cumin, turmeric and garam masala and fry for 1 minute. Add the ginger, chiles, tomatoes and salt to taste, and stir until well mixed. Add the chickpeas and their cooking liquid, and the mashed chickpeas. Bring to a boil, reduce the heat and simmer, uncovered, for 5 minutes.

CHOLE CHAAT

URAD DAL

THIS TYPE OF LENTIL IS USED IN THE SOUTH TO MAKE DOSAS AND IDLIS, BUT IN BENGAL, GUJARAT AND RAJASTHAN IT IS EATEN REGULARLY AS A LENTIL STEW. IT IS USUALLY COOKED WITH GINGER, ASAFOETIDA AND FENNEL SEEDS, AN AROMATIC COMBINATION OF SPICES.

The dal used for this recipe can be split, skins on, as shown here, or split and skins removed.

1 cup urad dal, skin on
1/4 teaspoon ground turmeric
4 ripe tomatoes, chopped
1 small onion, roughly chopped
2 tablespoons oil
1/2 teaspoon cumin seeds
1 teaspoon fennel seeds
2 inch piece of ginger, grated
2 dried chiles, broken into pieces
pinch of asafoetida
cilantro leaves

SERVES 4

PUT the dal in a heavy-bottomed saucepan and add 4 cups of water, the turmeric, chopped tomatoes and onion. Bring to a boil, then reduce the heat, cover and simmer for 40 minutes, or until the dal is cooked and feels soft when pressed between the thumb and index finger.

FOR the final seasoning (tarka), heat the oil in a small saucepan, add the cumin and fennel seeds and allow to pop. Add the ginger, chiles and asafoetida and fry over low heat for 30 seconds. Pour into the hot dal and simmer for another 5 minutes. Season with salt to taste. Garnish with cilantro leaves before serving.

DAL SAAG

COMBINING VEGETABLES WITH LENTILS IS POPULAR THROUGHOUT INDIA. TAKE CARE NOT TO OVERCOOK THIS DISH AFTER ADDING THE SPINACH, OTHERWISE YOU WILL LOSE ITS LOVELY, RICH GREEN COLOUR.

DAL SAAG

1 cup moong dal
2–3 tablespoons oil
1 teaspoon black mustard seeds
8 curry leaves
1/4 teaspoon asafoetida
1/4 teaspoon ground turmeric
1 teaspoon ground cumin
1 teaspoon ground coriander
1 inch piece of ginger, grated
2 green chiles, seeded and
  cut into 1/2 inch pieces
2 cups spinach leaves, roughly
  chopped
5 scallions, finely chopped

SERVES 4

PUT the moong dal in a heavy-bottomed saucepan, add 3 cups of water and bring to a boil. Reduce the heat and simmer for 30 minutes, or until the moong dal are soft and breaking up. The moong dal tend to soak up most of the liquid so you may need to add a little more.

FOR the final seasoning (tarka), heat the oil in a saucepan, add the mustard seeds, cover and allow to pop. Stir in the curry leaves, asafoetida, turmeric, cumin, coriander, ginger and chiles, then pour into the cooked dal.

STIR in the spinach and scallions and cook for 2 minutes, or until the spinach is just cooked. Season with salt to taste.

KALI DAL

DAL, WHICH IS BOTH THE NAME OF THE LENTILS, AND IN THIS CASE THE DISH, IS PART OF THE STAPLE DIET IN INDIA. THIS IS A SUMPTUOUS VERSION OF A SIMPLE DISH SERVED WITH ROTIS IN SIKH GURUDWARAS (TEMPLES). KALI MEANS BLACK AND THE GRAM IN THIS DISH HAVE A BLACK SKIN.

1 cup whole black gram
  (sabat urad)
1 onion, roughly chopped
2 garlic cloves, roughly chopped
2 inch piece of ginger, roughly
  chopped
1 green chile, roughly chopped
1/2 cup oil
2 tablespoons ground cumin
1 tablespoon ground coriander
2 teaspoons salt
1/4 teaspoon chili powder
3 tablespoons garam masala
  (page 284)
1/2 cup whipping cream

SERVES 6

PUT the whole black gram in a large, heavy-bottomed saucepan, add 8 cups of water and bring to a boil. Reduce the heat and simmer for 1 hour, or until the dal feels soft when pressed between the thumb and index finger. Most of the dal will split to reveal the creamy insides. Drain, reserving the cooking liquid.

BLEND the onion, garlic, ginger and chile together in a food processor to form a paste, or finely chop them together with a knife. Heat the oil in a frying pan and fry the onion mixture over high heat, stirring constantly, until golden brown. Add the cumin and coriander and fry for 2 minutes. Add the dal and stir in the salt, chili powder and garam masala. Pour 1 1/4 cups of the reserved dal liquid into the pan, bring to a boil, then reduce the heat and simmer for 10 minutes. Just before serving, stir in the cream and simmer for another 2 minutes to heat through.

A huge range of pulses and legumes are sold in the markets of India. These are eaten on a daily basis, often made into dal.

MASALA RAJMA

1 cup kidney beans
3 tablespoons oil
1/2 onion, finely chopped
2 Indian bay leaves (cassia leaves)
2 inch piece of cinnamon stick
2 garlic cloves, finely chopped
1/4 teaspoon ground turmeric
1/2 teaspoon ground coriander
1/2 teaspoon ground cumin
1/2 teaspoon garam masala
  (page 284)
3 dried chiles
1 inch piece of ginger, grated

SERVES 4

SOAK the kidney beans overnight in 5 cups of water in a large saucepan. Drain, return the beans to the saucepan with another 5 cups of water and bring to a boil. Boil for 15 minutes, then reduce the heat and simmer for 1 hour, or until the kidney beans are tender. Drain, reserving the liquid.

HEAT the oil in a heavy-bottomed saucepan over low heat. Add the onion, bay leaves, cinnamon and garlic and cook until the onion is lightly browned. Add the turmeric, coriander, cumin, garam masala, chiles and ginger and stir well. Add the beans with enough of their liquid to make a sauce. Bring to a boil and cook for 5 minutes, stirring constantly. Season with salt, to taste. If you wish, remove the chiles before serving.

MASALA RAJMA

KALI DAL

A woman binds curry leaves into neat bundles in the market.

PARIPPU

A DISH THAT INCLUDES LENTILS OF SOME SORT IS AN ESSENTIAL PART OF ANY INDIAN MEAL. THIS RECIPE IS FROM THE SOUTH AND IS FLAVORED WITH COCONUT AS WELL AS A TARKA OF FRIED ONION, CUMIN SEEDS, MUSTARD SEEDS AND CURRY LEAVES WHICH IS MIXED IN TOWARDS THE END OF COOKING.

1 cup masoor dal (red lentils)
1 onion, roughly chopped
1 ripe tomato, roughly chopped
1/4 cup creamed coconut, mixed
   with 1 cup water, or
   1 cup coconut milk (page 283)
2 green chiles, chopped
1/4 teaspoon ground turmeric
1/2 teaspoon ground cumin
1/2 teaspoon ground coriander
2 tablespoons oil
1 teaspoon cumin seeds
1/2 teaspoon black mustard seeds
1 onion, very finely chopped
10 curry leaves

SERVES 4

PUT the lentils in a heavy-bottomed saucepan with 2 cups of water. Add the roughly chopped onion, tomato, creamed coconut or coconut milk, green chiles, turmeric, ground cumin and coriander, and bring to a boil. Simmer and cook, stirring occasionally until the lentils are cooked to a soft mush (masoor dal does not hold its shape when it cooks). This will take 25 minutes. If all the water has evaporated before the lentils are cooked, add 1/2 cup of boiling water.

FOR the final seasoning (tarka), heat the oil in a small saucepan over low heat. Add the cumin seeds and mustard seeds, cover and allow the seeds to pop. Add the finely chopped onion and curry leaves and fry over low heat until the onion is golden brown. Pour the seasoned onions into the simmering lentils. Season with salt to taste, and cook for another 5 minutes.

RICE & GRAINS

PULAO

PULAO OR PILAF CAN BE PLAIN OR A FESTIVE, ELABORATE DISH WITH FRUIT, NUTS AND SPICES AS HERE. RICE DISHES THAT REFLECT THESE FLAVORS CAN BE FOUND AS FAR AFIELD AS SOUTHERN RUSSIA, PERSIA AND MOROCCO, A LEGACY OF RECIPES TRAVELING WITH CONQUERORS AND TRADERS.

1 lb. basmati rice
1 teaspoon cumin seeds
4 tablespoons ghee or oil
2 tablespoons chopped almonds
2 tablespoons golden raisins
2 onions, finely sliced
2 cinnamon sticks
5 cardamom pods
1 teaspoon sugar
1 tablespoon ginger juice
  (page 280)
15 saffron threads, soaked in
  1 tablespoon warm milk
2 Indian bay leaves (cassia leaves)
1 cup coconut milk (page 283)
2 tablespoons fresh or frozen peas
rosewater (optional)

SERVES 6

WASH the rice in a strainer under cold, running water until the water from the rice runs clear. Drain the rice and put in a saucepan, cover with water and soak for 30 minutes. Drain.

PLACE a small frying pan over low heat and dry-roast the cumin seeds until aromatic.

HEAT the ghee or oil in a karhai or heavy-bottomed frying pan and fry the almonds and raisins until browned. Remove from the pan, fry the onion in the same ghee until dark golden brown, then remove from the pan.

ADD the rice, roasted cumin seeds, cinnamon, cardamom, sugar, ginger juice, saffron and salt to the pan and fry for 2 minutes, or until aromatic.

ADD the bay leaves and coconut milk to the pan, then add water until the level is 2 inches above the rice. Bring to a boil, cover and cook over medium heat for 8 minutes, or until most of the water has evaporated.

ADD the peas to the pan and stir well. Reduce the heat to very low and cook until the rice is cooked through. Stir in the fried almonds, raisins and onions, reserving some for garnishing. Drizzle with a few drops of rosewater if you would like a more aromatic dish.

A woman sorts through her rice by tossing it in the air to get rid of any chaff. In India rice often has to be picked over before use.

UPAMA

2 tablespoons chana dal
4 tablespoons ghee or oil
1/2 cup cashew nuts
1 teaspoon black mustard seeds
15 curry leaves
1/2 onion, finely chopped
1 cup coarse semolina
lime juice

SERVES 4

SOAK the dal in plenty of water for 3 hours. Drain, then put in a saucepan with 2 cups of water. Bring to a boil and cook for 2 minutes. Drain the dal, then dry in a kitchen towel. Brush a little of the ghee onto the cashew nuts and toast them in a frying pan over low heat until they are golden.

HEAT the remaining ghee in a heavy-bottomed frying pan and add the mustard seeds and cooked dal. Cook until the seeds start to pop, then add the curry leaves and onion and cook until the onion softens. Add the semolina. Toss everything together and when the semolina is hot and the grains are brown and coated in oil, sprinkle with 2 cups of boiling water, 1/2 cup at a time, tossing and stirring after each addition, until the water is absorbed. Season with salt to taste. Sprinkle with lime juice and cashews.

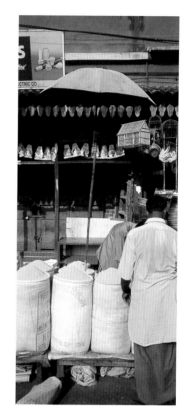

KHICHHARI

KHICHHARI OR KITCHERI IS THE PRECURSOR TO KEDGEREE, A DISH TAKEN UP WITH MUCH ENTHUSIASM BY THE BRITISH IN INDIA. THERE ARE MANY RECIPES FOR KHICHHARI AND THE LENTILS CAN BE YELLOW AS HERE OR MOONG DAL. EAT IT WITH YOGURT OR CHUTNEYS AND BREADS.

1/3 cup toor dal (yellow lentils)
1 1/2 cups basmati rice
3 tablespoons ghee
1 teaspoon cumin seeds
6 cloves
1/2 cinnamon stick
2 onions, finely chopped
2 garlic cloves, finely chopped
1 inch piece of ginger, finely
   chopped
1 teaspoon garam masala
   (page 284)
3 tablespoons lemon juice
1 teaspoon salt

SERVES 6

SOAK the dal in 2 cups water in a large saucepan for 2 hours. Wash the rice in a strainer under cold water until the water from the rice runs clear. Drain.

HEAT the ghee in a heavy-bottomed saucepan over low heat and fry the cumin seeds, cloves and cinnamon for a few seconds. Increase the heat to medium, add the onions, garlic and ginger and cook until they soften and begin to brown.

ADD the rice and dal and toss to thoroughly coat in ghee. Add the garam masala, lemon juice, salt and 3 cups of boiling water. Bring to a boil, then reduce the heat to very low, cover tightly and cook for 15 minutes. Remove from the heat and gently fluff up with a fork. Cover the saucepan with a clean cloth and allow to rest for 10 minutes. Fluff up again and season with salt to taste.

KHICHHARI

Cook the meat and then put the rice and saffron mixture on top. Use a rope of dough to seal on the lid and keep in the flavours.

LAMB BIRYANI

THIS IS A RICE AND LAMB DISH IN WHICH BOTH INGREDIENTS ARE COOKED TOGETHER IN A SEALED CONTAINER. YOU CAN COOK THE LAMB WITHOUT BROWNING IT FIRST AND, IN FACT, THIS IS THE TRADITIONAL METHOD. HOWEVER, BROWNING THE MEAT ADDS EXTRA FLAVOR.

2 lb. boneless lamb leg or shoulder, cut into 1 inch cubes
3 inch piece of ginger, grated
2 garlic cloves, crushed
2 tablespoons garam masala (page 284)
$1/2$ teaspoon chili powder
$1/2$ teaspoon ground turmeric
4 green chiles, finely chopped
$1/3$ cup chopped cilantro leaves
$1/4$ cup chopped mint leaves
1 lb. basmati rice
4 onions, thinly sliced
$1/4$ teaspoon salt
$1/2$ cup oil
$1/2$ cup unsalted butter, melted
1 cup plain yogurt (page 280)
$1/2$ teaspoon saffron strands, soaked in 2 tablespoons hot milk
3 tablespoons lemon juice

SEALING DOUGH
$1 1/3$ cups whole wheat flour
1 teaspoon salt

SERVES 6

MIX the lamb cubes in a bowl with the ginger, garlic, garam masala, chili powder, turmeric, chiles, cilantro and mint. Cover and marinate in the fridge overnight.

WASH the rice in a strainer under cold, running water until the water from the rice runs clear. Put the sliced onion in a strainer, sprinkle with the salt and allow to rest for 10 minutes to drain off any liquid that is released. Rinse and pat dry.

HEAT the oil and butter in a large, heavy-bottomed saucepan, add the onions and fry for 10 minutes or until golden brown. Drain through a strainer, reserving the oil and butter.

REMOVE the lamb from the marinade, reserving the marinade, and fry in batches in a little of the oil and butter until the lamb is well browned all over. Transfer to a 'degchi' (thick-bottomed pot) or heavy casserole and add the browned onion, any remaining marinade and the yogurt, and cook everything over low heat for 30–40 minutes, or until the lamb is tender.

IN a separate saucepan, boil enough water to cover the rice. Add the rice to the saucepan. Return the water to a boil, cook the rice for 5 minutes, then drain well and spread the rice evenly over the meat. Pour 2 tablespoons of the leftover oil and ghee over the rice and drizzle with the saffron and milk.

TO MAKE the sealing dough, preheat the oven to 425°F. Make a dough by mixing the flour and salt with a little water. Roll the dough into a sausage shape and use to seal the lid onto the rim of the pot or casserole, pressing it along the rim where the lid meets the pot. Put the pot over high heat for 5 minutes to bring the contents to a boil, then transfer it to the oven for 40 minutes. Remove the pot and break the seal of dough.

YAKHNI PULAO

THIS RICE DISH IS PARTICULARLY DELICIOUS WHEN COOKED IN HOME-MADE STOCK (YAKHNI) BUT YOU CAN, OF COURSE, USE STORE-BOUGHT STOCK. YAKHNI PULAO IS DELICATELY FLAVORED WITH WHOLE SPICES AND GOES WELL NOT ONLY WITH INDIAN DISHES, BUT WITH OTHER CASSEROLES.

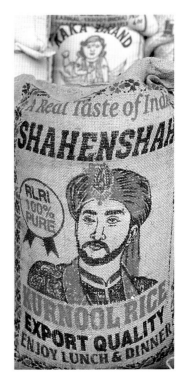

Rice is a staple across most of India. Hundreds of varieties exist, each with its own flavor, aroma and texture.

1 cup basmati rice
2 cups chicken stock
6 tablespoons ghee or oil
5 cardamom pods
2 inch piece of cinnamon stick
6 cloves
8 black peppercorns
4 Indian bay leaves (cassia leaves)
1 onion, finely sliced

SERVES 4

WASH the rice in a strainer under cold running water until the water from the rice runs clear. Drain.

HEAT the stock to near boiling point in a saucepan.

MEANWHILE, heat 2 tablespoons of the ghee or oil over medium heat in a large, heavy-bottomed saucepan. Add the cardamom, cinnamon, cloves, peppercorns and bay leaves and fry for 1 minute. Reduce the heat to low, add the rice and stir constantly for 1 minute. Add the heated stock and some salt to the rice and bring rapidly to a boil. Cover and simmer over low heat for 15 minutes. Allow the rice to rest for 10 minutes before uncovering. Lightly fluff up the rice before serving.

MEANWHILE, heat the remaining ghee or oil in a frying pan over low heat and fry the onion until soft. Increase the heat and fry until the onion is dark brown. Drain on paper towels, then use as garnish.

SHRIMP PULAO

1 cup basmati rice
3/4 lb small shrimp
3 tablespoons oil
1 onion, finely chopped
1 inch piece of cinnamon
6 cardamom pods
5 cloves
4 Indian bay leaves (cassia leaves)
1 lemongrass stalk, finely chopped
4 garlic cloves, crushed
2 inch piece of ginger, grated
1/4 teaspoon ground turmeric

SERVES 4

WASH the rice in a strainer under cold running water until the water from the rice runs clear. Drain. Peel and devein the shrimp, then wash thoroughly and pat dry with paper towels.

HEAT the oil in a karhai or heavy-bottomed frying pan over low heat and fry the onion, cinnamon, cardamom, cloves, bay leaves and lemongrass until the onion is lightly browned. Stir in the garlic, ginger and turmeric. Add the shrimp and stir until the shrimp turn pinkish. Add the rice and fry over medium heat for 2 minutes. Add 2 cups of boiling water and some salt and bring to a boil. Reduce the heat and simmer for 15 minutes. Remove from the heat, cover tightly with a lid and allow to rest for 10 minutes. Fluff up the rice before serving.

SHRIMP PULAO

Paddy fields in Kerala.

Fresh yogurt is made and sold daily in India. It is left to set in earthenware pots which help to absorb any excess moisture.

YOGURT RICE

THIS IS A POPULAR DISH TO PREPARE FOR TAKING ON JOURNEYS AS THE DISH IS SERVED COLD AND THE ACID IN THE YOGURT ACTS AS A PRESERVATIVE. THE FLAVORS WILL NOT BE AS STRONG IF YOU SERVE THE RICE STRAIGHT FROM THE FRIDGE, SO BRING IT BACK TO ROOM TEMPERATURE.

2 tablespoons urad dal
2 tablespoons chana dal
1 cup basmati rice
2 tablespoons oil
1/2 teaspoon mustard seeds
12 curry leaves
3 dried chiles
1/4 teaspoon ground turmeric
pinch of asafoetida
2 cups plain yogurt (page 280)

SERVES 4

SOAK the dals in 1 cup boiling water for 3 hours. Wash the rice in a strainer under cold running water until the water from the rice runs clear. Drain.

PUT the rice and 2 cups water in a saucepan and bring rapidly to a boil. Stir, cover, reduce the heat to a slow simmer and cook for 10 minutes. Leave for 15 minutes before fluffing up with a fork.

DRAIN the dals and pat dry with paper towels. For the final seasoning (tarka), heat the oil in a small saucepan over low heat, add the mustard seeds, cover and shake the saucepan until the seeds start to pop. Add the curry leaves, chiles and the dals and fry for 2 minutes, stirring occasionally. Stir in the turmeric and asafoetida.

PUT the yogurt in a large bowl, pour the fried dal mixture into the yogurt and mix thoroughly. Mix the rice into the spicy yogurt. Season with salt to taste. Cover and refrigerate. Serve cold, but before serving, stand the rice at room temperature for 10 minutes. Serve as part of a meal. Yogurt rice goes very well with meat dishes.

ANDHRA-STYLE CHICKEN PULAO

3 lb. chicken or chicken pieces
2 lb. basmati rice
3 onions, sliced
1/2 teaspoon salt
1/2 cup oil
3/4 cup ghee
2 inch piece of cinnamon stick
2 cardamom pods
3 cloves
2 star anise
2 stalks of curry leaves
1 inch piece of ginger, grated
6 garlic cloves, crushed
4–6 green chiles, slit lengthwise
1 2/3 cups buttermilk
4 ripe tomatoes, diced
3/4 cup coconut milk (page 283)
4 cups chicken stock
1 lemon, cut into wedges

SERVES 8

IF USING a whole chicken, cut it into 16 pieces by removing both legs and cutting between the joint of the drumstick and thigh. Cut each of these in half through the bone with a cleaver or poultry shears (make sure there are no bone shards). Cut down either side of the backbone and remove the backbone. Turn the chicken over and cut through the cartilage down the center of the breastbone. Cut each breast into 3 pieces and cut off the wings. Trim off the wing tips. Trim off any excess fat or skin from the pieces.

WASH the rice in a strainer under cold, running water until the water from the rice runs clear. Drain well. Put the sliced onions in a strainer, sprinkle with the salt and leave for 10 minutes to drain off any liquid that is released. Rinse and pat dry.

HEAT the oil and ghee over medium heat in a large, ovenproof 'degchi' (thick-bottomed pot), or heavy casserole. Add the cinnamon, cardamom and cloves and heat until they begin to crackle. Reduce the heat to low and add the star anise and the curry leaves from one stem. Add the sliced onions and cook until golden brown. Add the ginger and garlic and cook until golden. Add the chicken, increase the heat to medium and fry until the pieces are browned on all sides. Add the slit chiles, the remaining curry leaves, the buttermilk and some salt. Cook for 12 minutes, or until the chicken is cooked through and the liquid is reduced by half. Add the diced tomatoes and the coconut milk. Cook until the tomatoes are tender, then add the stock and bring to a boil.

PREHEAT the oven to 425°F. Add the drained rice to the chicken and stir it in well. Check the seasoning, adjust if necessary, and cook for 10 minutes, or until nearly all the liquid is absorbed.

REMOVE the pot from the heat, cover it with a clean wet cloth, then a tight-fitting lid, and put it in the oven for 15 minutes, until the rice is cooked through. Serve hot with lemon wedges.

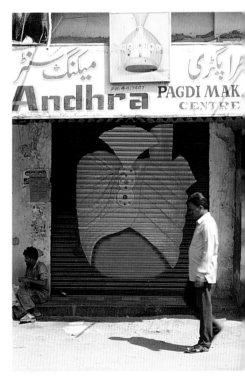

A shop which makes ceremonial headdresses in Hyderabad, Andhra Pradesh.

Sevian or vermicelli made from wheat flour are available as skeins of noodles or as bunches of straight lengths. Sometimes they are sold toasted.

SEVIAN KHEEMA

1 teaspoon cumin seeds
3 tablespoons ghee or oil
1 red onion, finely chopped
3 garlic cloves, crushed
1 inch piece of ginger, grated
1/2 lb. ground lamb or beef
1 teaspoon ground black pepper
1/2 lb. sevian, broken into small
  pieces
3 tablespoons lime or lemon juice

SERVES 4

PLACE a small frying pan over low heat, dry-roast the cumin until aromatic, then grind to a fine powder using a spice grinder or pestle and mortar.

HEAT 1 tablespoon ghee in a karhai or heavy-bottomed frying pan and fry the onions, garlic and ginger for 3–4 minutes. Add the cumin, cook for 1 minute, then add the meat and cook for 8 minutes, or until the meat is dry, breaking up any lumps with the back of a fork. Season with the black pepper and salt to taste, and remove from the pan.

HEAT the remaining ghee in the pan and fry the sevian for 1–2 minutes. Add the meat and fry for 1 minute. Add 1/2 cup of water and cook until the sevian are tender, adding more water if necessary. The dish should be dry, so don't add too much at once. When cooked, sprinkle with the juice.

IDIYAPPAM

IN THIS DISH FROM KERALA, THE RICE NOODLES ARE OFTEN MADE AT HOME. HOWEVER, THIS IS QUITE

LABOR INTENSIVE SO WE HAVE USED RICE STICKS OR VERMICELLI AS A CONVENIENT SUBSTITUTE.

IDIYAPPAM

1/2 lb. rice sticks or vermicelli
4 tablespoons oil
1/3 cup cashew nuts
1/2 onion, chopped
3 eggs
1 cup fresh or frozen peas
10 curry leaves
2 carrots, grated
2 leeks, finely shredded
1 red pepper, diced
2 tablespoons tomato ketchup
1 tablespoon soy sauce
1 teaspoon salt

SERVES 4

SOAK the rice sticks in cold water for 30 minutes, then drain and put in a saucepan of boiling water. Remove from the heat and leave in the saucepan for 3 minutes. Drain and refresh in cold water.

HEAT 1 tablespoon oil in a frying pan and fry the cashews until golden. Remove, add the onion to the pan, fry until dark golden, then drain on paper towels. Cook the eggs in boiling water for 10 minutes to hard-boil, then cool them immediately in cold water. When cold, peel them and cut into wedges. Cook the peas in boiling water until tender.

HEAT the remaining oil in a frying pan and briefly fry the curry leaves. Add the carrots, leeks and red pepper and stir for 1 minute. Add the ketchup, soy sauce, salt and rice sticks and mix, stirring constantly to prevent the rice sticks from sticking to the pan. Serve on a platter and garnish with the peas, cashews, fried onions and egg wedges.

BREADS

Slap the chapati backward and forward to get rid of any excess flour. Press it with a kitchen towel to make it puff up as it cooks.

CHAPATIS

CHAPATIS ARE THE MOST BASIC FORM OF UNLEAVENED BREAD. THEY SHOULD BE COOKED ON A HIGH HEAT TO PREVENT THEM BECOMING TOUGH. IF YOU WANT TO MAKE THEM OFTEN, BUY A FLAT GRIDDLE. IF YOU CAN'T BUY CHAPATI FLOUR, USE EQUAL AMOUNTS OF WHOLE WHEAT AND MAIDA (PLAIN FLOUR).

$1^2/_3$ cups atta (chapati flour)
$^1/_2$ teaspoon salt
$^1/_2$ cup ghee or clarified butter

MAKES 8

SIFT the atta and salt into a bowl and make a well in the center. Add $^1/_2$ cup of tepid water, or enough to mix to form a soft, pliable dough. Turn the dough out onto a floured work surface and knead for 5 minutes. Place in an oiled bowl, cover and allow to rest for 30 minutes.

PUT a tava or griddle, or a heavy-bottomed frying pan over medium heat and allow it to heat up. Divide the dough into eight equal portions. Working with one portion at a time and keeping the rest covered, on a lightly floured surface roll out each portion to form a 6 inch diameter circle. Keep the rolled chapatis covered with a damp cloth while you roll them and cook them. Remove the excess surface flour on the chapati prior to cooking by holding the chapati in the palms of your hands and gently slapping it from one hand to the other. If you leave the flour on it may burn.

PLACE each chapati on the tava, leave it for 7–10 seconds to brown, then turn it over to brown on the other side. Depending on the hotness of the griddle, the second side should take 15 seconds. Turn over the chapati again and, using a folded kitchen towel, apply gentle pressure to the chapati in several places to heat it and encourage it to puff up like a balloon. It is this puffing up process that gives the chapati its light texture. Smear the hot chapati with a little of the ghee or butter, and leave stacked and covered with a kitchen towel until all the chapatis are cooked.

NAAN

PERHAPS THE MOST FAMOUS LEAVENED BREAD FROM NORTH INDIA, TRADITIONALLY THIS BREAD IS COOKED ON THE WALLS OF A TANDOOR (CLAY OVEN). IT IS NOT EASY TO RECREATE THE INTENSE HEAT IN A DOMESTIC OVEN SO THE TEXTURE IS SLIGHTLY DIFFERENT BUT THE TASTE IS DELICIOUS.

4 cups maida or all-purpose flour
1 1/4 cups milk
1 package dry yeast or 0.6 oz.
    fresh yeast
2 teaspoons kalonji (nigella seeds),
    (optional)
1/2 teaspoon baking powder
1/2 teaspoon salt
1 egg, beaten
2 tablespoons oil or ghee
3/4 cup plain yogurt (page 280)

MAKES 10

SIFT the maida into a large bowl and make a well in the center. Warm the milk over low heat in a saucepan until it is hand hot (the milk will feel the same temperature as your finger when you dip your finger into it). If you are using fresh yeast, mix it with a little milk and a pinch of maida and set it aside to activate and go frothy.

ADD the yeast, kalonji, baking powder and salt to the maida. In another bowl, mix the egg, oil and yogurt. Pour into the maida with 1 cup of the milk and mix to form a soft dough. If the dough seems dry add the remaining 1/4 cup of milk. Turn out onto a floured work surface and knead for 5 minutes, or until smooth and elastic. Put in an oiled bowl, cover and leave in a warm place to double in size. This will take several hours.

PREHEAT the oven to 400°F. Place a roasting pan half-filled with water at the bottom of the oven. This provides moisture in the oven which prevents the naan from drying out too quickly.

PUNCH down the dough, knead it briefly and divide it into 10 portions. Using the tips of your fingers, spread out one portion of dough to the shape of a naan bread. They are traditionally tear-drop in shape, so pull the dough on one end. Put the naan on a greased baking sheet. Bake on the top shelf for 7 minutes, then turn the naan over and cook for another 5 minutes. While the first naan is cooking, shape the next one. If your sheet is big enough, you may be able to fit two naan at a time. Remove the cooked naan from the oven and cover with a cloth to keep it warm and soft.

REPEAT the cooking process until all the dough is used. You can only use the top shelf of the oven because the naan won't cook properly on the middle shelf. Refill the baking sheet with boiling water when necessary.

Make sure that the naan dough is very soft but not sticky. Shape it by pulling it into the right shape with your hands.

PARATHAS

THIS FRIED UNLEAVENED BREAD IS OFTEN EATEN ON SPECIAL OCCASIONS. IT IS BEST COOKED ON A TAVA OR IRON GRIDDLE. IF YOU CAN'T FIND CHAPATI FLOUR, YOU CAN USE EQUAL AMOUNTS OF WHOLE WHEAT AND MAIDA (PLAIN FLOUR) INSTEAD.

The ghee folded and rolled into the parathas will separate out the layers as they cook. Try to keep the shape neat as you roll.

1^1/$_2$ cups atta (chapati flour)
^{1}/$_2$ teaspoon salt
1 tablespoon oil or ghee
oil or ghee for cooking
   and brushing

MAKES 6

SIFT the atta and the salt into a bowl and make a well in the center. Add ^{1}/$_2$ cup of tepid water and the oil or ghee and mix to form a soft pliable dough. Turn the dough out onto a floured work surface and knead for 5 minutes, then place in an oiled bowl, cover and allow to rest for 30 minutes. Divide the dough into six equal portions.

ROLL each portion into a 6 inch diameter circle. Using a pastry brush, cover the surface of each paratha with a very thin coating of oil or ghee. Fold each into a semicircle and brush thinly with oil. Fold into quarters and roll out each quarter to roughly three times its original size. Cover the rolled-out parathas with a cloth and cook them one at a time.

PLACE a tava, griddle or a heavy-bottomed frying pan over medium heat and allow it to heat up. Lightly brush the surface of the tava or griddle with oil. Remove the excess surface flour on each paratha prior to cooking by holding it in the palms of your hands and gently slapping it from one hand to the other. If you leave the flour on, it may burn.

PUT a paratha on the tava and cook for 1 minute. Turn it over and cook for another minute, or until the surface has brown flecks. This cooking process should be quick to ensure that the parathas remain soft. Repeat until all the parathas are cooked. Cover the cooked ones with a cloth.

PARATHAS must be served warm and can be reheated in a microwave oven, or wrapped in foil and heated in a conventional oven at 350°F for 10 minutes.

RUMALI ROTI

RUMALI ROTI is a large, thin bread whose name means "handkerchief bread." Rumali roti is made from wheat flour. In order to stretch out the dough to the desired thickness and size, it has to be tossed in the air, in much the same way as for making a pizza base *(left and center left)*, until it is the size of a man's handkerchief. The dough is cooked on a convex tava for a few minutes on each side, until the surface begins to blister *(center right and right)*. The rumali roti is then folded on the tava before serving.

PARATHAS

PARATHA is a flaky bread made with dough which is either rolled and folded, like puff pastry, to incorporate ghee or oil into its layers of dough, or twisted and coiled to achieve the same result. These parathas, made in Kerala, use the coiled method. First the dough is shaped into a circle by pushing it out with the heel of the hand on a flat surface *(left and center)*, after which it is greased and twisted up into a tight tube by holding it in the air and twirling it *(right)*. This tube is coiled up, thus incorporating the ghee or oil between each fold of the paratha.

Next, the coiled dough *(left)* is flattened out again, drizzled with more ghee, and cooked on a greased griddle *(center)* until it is browned on each side and cooked through. The parathas are stacked in a pile (they are usually bought more than one at a time) and the cook places his or her hands on either side of the pile and claps them together, turning the pile at the same time. This turns the parathas into a soft, flaky mass and splits the dough back into its coils. The parathas are sold folded into a newspaper that is lined with a banana leaf *(right)*.

PAPPADAMS or padad are often made by small companies. The company shown here operates on a rooftop in Delhi, the perfect environment for drying the pappadams in the hot sun. A dough *(left)* is made by kneading together besan flour, rice flour and water, along with a generous amount of dried chile flakes for seasoning. The dough is then forced through an extruder *(center left)* to make it smooth and to remove any

BREADS

IN INDIA, ROTI IS THE GENERIC NAME FOR BREAD OR BREAD-LIKE ACCOMPANIMENTS. THERE IS A GREAT VARIETY AND THEY ARE BAKED, GRILLED, ROASTED OR FRIED. THERE IS NO RULE REGARDING WHICH TYPE OF ROTI GOES WITH WHICH DISH.

Roti are popular all over India, especially in northern and central areas where wheat and grains are staples rather than rice. Although it is a common assumption that rice is part of every Indian meal, there are actually vast areas of India that don't have the right climate or terrain for rice growing. Therefore, these areas produce different grains and have a large repertoire of roti which commonly accompany meals.

In northern and central India, roti are eaten with every meal instead of rice. Throughout the rest of India, roti as well as rice are eaten with main meals every day. Roti function both as part of the meal and as a handy eating tool because they are used to scoop up the more liquid dishes including dal, or to pick up pieces of meat. Roti are also utilized as wrappers for grilled meats, or as edible plates, with accompaniments piled on top, at roadside stands.

COOKING ROTI

Roti made from wheat are generally cooked in one of four ways: on a tava (a flat, convex or concave griddle) without the use of fat, or on a tava using a little ghee or oil, or deep-fried in a karhai, or baked in a tandoor or oven. Each of the first three methods gives a different result using essentially the same unleavened dough. Sometimes, as for parathas, the dough is layered with ghee to give a more flaky texture. At other times, it may be covered as it cooks to create a softer texture. Baked roti are made from leavened dough.

KULCHA, a specialty of Hyderabad, is baked in a wood-fired oven, rather like a tandoor, set in the floor of the bakery. The breads are baked and sold twice daily, once in the morning and once in the early afternoon. A leavened dough is made using maida and ghee. This is kneaded *(far left)*, then shaped by hand, either into a square *(left)* marked with a cross made of thumbprints in the dough, or a round bun-like disc

excess moisture. As the dough emerges from the extruder, it is broken off into small balls, each big enough for one pappadam. The dough is rolled to a very thin disc by hand *(center)*, each roller making only one or two quick passes over the dough. The discs of dough are then arranged on straw mats *(center right and right)* and left in the hot sun until completely dry and brittle. They are then stacked in piles to be sold.

UNLEAVENED ROTI

Unleavened roti cooked on a tava include chapatis, rumali, and phulkas (a type of chapati which is made to puff up by briefly cooking it on hot coals) as well as roti flavored with spinach. Those cooked with fat are parathas, either plain or stuffed with a range of fillings. The most common of the deep-fried bread is the puri, which ranges from the tiny mouthfuls (gol goppas) used to make chaat, such as pani puri, to bigger ones eaten with meals. Pappadams are also a deep-fried accompaniment to meals, though unlike the softer roti they are made from a dough of ground beans and form a very thin, crisp disc with a bubbled surface.

LEAVENED ROTI

Leavened breads rely on the intense, all-round heat of an oven or tandoor to make them rise and cook in minutes. The breads are stuck to the oven wall for a few minutes only. They include naan, kulcha and sheermal. Baked breads are common to areas such as the Punjab, Hyderabad and Kashmir where ovens or tandoors (often communal) are commonly used. These ovens have been present in the Indus valley in northern India since the 2nd century BC and were introduced by the Moghuls, though they are now very much associated with the Punjab. In other areas of India, baked breads are generally produced by restaurants as domestic kitchens do not have suitable ovens.

Other bread-like accompaniments include cakes and pancakes made of rice and gram batters, either steamed or cooked on griddles, such as idlis, appams and dosas.

FLOURS FOR ROTI

The flours most commonly used for rotis are maida, an all-purpose white flour, and atta, a mix of whole wheat and all-purpose white flours. Other flours are made from legumes such as bengal gram or chickpeas (besan flour), mung beans (mung flour) and urad dal (urad flour) amongst others. These are used regionally, depending where they are grown.

marked with three vertical lines *(center left, top and bottom)*. The shaped breads are then covered with a cloth and left to rise. Each bread is cooked by slapping it onto the red hot wall of the oven for a few minutes *(center right)*. It is then removed using an iron rod *(right)* when the crust is crisp but the inside soft and doughy, before being eaten warm from the oven *(far right)*.

SHEERMAL a leavened, baked bread whose name "sheer" means milk. Its yellow colour comes from a glaze of melted butter and saffron which is painted on before baking.

APPAM this spongy pancake is made from a batter of ground rice and urad dal. Though not strictly a bread, it is served with meals in south India and used to soak up gravies.

CHAPATI this common unleavened bread is made with atta or chapati flour. Similar to roti, chapati is made fresh for each meal in many homes. It is cooked without fat on a tava.

NAAN a leavened bread made from a maida dough enriched with yogurt, ghee and egg and baked on the wall of a tandoor. Probably India's best-known oven-baked bread.

IDLI a steamed rice cake which is eaten either as a snack or as an accompaniment to breakfast dishes in the south. Some contain rice and urad dal, others are made from semolina (rava).

KULCHA a baked bread which is a specialty of Hyderabad. Some are round, marked with lines and others are squares marked with a cross. Often stuffed with paneer or onion.

PHULKA a chapati which is put on hot coals once it has been cooked on a tava. The intense heat causes the center to steam and puff up. Phulkas are often eaten with Punjabi dishes.

ROTI this is the plainest flat bread and is cooked on a tava. It is made from a basic atta (chapati) flour dough and water and is freshly cooked for each meal with which it is to be served.

RUMALI ROTI a huge, thin, soft sheet of unleavened bread, said to be the size of a man's handkerchief after which it is named. It is cooked on a convex tava and served folded.

PURI a puff of deep-fried, unleavened bread. Rather than crisp and hard when fried, these should be very soft. Small versions, often sold ready-made, are called pani puri.

PAPPADAM dried disks of dough made from legume flours. Bought in their dried form and then fried. In northern India they are often flavored with chile, in the south they are usually plain.

PARATHA a flaky bread made by incorporating ghee or oil into an unleavened dough, by folding or coiling the dough and trapping the fat between the layers. A popular bread all over India.

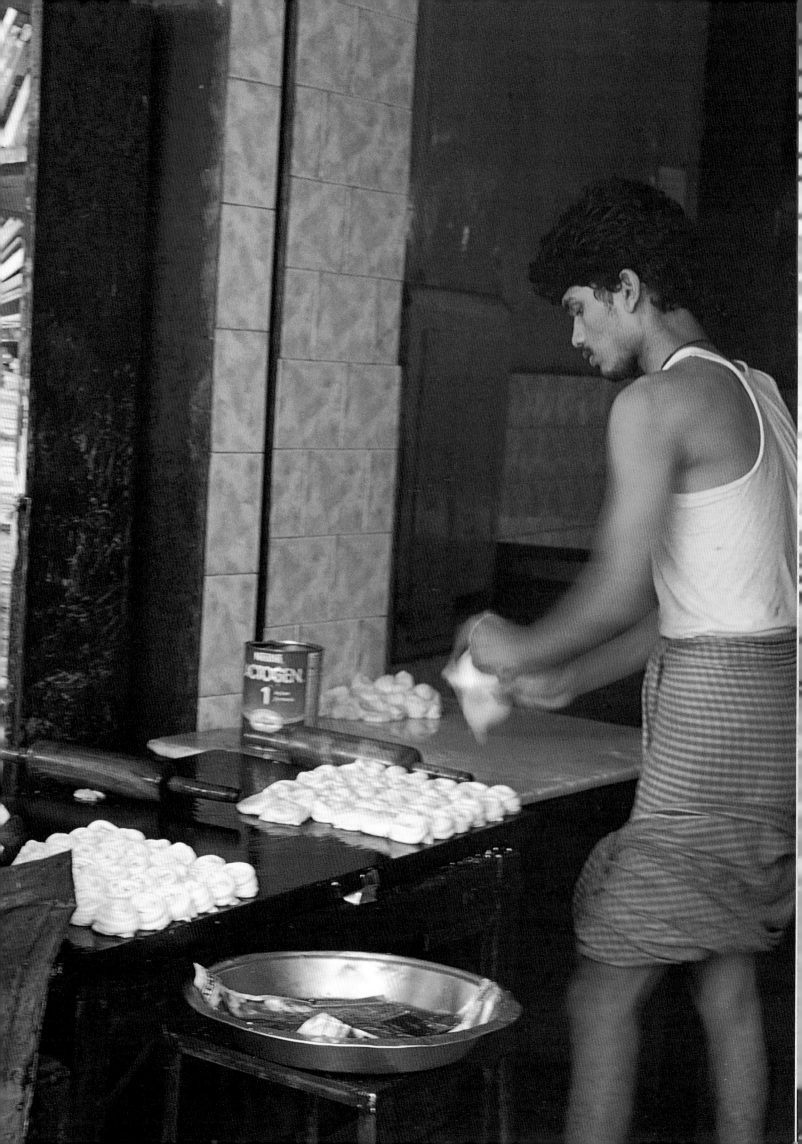

PURIS

PURIS AND PURI CRISPS ARE SIMPLE TO MAKE EVEN FOR A LARGE GROUP OF PEOPLE. THE DOUGH SHOULD BE PREPARED AHEAD OF TIME AND ALLOWED TO REST. THE OIL SHOULD BE HOT SO THE PURIS PUFF UP WELL, BUT NOT SO HOT THAT YOU BURN THE OUTSIDE AND UNDERCOOK THE INSIDE.

3 cups maida or all-purpose flour
1 cup fine semolina
oil for deep-frying

MAKES 12 LARGE PURI OR
35 CRISPS

MIX the maida and semolina with 1/2 cup of water into a dough and knead well until firm. If necessary, add more flour to make it a really firm dough. Cover and leave for 1 hour.

TO MAKE puri, knead the dough again, then divide into 12 balls. Roll each dough ball out, making each into a very thin circle about 4 inches in diameter.

FILL a karhai or heavy-bottomed saucepan a third full with oil and heat to 350°F. Test the temperature by putting a small piece of the dough into the oil. If the dough rises to the surface in a couple of seconds, the oil is ready. Put a puri into the hot oil, then 5 seconds after it rises to the surface gently push it down, using the back of a spoon, to keep it submerged in the hot oil until it puffs up—this will also take 5 seconds. Turn over and cook until the other side is lightly browned. Remove from the oil and drain on a wire rack. This whole frying process should take 15–20 seconds for each puri. Continue until all the puris are cooked.

TO MAKE puri crisps, roll out the kneaded dough, not too thinly, then cut out 1 1/2 inch diameter circles with a pastry cutter and set them aside on a baking sheet.

FILL a karhai or heavy-based saucepan a third full with oil and heat until a small ball of dough will rise to the surface in a few seconds. Deep-fry the puri crisps in batches until golden and puffed. Drain on paper towels. If you have any remaining pastry, cut it into pieces and deep-fry to make irregular-shaped crisps.

Roll out the puris until they are quite thin so that as they fry and puff up they split into two very light layers.

SAAG ROTI

A SIMPLE ROTI WITH A SPINACH BASE IS NOT ONLY INTERESTING AND TASTY, BUT NUTRITIOUS AS WELL. MAKE IT WITH SOME CHOPPED BROWNED ONION FOR AN AROMATIC ALTERNATIVE. YOU CAN USE EQUAL AMOUNTS OF WHOLE WHEAT AND MAIDA IF YOU CAN'T BUY CHAPATI FLOUR.

4 cups spinach leaves, stems
    removed
1 lb. atta (chapati flour)
1 teaspoon salt
1 teaspoon ghee or oil
ghee or oil for cooking

MAKES 20

COOK the spinach briefly in a little simmering water until it is just wilted, then refresh in cold water. Drain thoroughly, then finely chop. Squeeze out any extra water by putting the spinach between two plates and pushing them together.

SIFT the atta and salt into a bowl and make a well in the center. Add the spinach, ghee and 1 cup of tepid water and mix to form a soft, pliable dough. Turn out the dough onto a floured work surface and knead for 5 minutes. Place in an oiled bowl, cover and allow to rest for 30 minutes.

DIVIDE the dough into 20 balls. Working with one portion at a time and keeping the rest covered, on a lightly floured surface evenly roll out each portion to a very thin 5 inch circle.

HEAT a tava, griddle or heavy-bottomed frying pan until hot, oil it lightly with ghee or oil and cook one roti at a time. Cook each on one side, covered with a saucepan lid (this will help keep them soft), for 1 minute. Turn it over, cover again and cook the other side for 2 minutes. Check the roti a few times to make sure it doesn't overcook. The roti will blister a little and brown in some places. Remove the roti and keep it warm under a kitchen towel. Cook the remaining roti.

Make sure that the spinach is evenly distributed throughout the dough. Cover the roti with a lid to keep it soft as it cooks.

STUFFED PARATHAS

STUFFED PARATHAS ARE VERY MUCH A FESTIVE FOOD. AFTER STUFFING THEM, ROLL THEM OUT CAREFULLY SO THE FILLING DOESN'T OOZE OUT. IF YOU CAN'T GET HOLD OF CHAPATI FLOUR YOU CAN USE EQUAL AMOUNTS OF WHOLE WHEAT AND MAIDA.

4 cups atta (chapati flour)
1 teaspoon salt
4 tablespoons oil or ghee
1/2 lb. potatoes, unpeeled
1/4 teaspoon mustard seeds
1/2 onion, finely chopped
pinch of ground turmeric
pinch of asafoetida
ghee or oil for shallow-frying
extra ghee or oil for brushing
  on the dough

MAKES 14

SIFT the atta and salt into a bowl and make a well in the center. Add 2 tablespoons of the oil or ghee and about 1 1/4 cups tepid water and mix to a soft, pliable dough. Turn out onto a floured surface, knead for 5 minutes, then place in an oiled bowl. Cover and allow to rest for 30 minutes.

SIMMER the potatoes for 15–20 minutes or until cooked. Cool slightly, then peel and mash. Heat the remaining oil or ghee in a saucepan over medium heat, add the mustard seeds, cover and shake the saucepan until the seeds start to pop. Add the onion and fry for 1 minute. Stir in the turmeric and asafoetida. Mix in the potatoes and cook over low heat for 1–2 minutes, or until the mixture leaves the side of the saucepan. Season with salt to taste, and allow to cool.

DIVIDE the dough into 14 portions and roll each into a 6 inch circle. Spread 1 teaspoon of the potato filling evenly over one half of each circle of dough and fold into a semicircle. Rub oil on half the surface area, then fold over into quarters. Roll out until doubled in size. Cover the parathas with a cloth, then cook them one at a time.

HEAT a tava, griddle or a heavy-bottomed frying pan over medium heat. Oil the surface of the tava or griddle. Remove the excess flour on each paratha prior to cooking by holding it in the palms of your hands and gently slapping it from one hand to the other. If you leave the flour on it may burn.

COOK each paratha for 2–3 minutes, then turn over and cook for 1 minute, or until the surface has brown flecks. Cooking should be quick to ensure the parathas remain soft. Cover the cooked parathas with a cloth. Parathas must be served warm. They can be reheated in a microwave, or wrapped in aluminum foil and heated in a conventional oven at 350°F for 10 minutes.

Fold the filling into the parathas and then gently roll them out so that the filling stays in place.

Pour the idli mixture into the steamer. The consistency should be such that it finds its own level and cooks to a neat shape.

QUICK IDLIS

IDLIS

1 1/4 cups urad dal
1/2 cup rice flour (rava-idli)
1 teaspoon fenugreek seeds
1 teaspoon salt

MAKES 20

PUT the the dal in a bowl, cover with water and soak for at least 4 hours, or overnight.

DRAIN the dal, then grind in a food processor or blender with a little water, to form a fine paste.

COMBINE the rice flour, fenugreek seeds and salt in a large bowl and mix in enough water to make a thick, pourable batter. Mix the batters together. Cover with a cloth and leave in a warm place for 8 hours, until the batter ferments and bubbles. The batter will double in volume.

POUR the mixture into a greased idli mold, filling the cups almost to the brim. Cover and steam the idlis over simmering water for 10–15 minutes, until they are firm and puffed. Traditionally, the idlis are eaten with sambhar (page 53) or with podi (page 242), or as a side dish for dishes that have plenty of sauce.

QUICK IDLIS

1/3 cup chana dal
1 inch piece of ginger, finely chopped
1 1/4 cups plain yogurt (page 280)
2 tablespoons oil
1 teaspoon black mustard seeds
10 curry leaves
1 green chile, seeded and finely chopped
2 1/2 cups fine semolina
1/2 cup grated coconut (page 283)
1/4 teaspoon baking soda
2 teaspoons salt

MAKES 16

PUT the dal in a bowl, cover with water and soak for at least 4 hours, or overnight. Drain and blend with the ginger, yogurt and 2/3 cup of water in a food processor or blender, to form a thin paste.

HEAT the oil in a frying pan, add the mustard seeds, cover and shake the pan until the seeds start to pop. Add the curry leaves and chile and fry for 1 minute. Add the semolina and grated coconut and stir for 2 minutes, or until they start to brown.

MIX both the mixtures together and stir in the baking soda and salt. Leave for 1 hour, until the mixture thickens and becomes fluffy. Add 2 1/2 cups of water to make a thick, pourable batter. Pour the mixture into a greased idli mold, filling the cups almost to the brim.

COVER and steam the idlis over simmering water for 10 minutes, or until they are firm and puffed.

DOSAS

THESE ARE LARGE, SPONGY, RICE PANCAKES WITH A CRISP SURFACE. THEY ARE TRADITIONALLY EATEN WITH SAMBHAR FOR BREAKFAST. FOR THE BEST RESULT, RICE FLOUR THAT IS SPECIALLY MADE FOR MAKING DOSAS SHOULD BE SOUGHT OUT AS IT IS GROUND TO THE RIGHT CONSISTENCY.

1/2 cup urad dal
1 teaspoon salt
1 3/4 cups rice flour
oil for cooking

MAKES 20

PUT the dal in a bowl and cover with water. Soak for at least 4 hours or overnight.

DRAIN, then grind the dal with the salt and a little water in a food processor, blender or pestle and mortar to form a fine paste. Mix the paste with the rice flour, add 4 cups of water and mix well. Cover with a cloth and leave in a warm place for 8 hours, or until the batter ferments and bubbles. The batter will double in volume.

HEAT a tava or a nonstick frying pan over medium heat and leave to heat up. Don't overheat it—the heat should always be medium. Lightly brush the surface of the tava or frying pan with oil. Stir the batter and pour a ladleful into the middle of the griddle and quickly spread it out with the back of the ladle or a flexible-bladed knife, to form a thin pancake. Don't worry if the dosa is not perfect—they are very hard to get exactly right. Drizzle a little oil or ghee around the edge to help it crisp up. Cook until small holes appear on the surface and the edges start to curl. Turn over with a spatula and cook the other side. (The first dosa is often a disaster but it will season the pan for the following ones.)

REPEAT with the remaining mixture, oiling the pan between each dosa. Roll the dosas into big tubes and keep warm. Dosas are often filled with potato masala filling (page 245) and served with sambhar (page 53) and chutneys, or with curries.

Spread the dosa batter out as thinly as you can. This will take a little practice. Drizzle the edge with oil to help it crisp up.

SIDE DISHES

Jaggery comes in different varieties and broken into varying sized lumps.

MANGO CHUTNEY

MANGO SALAD

THIS IS A SCRUMPTIOUS SALAD TO BE SERVED WITH ANY MEAL. TO CHOOSE RIPE MANGOES, CHECK THAT THEY ARE ONLY SLIGHTLY SOFT WHEN YOU TOUCH THEM, THEN SMELL THEM TO SEE WHETHER THEY HAVE THAT WONDERFUL MANGO AROMA.

5 cups grated coconut (page 283)
2 dried chiles, seeded and
    chopped
1 tablespoon grated jaggery or light
    brown sugar
2 cups ripe mango flesh, cubed
1 tablespoon oil
1/2 teaspoon coriander seeds
1/2 teaspoon black mustard seeds
6 curry leaves

SERVES 4

PUT the coconut, chiles and jaggery in a blender and add enough water to make a thick, coarse paste. If you don't have a blender, crush everything together in a pestle and mortar, adding a little water as you go.

TRANSFER the paste to a bowl and toss the mango through. Season with salt, to taste, then refrigerate. Heat the oil in a small frying pan over low heat and add the coriander, mustard seeds and curry leaves. Cover and shake the pan until the seeds start to pop. Pour the oil and seeds over the mango mixture and stir.

MANGO CHUTNEY

THIS IS A WONDERFUL MANGO CHUTNEY THAT IS NOT TOO HOT AND IS VERY SIMPLE TO MAKE. IT IS ONE THAT IS FAMILIAR TO MOST PEOPLE AND GOES WITH ALMOST EVERYTHING. SWEET CHUTNEY BRINGS A CONTRASTING FLAVOR TO SAVORY DISHES AND ALSO GOES WELL WITH PAPPADAMS.

1 tablespoon oil
2 garlic cloves, crushed
1 teaspoon grated ginger
2 cinnamon sticks
4 cloves
1/2 teaspoon chili powder
2 lb. fresh or frozen ripe mango
    flesh, roughly chopped
1 1/2 cups clear vinegar
1 cup sugar

MAKES 2 CUPS

HEAT the oil in a heavy-bottomed saucepan over medium heat, add the garlic and ginger and fry for 1 minute. Add the remaining ingredients and bring to a boil.

REDUCE the heat to low and cook for 1 hour, or until the mango is thick and pulpy, like jam. It should fall in sheets off the spoon when it is ready. Add salt, to taste, and more chili if you wish. Remove the whole spices.

POUR the chutney into hot sterilized jars (wash the jars in boiling water and dry them thoroughly in a warm oven). Seal the jars and allow to cool completely. Store in a cool place, or in the fridge after opening.

LACCHA

THIS SPECIALTY FROM DELHI IS A TOMATO AND ONION ACCOMPANIMENT THAT IS ALMOST LIKE A SALAD. IT IS EASY TO PREPARE AND GOES PARTICULARLY WELL WITH TANDOORI MEATS AND BREADS SUCH AS CHAPATIS, PURIS OR NAAN.

Cucumbers in India come with both green and yellow skins.

1 red onion, finely sliced into rings
1/2 teaspoon salt
1/2 teaspoon cumin seeds
1/4 teaspoon chili powder
2 tomatoes, thinly sliced
1 lb. cucumber, peeled
   and thinly sliced
3 tablespoons lemon juice

SERVES 6

MIX the onion with the salt and allow to drain in a strainer or colander for 10 minutes. Rinse under cold water, then drain and put in a bowl.

PLACE a small frying pan over low heat and dry-roast the cumin seeds until aromatic. Grind the roasted seeds to a fine powder using a spice grinder or pestle and mortar. Add the cumin and chili powder to the onion and mix well.

ARRANGE the tomato slices on a plate and top with a layer of cucumber, then onion. Sprinkle with the lemon juice and season with salt and black pepper to taste.

RAITA

A RAITA IS SIMILAR TO A PACHADI WHICH IS POPULAR IN SOUTHERN INDIA. BOTH HAVE A YOGURT OR CURD BASE WITH VARYING VEGETABLES OR FRUITS ADDED. A YOGURT DISH IS SERVED WITH ALMOST EVERY INDIAN MEAL AS A CONTRAST TO HOT OR SPICY DISHES.

RAITA

1 lb. cucumber, grated
1 large, ripe tomato, finely chopped
1 1/4 cups plain yogurt (page 280)
1/2 tablespoon oil
1 teaspoon black mustard seeds
1 tablespoon cilantro leaves
   (optional)

SERVES 4

PUT the cucumber and tomato in a strainer for 20 minutes to drain off any excess liquid. Mix them in a bowl with the yogurt and season with salt, to taste.

FOR the final seasoning (tarka), heat the oil in a small saucepan over medium heat, add the mustard seeds, then cover and shake the saucepan until the seeds start to pop. Pour the seeds and oil over the yogurt. Serve sprinkled with the cilantro leaves if you wish.

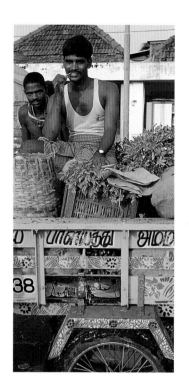

RADISH SALAD

USE THE SMALLEST RADISHES THAT YOU CAN FIND FOR THIS SALAD. COMBINING THE RADISHES WITH PEANUTS GIVES A CRUNCHY TEXTURE AND HOT FLAVOR. IT SERVES AS A FRESH-TASTING ACCOMPANIMENT TO MOST COOKED DISHES.

1 1/2 cups small radishes
1 tablespoon oil
1/4 teaspoon cumin seeds
1/4 teaspoon black mustard seeds
pinch of asafoetida
1/4 teaspoon ground turmeric
1/4 teaspoon salt
1 tablespoon lemon juice
2/3 cup roasted peanuts,
  roughly chopped

SERVES 4

WASH the radishes and trim the ends. Cut each radish into four or eight pieces.

HEAT the oil in a small saucepan over medium heat, add the cumin and mustard seeds, then cover and shake the saucepan until the seeds start to pop.

ADD the asafoetida, turmeric and salt to the saucepan, then remove from the heat, add the lemon juice and allow to cool. Just before serving, arrange the radishes and the peanuts in a bowl, pour the dressing over the top and mix thoroughly.

CARROT SALAD

CARROT SALADS ARE POPULAR THROUGHOUT INDIA. IN THIS ONE, THE SPICES ARE HEATED IN THE OIL IN ORDER FOR THEIR FLAVOR TO PERMEATE THE DRESSING. THIS SALAD GETS MORE FLAVOURFUL IF IT IS ALLOWED TO REST FOR HALF AN HOUR BEFORE SERVING.

1 tablespoon oil
1/4 teaspoon black mustard seeds
1/4 teaspoon cumin seeds
pinch of ground turmeric
1/4 teaspoon salt
1/4 teaspoon sugar
1 1/2 tablespoons lemon juice
1 lb. carrots, finely grated
cilantro leaves

SERVES 4

HEAT the oil in a small saucepan over medium heat, add the mustard and cumin seeds, then cover and shake the saucepan until the seeds start to pop.

ADD the turmeric, salt and sugar to the saucepan, then remove the saucepan from the heat and allow the spices to cool for 5 minutes. Mix in the lemon juice, then toss the carrots through. Cover and leave for 30 minutes. Garnish with cilantro leaves just before serving.

CARROT SALAD

CHURRI

THIS IS A VERY REFRESHING SIDE DISH WHICH IS TRADITIONALLY USED AS AN ACCOMPANIMENT TO BIRYANI BUT IT IS VERSATILE AND CAN BE SERVED WITH MOST DISHES. THE YOGURT AND BUTTERMILK HAVE A COOLING EFFECT WHEN CHURRI IS EATEN WITH HOT OR SPICY DISHES.

1 teaspoon cumin seeds
1/2 cup mint leaves, roughly chopped
1/2 cup cilantro leaves, roughly chopped
1 inch piece of ginger, roughly chopped
2 green chiles, roughly chopped
1 1/4 cups plain yogurt (page 280)
1 1/4 cups buttermilk
1 onion, thinly sliced

SERVES 4

PLACE a small frying pan over low heat and dry-roast the cumin seeds until aromatic. Grind the seeds to a fine powder in a spice grinder or pestle and mortar.

CHOP the mint, cilantro, ginger and chiles to a fine paste in a blender, or chop together finely with a knife. Add the yogurt and buttermilk and a pinch of salt to the mixture and blend until all the ingredients are well mixed. Check the seasoning, adjust if necessary, then mix in the sliced onion and the ground cumin, reserving a little cumin to sprinkle on top.

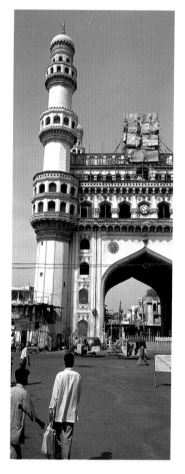

The Charminar, Hyderabad.

CARROT PACHADI

THIS DELIGHTFUL CARROT SIDE DISH IS SIMILAR TO RAITA, PACHADI BEING THE SOUTHERN INDIAN TERM FOR A YOGURT-BASED ACCOMPANIMENT. THIS GOES PARTICULARLY WELL WITH BIRYANI AND PULAO BUT IS SUITABLE FOR SERVING WITH MANY OTHER DISHES AS THE YOGURT IS SOOTHING.

1 tablespoon oil
1 teaspoon black mustard seeds
2–3 dried chiles
1/4 teaspoon asafoetida
1 stalk of curry leaves
2 1/2 cups plain yogurt (page 280)
4 carrots, finely grated
cilantro leaves

SERVES 4

HEAT the oil in a small saucepan over medium heat, add the mustard seeds and chiles, then cover and shake the saucepan until the seeds start to pop. Remove from the heat and immediately stir in the asafoetida and curry leaves.

WHISK the yogurt to remove any lumps, then mix in the grated carrots. Mix in the mustard seeds, chiles, asafoetida, curry leaves along with the oil, then season with salt, to taste. Garnish with cilantro leaves.

CARROT PACHADI

KOSAMBRI

KOSAMBRI ARE SALAD-LIKE DISHES FROM MYSORE. THIS ONE USES A COMBINATION OF CARROTS OR RADISHES AND DAL BUT THERE ARE MANY VARIATIONS. THIS IS AN EXCELLENT COMBINATION OF INGREDIENTS AND CAN BE SERVED ALONGSIDE MOST INDIAN DISHES.

EGGPLANT SAMBAL

1/3 cup moong dal
11/3 cups carrots or white radishes, finely grated
1/3 cup grated coconut (page 283)
3/4 cup cilantro leaves
1/2 tablespoon oil
1/2 teaspoon yellow mustard seeds
2 dried chiles
2 tablespoons lemon juice

SERVES 4

SOAK the dal in plenty of boiling water for 3 hours, then drain.

COMBINE the dal, carrots or radishes, coconut and the cilantro leaves in a salad bowl. Heat the oil in a small saucepan over medium heat, add the mustard seeds, then cover and shake the saucepan until the seeds start to pop. Add the chiles, remove from the heat and add the lemon juice. When cold, pour over the remaining ingredients and toss well. Season with salt to taste.

EGGPLANT SAMBAL

EGGPLANT IS ALSO KNOWN BY ITS INDIAN NAME BRINJAL. FOR THIS RECIPE, IT IS PREFERABLE TO USE THE LONG, THIN, ASIAN EGGPLANT. USE THE SAMBAL AS AN ACCOMPANIMENT OR EAT IT AS A DIP WITH PIECES OF INDIAN BREAD.

2 medium eggplant
1/2 tablespoon oil
1/2 teaspoon ground turmeric
3 tablespoons lime juice
2 red chiles, seeded and finely diced
1 small red onion, finely diced
4 tablespoons plain yogurt (page 280)
cilantro leaves

SERVES 4

PREHEAT the oven to 400°F. Slice each eggplant in half and brush the cut halves with the oil and ground turmeric. Place the eggplant in a roasting pan and roast them for 30 minutes, or until they are browned all over and very soft.

SCOOP the eggplant pulp into a bowl. Mash the pulp with the lime juice, chiles and onion, reserving some chile and onion for garnish. Season with salt to taste, then fold in the yogurt. Garnish with the cilantro leaves and remaining onion and chile.

POUSSIN PICKLE

THIS RECIPE USES POUSSIN (BABY CHICKENS) AS THEY ARE AVAILABLE ALL YEAR ROUND. HOWEVER, IN NORTHERN INDIA, WHEN THE GAME SEASON IS UNDER WAY, PARTRIDGE WOULD BE USED. THE PICKLE IS AN IDEAL ACCOMPANIMENT TO MOST DISHES OR CAN BE EATEN WITH BREADS.

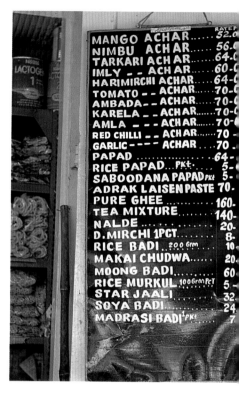

2 x 1³/₄ lb. poussin or 1 partridge
6 garlic cloves, roughly chopped
2 inch piece of ginger, roughly
   chopped
1²/₃ cups mustard oil or oil
2 Indian bay leaves (cassia leaves)
12 dried chiles
20 black peppercorns
1 teaspoon kalonji (nigella seeds)
3 teaspoons coriander seeds
1 teaspoon cumin seeds
2 teaspoons yellow mustard seeds
¹/₄ teaspoon ground turmeric
1 teaspoon garam masala
   (page 284)
pinch of asafoetida
1 tablespoon salt
¹/₂ cup jaggery or soft brown sugar
1²/₃ cups dark vinegar

MAKES 4 CUPS

CUT each poussin or partridge into six pieces by removing both legs and cutting between the joint of the drumstick and thigh. Cut down one side of each backbone, leaving it attached to one side. Turn each poussin or partridge over and cut through the cartilage down the center of each breastbone. Remove all the wing tips. Trim any excess fat or skin.

CHOP the garlic and ginger finely in a food processor, or grate the ginger and crush the garlic and mix them together. Heat the mustard oil in a heavy-bottomed saucepan over medium heat until smoking. Reduce the heat to low, then add the garlic and ginger mixture, bay leaves, dried chiles, peppercorns, kalonji, coriander, cumin and mustard seeds, turmeric, garam masala and asafoetida to the saucepan. Gently shake the saucepan until the seeds start to sizzle and pop. Add the poussin pieces and salt, stir well and fry over medium heat for 20 minutes, stirring occasionally until the poussin are browned all over and cooked through. Remove the poussin pieces from the saucepan with a slotted spoon and place in a bowl. Allow the saucepan of spiced oil to cool.

PUT the jaggery and vinegar in a saucepan and bring to a boil, reduce the heat and cook over medium heat for 10–15 minutes, until the jaggery has completely dissolved and the vinegar has reduced by a third. Allow to cool.

WHEN the vinegar has cooled, mix it with the cooled oil, stir in the poussin pieces and mix well. Store the pickle in special ceramic pickling pots or sterilized jars (wash the jars in boiling water and dry in a warm oven). Marinate for 3–5 days, shaking the bottle carefully at least twice daily so that the poussin can absorb all the flavors. It will now be ready for serving. Store in a cool place, or in the fridge after opening.

Pickles (achar) and chutneys (chatnis) are popular all over India. Shops and stalls usually sell a bewildering variety.

PINEAPPLE CHUTNEY

THIS QUICK AND SIMPLE FRESH PINEAPPLE CHUTNEY CAN BE ENJOYED AS PART OF ANY MAIN MEAL

INCLUDING MEAT AND POULTRY OR FISH AND SEAFOOD DISHES. THE ACIDITY OF THE PINEAPPLE WILL

CUT THROUGH ANY RICH DISHES AND MAKE A REFRESHING CONTRAST.

2 small or 1 large pineapple,
   slightly green
1 teaspoon salt
1 red onion, thinly sliced into
   half rings
4 red chiles, seeded and finely
   chopped
4 garlic cloves, finely chopped
2 teaspoons ginger juice
   (page 280)
1/4 cup confectioners' sugar, or to
   taste
6 tablespoons lime juice, or to taste

SERVES 6

PEEL the pineapple by cutting down the outside in strips. Remove any remaining eyes, then slice the pineapple lengthwise and remove the tough central core.

RUB the pineapple with the salt and allow it to rest for a few minutes in a colander to draw out some of the juices. Rinse, then chop into small chunks and drain well on paper towels.

MIX all the ingredients together in a bowl, adding enough sugar, lime juice, pepper and salt to achieve a balanced flavor. Chill and serve.

PODI

PODI

PODI IS A COARSE POWDER USED AS A DIP OR AS A SEASONING. EAT IT WITH IDLI OR USE IT AS A

SCATTER SEASONING FOR STEAMED VEGETABLES OR SALADS. THIS WILL MAKE ENOUGH TO LAST A

LONG TIME SO STORE IT IN A JAR AND USE IT AS YOU NEED IT (YOU CAN MAKE HALF IF YOU WISH).

1/2 cup urad dal
1/2 cup chana dal
1/3 oz. dried chillies
75 g sesame seeds
1/2 teaspoon sugar
1/2 teaspoon salt
1 tablespoon ghee

MAKES 7 OZ.

PLACE a small frying pan over low heat and dry-roast the urad dal, stirring constantly until brown. Remove from the pan and repeat with the chana dal, dried chiles and sesame seeds. Grind the roasted mixture to a powder with the sugar and salt, using a spice grinder or pestle and mortar. Cool completely and store in a jar or an airtight container.

WHEN ready to serve, heat the ghee in a frying pan and add 2 teaspoons of podi per person. Toss together until well mixed.

POTATO MASALA

THIS FILLING IS TRADITIONALLY ROLLED IN DOSAS TO MAKE MASALA DOSA, WHICH IS SERVED FOR BREAKFAST OR AS A SNACK IN SOUTHERN INDIA. HOWEVER, IT ALSO MAKES AN EXCELLENT SPICY POTATO SIDE DISH.

2 tablespoons oil
1 teaspoon black mustard seeds
10 curry leaves
1/4 teaspoon ground turmeric
1/2 inch piece of ginger, grated
2 green chiles, finely chopped
2 onions, chopped
1 lb. waxy potatoes, cut into
  1 inch cubes
1 tablespoon tamarind paste
  (page 280)

SERVES 4

HEAT the oil in a heavy-based frying pan, add the mustard seeds, cover and when they pop add the curry leaves, turmeric, ginger, chiles and onions and cook, uncovered, until the onions are soft.

ADD the potato cubes and 1 cup of water to the pan, bring to a boil, cover and cook until the potatoes are tender and almost breaking up. If there is any liquid left in the pan, simmer, uncovered, until it evaporates. If the potatoes aren't cooked and there is no liquid left, add a little more and continue to cook. Add the tamarind and season with salt to taste.

PAPAYA MUSTARD PICKLE

THIS IS A WONDERFUL PICKLE SUITABLE FOR SERVING WITH ROAST LAMB RAAN OR WITH PIECES OF ROTI AND A QUICK DAL CURRY OR SAMBAR. MAKE SURE YOU USE A GREEN PAPAYA AND NOT A RIPE ONE, OTHERWISE THE FLESH WILL DISINTEGRATE WHEN YOU COOK IT.

PAPAYA MUSTARD PICKLE

5 red chiles, seeded and chopped
1 large red onion, chopped
3 inch piece of ginger, grated
3 garlic cloves, chopped
4 tablespoons black mustard seeds
2 cups clear vinegar
1 tablespoon oil
3 green chiles, seeded
  and chopped
3/4 cup sugar
1/4 teaspoon salt
1/4 teaspoon ground turmeric
1 lb. green papaya, cut into
  1/2 inch cubes

MAKES 4 CUPS

CHOP the red chiles, onion, ginger, garlic, mustard seeds and 1/2 cup of vinegar together in a food processor or pestle and mortar to form a paste. The mustard seeds will not break up completely.

HEAT the oil in a large heavy-bottomed saucepan and cook the paste and remaining vinegar until aromatic and reduced. Add the green chiles and sugar and stir until the sugar is dissolved. Add the salt, turmeric and papaya and simmer for 2 minutes, making sure the papaya stays firm.

POUR the pickle into sterilized jars (wash the jars in boiling water and dry in a warm oven) and allow to cool completely. Store in a cool place, or in the fridge after opening.

SWEET TOMATO CHUTNEY

THIS IS AN EASY STORE-CUPBOARD CHUTNEY. IT IS AN ESPECIALLY HANDY RECIPE IF YOU HAVE AN ABUNDANCE OF VERY RIPE TOMATOES (YOU WILL NEED 1$^3/_4$ LB. PEELED FRESH TOMATOES). IF YOU CAN'T FIND CLEAR VINEGAR AT INDIAN FOOD SHOPS OR SUPERMARKETS, USE WHITE VINEGAR.

8 garlic cloves, roughly chopped
2 inch piece of ginger, roughly
  chopped
2 x 14 oz. cans diced tomatoes
1$^1/_4$ cups clear vinegar
1$^1/_2$ cups jaggery or light brown
  sugar
2 tablespoons golden raisins
2 teaspoons salt
$^3/_4$ teaspoon cayenne pepper
chili powder (optional)

MAKES 2 CUPS

COMBINE the garlic, ginger and a can of tomatoes in a blender or food processor and blend until smooth. If you don't have a blender, crush the garlic, grate the ginger and push the tomatoes through a strainer before mixing them all together.

PUT the other can of tomatoes, the vinegar, sugar, golden raisins and salt in a large, heavy-bottomed saucepan. Bring to a boil and add the garlic and ginger mixture. Reduce the heat and simmer gently for 1$^1/_2$–1$^3/_4$ hours, stirring occasionally, until the mixture is thick enough to fall off a spoon in sheets. Make sure the mixture doesn't catch on the bottom.

ADD the cayenne pepper. For a hotter chutney, add a little chili powder. Allow to cool, then pour into sterilized jars (wash two 1-cup jars in boiling water and dry them in a warm oven). Store in a cool place, or in the fridge after opening.

Shelled tamarind husk and pulp.

TAMARIND AND RAISIN CHUTNEY

2 teaspoons fennel seeds
1 cup tamarind paste (page 280)
$^1/_3$ cup pitted dates, chopped
$^1/_4$ cup raisins
1 teaspoon chili powder
$^3/_4$ cup jaggery or light brown sugar
1 tablespoon oil
$^1/_2$ teaspoon black mustard seeds
6 green chiles, slit in half and
  seeded but left whole

MAKES 1 CUP

PLACE a small frying pan over low heat and dry-roast the fennel seeds, stirring constantly until aromatic. Grind the seeds to a fine powder using a spice grinder or pestle and mortar. Mix the ground fennel with the tamarind, dates, raisins, chili powder, jaggery and a pinch of salt.

HEAT the oil in a large, heavy-bottomed saucepan over medium heat, add the mustard seeds, then cover and shake the saucepan until they start to pop. Add the date mixture and chiles, bring to a boil and cook for 3 minutes, until the mixture starts to thicken. Reduce the heat and simmer for 40 minutes until the chutney is thick enough to fall off a spoon in sheets. Cool, then put in a sterilized jar (wash the jar in boiling water and dry in a warm oven). Store in a cool place. Refrigerate after opening.

TAMARIND AND RAISIN
CHUTNEY

LEMON PICKLE

PICKLES ARE VERY MUCH A PART OF AN INDIAN MEAL. ALTHOUGH THERE ARE MANY VARIETIES OF COMMERCIALLY MANUFACTURED PICKLES AVAILABLE, A HOMEMADE ONE IS FAR SUPERIOR. CHOOSE THIN-SKINNED LEMONS FOR THIS IF YOU CAN. YOU CAN ALSO USE INDIAN LIMES FOR THIS RECIPE.

1 lb. thin-skinned lemons
1/2 teaspoon ground turmeric
2 tablespoons salt
1/2 teaspoon fenugreek seeds
1 teaspoon yellow mustard seeds
1/2 tablespoon chili powder
2 tablespoons oil

MAKES 2 CUPS

WASH the lemons, place them in a saucepan with 2 cups of water and the turmeric and bring slowly to a boil, skimming off any impurities that rise to the top. Boil for 8 minutes, then remove from the heat and drain well.

CUT each lemon into eight sections and remove any pips. By this time, the lemon flesh will have turned to a pulp. Sprinkle the lemons with the salt and pack them into a 2-cup glass jar which has been sterilized (wash the jar in boiling water and dry in a warm oven). Put the lid on tightly and keep the lemons in the jar for 1 week, turning the jar over every day. If the lid of the jar is too narrow to balance upside down, store the jar on its side and roll it over every day instead.

PLACE a small frying pan over low heat and dry-roast the fenugreek and mustard seeds until aromatic and starting to pop, shaking the pan occasionally to prevent them burning. Grind the roasted seeds to a fine powder using a spice grinder or pestle and mortar.

TRANSFER the lemons to a bowl and mix in the ground spices and the chili powder. Clean the jar and sterilize it again. Put the lemons and any juices back into the jar and pour the oil over the top to act as an air barrier and stop the top layer from discoloring. Store in a cool place, or in the fridge after opening.

Boiling the lemons will soften both the rind and flesh. Skim off any impurities that appear on the surface of the water.

A coconut farm in Kerala.

A grinding stone is used in India instead of a pestle and mortar. The grinding stone is rubbed back and forth over ingredients.

FRESH COCONUT CHUTNEY

CHUTNEY MADE WITH FRESH COCONUT IS SERVED WITH IDLIS AND DOSAS FOR BREAKFAST, OR AS A SNACK. THE CURRY LEAVES AND TAMARIND GIVE A DISTINCTIVE INDIAN FLAVOR.

1 teaspoon chana dal
1 teaspoon urad dal
1/2 fresh coconut, grated
2 green chiles, seeded and
  finely chopped
1/2 teaspoon salt
1 tablespoon oil
1 teaspoon black mustard seeds
5 curry leaves
1 teaspoon tamarind paste
  (page 280)

SERVES 4

SOAK the dals in cold water for 2 hours, then drain well.

PUT the grated coconut, chiles and salt in a food processor and blend to a fine paste. If you don't have a food processor, either finely chop everything together with a knife or pound them in a pestle and mortar.

HEAT the oil in a small saucepan and add the mustard seeds and dals, then cover and shake the saucepan until they start to pop. Add the curry leaves and fry for 1 minute, or until the dal browns. Add these ingredients to the coconut with the tamarind and mix well.

MINT AND CILANTRO CHUTNEY

MINT AND CILANTRO CHUTNEY

THIS REFRESHING MINT AND CILANTRO CHUTNEY IS PERFECT FOR SERVING WITH NIMKI, SAMOSAS OR SINGHARAS. HOWEVER, IT CAN BE SERVED WITH JUST ABOUT ANY INDIAN MEAL.

1 1/2 cups mint leaves
1 cup cilantro leaves
1 green chile
1 tablespoon tamarind paste
  (page 280)
1/2 teaspoon salt
1 1/2 teaspoons sugar
3 tablespoons plain yogurt
  (page 280), (optional)

SERVES 4

WASH the mint and cilantro leaves. Discard any tough stems but keep the young soft ones for flavor. Blend all the ingredients together in a blender or food processor, or chop everything finely and pound it together in a pestle and mortar. Taste the chutney and add more salt if necessary. If you want a creamier, milder chutney, stir in the yogurt.

SWEETS & DRINKS

The Writers building, Kolkata (Calcutta).

ROSSOGOLLAS

KOLKATA (CALCUTTA) IS THE CITY WHERE THE BEST BENGALI SWEETS CAN BE FOUND. ROSSOGOLLAS OR RASGULLAS ARE SWEETENED MILK BALLS IN SYRUP, SAID TO HAVE BEEN INVENTED BY AN OLD FIRM, K.C. DAS, WHICH SPECIALIZES IN SWEETS. MAKE THE CHENNA BEFORE YOU START.

1 quantity chenna
(page 279)
3 tablespoons chopped nuts
(optional)

SYRUP
2 lb. sugar
3 tablespoons milk
rosewater (optional)

SERVES 6

DIVIDE the chenna dough into 30 portions and roll each into a ball. If you are using the nuts, make a hollow in each ball, add a few chopped nuts to the center, then re-roll as a ball.

MAKE a thin syrup by combining the sugar with 6 cups of water in a heavy-bottomed saucepan and simmering the mixture over low heat until it is slightly thickened. The syrup should feel sticky and greasy. Add the milk to the boiling syrup to clarify it—this will force any impurities to rise to the surface. Skim off the impurities with a spoon.

DROP the rossogollas into the clean boiling syrup, reduce the heat and simmer for 10 minutes, or until they float. Sprinkle a little water on the boiling syrup every 2 minutes to stop it reducing too much and foaming. When the rossogollas are cooked, they will float on the surface.

REMOVE from the heat and allow to cool in the syrup. If you would like a rose flavor, add a few drops of rosewater. Keep the rossogollas refrigerated until required. Serve with a little of the syrup poured over them.

Make a dent in each ball and fill it with nuts before smoothing the balls into shape. Gently poach them in the sugar syrup.

KARANJI

THESE MINI, COCONUT-FILLED, DEEP-FRIED SWEET PASTRIES ARE EATEN AS A SNACK AT AFTERNOON TEA TIME. BECAUSE THEY CAN BE STORED FOR A WEEK, THEY ARE GOOD TO HAVE ON HAND FOR SERVING TO HUNGRY, UNEXPECTED VISITORS AT ANY TIME OF THE DAY.

1³/₄ cups maida or
   all-purpose flour
4 tablespoons oil or ghee
oil for deep-frying

FILLING
10 cardamom pods
¹/₃ cup sugar
2 inch piece of cinnamon stick
3 cups grated coconut (page 283)

MAKES 30

SIFT the maida into a bowl. Add the oil or ghee and rub it in with your fingers until the mixture resembles bread crumbs. Add 5 tablespoons lukewarm water, a little at a time, and, using a flexible-bladed knife, blend the dough together. Turn out onto a floured surface and knead for 5 minutes, until smooth and pliable. Cover and leave at room temperature for 15 minutes. Don't refrigerate or the oil will congeal, making it difficult to roll.

TO MAKE the filling, remove the cardamom seeds from the pods and coarsely crush them in a pestle and mortar. In a heavy-bottomed saucepan, combine the sugar, cinnamon and ³/₄ cup of water. Heat gently until the sugar has dissolved. Bring to a boil, add the coconut, then stir over low heat until the liquid has evaporated and the mixture comes together. The mixture should not be bone dry. Remove from heat, add the cardamom and allow to cool.

ON a lightly floured surface, roll out a third of the pastry to an 11 inch diameter round. Using a 3 inch cutter, cut out 10 rounds of pastry. Place ¹/₂ tablespoon of the filling in the center of each round, then moisten the edges with water. Seal into a semicircle and crimp the edge. Repeat until all the pastry and filling has been used. Cover until ready to fry.

FILL a karhai or deep, heavy-bottomed saucepan a third full with oil and heat. Add a small piece of pastry and if it rises to the surface in a couple of seconds the oil is ready for use. Put in a few karanjis at a time and fry for 30–60 seconds, until lightly browned. Turn them over and brown them on the other side. Remove from the saucepan and place on a cooling rack for 5 minutes before draining on paper towels. When cold, store in an airtight container for up to a week.

Cut rounds from the pastry with a cutter and then fill them with the coconut mixture. Seal firmly so they don't leak when cooked.

KULFI

YOUNG AND OLD TAKE GREAT DELIGHT IN THESE FLAVORED ICES WHICH ARE SOLD IN INDIA AT ROADSIDE STANDS. THEY ARE NOT GENERALLY MADE IN HOUSEHOLDS AS THEY ARE TIME-CONSUMING.

8 cups milk
10 cardamom pods, lightly crushed
6 tablespoons sugar
1 tablespoon almonds, blanched and finely chopped
2 tablespoons unsalted pistachio nuts, skins removed, finely chopped
edible silver leaf (varak), (optional)

MAKES 12

PUT the milk and cardamom pods in a heavy-bottomed saucepan and bring to a boil. Reduce the heat to low and simmer, stirring frequently, for 2 hours, until the milk has reduced to a third of the original amount, approximately 3 cups. Whenever a thin skin forms on top, stir it back in.

ADD the sugar to the pan, simmer for 5 minutes, then strain into a shallow plastic freezer box. Add the almonds and half the pistachios, then cool. Put twelve 3-cup kulfi molds or dariole molds in the freezer to chill.

PLACE the kulfi mixture in the freezer and every 20 minutes, using an electric mixer or a fork, give the ice cream a good stir to break up the ice crystals. When the mixture is quite stiff, divide it among the molds and freeze until hardened completely. Dip the molds in hot water and turn out the kulfi. Sprinkle with the remaining pistachios and decorate with a piece of silver leaf.

Kulfi are flavored ices made in specially shaped molds. When the mixture has hardened, fill the conical molds, then freeze.

CARROT HALVA

THIS IS A VERY SIMPLE INDIAN SWEET. THE ONLY SECRET TO MAKING IT LOOK AUTHENTIC IS TO USE REALLY BRIGHT-ORANGE CARROTS TO GIVE A GOOD COLOR. CARROT HALVA IS TRADITIONALLY MADE IN THE WINTER MONTHS AND IS BEST EATEN HOT WITH A DOLLOP OF CREAM.

2 lb. carrots, coarsely grated
4 cups milk
1/3 cup ghee
1 cup sugar
2/3 cup raisins
1 teaspoon cardamom seeds, finely ground
1/2 cup slivered almonds
ground cardamom

SERVES 8

PUT the grated carrots and milk in a heavy-bottomed saucepan over low heat and bring to a simmer. Cook, stirring until the carrots are tender and the milk evaporates. This must be done slowly or the mixture will burn. Add the ghee and cook until the carrots start to brown.

ADD the sugar and cook until the mixture is thick and dry. Add the raisins, cardamom and almonds. Serve hot in small bowls, with whipping cream or ice cream, and sprinkle with ground cardamom.

CARROT HALVA

ANGOORI PETHA pieces of winter melon which have been candied in sugar syrup until they are translucent. Angoori means they are still syrupy rather than completely dry.

KUBANI METHA an apricot dessert from Hyderabad made with soaked, dried apricots, cardamom, cinnamon, rose and vanilla extract, and pistachio nuts. It is served with cream.

AMRITA KUMBHA made from sandesh, shaped into little pots and filled with paneer. The name means "pot of nectar." The sweet is named after a "pot" fought over by Hindu gods and demons.

BADAM CHOP a sandwich made from two pieces of almond-based dough filled with malai and decorated with whole almonds and chopped pistachios. A very rich sweet.

LAL DOI red yogurt which is sweetened and served in little pots. One of Kolkata's (Calcutta) famous sweets, it was endorsed by the winner of the Nobel prize, author Rabindranath Tagore.

KHEER MOHAN balls made from chenna that is flavored with saffron. They are cooked in sugar syrup and then split in half. The filling is malai flavored with pistachio and saffron.

HALVA means sweets in Arabic and refers to thick mixtures made from vegetables or grains. This version is sooj halva made with toasted semolina, sugar syrup and either fruit or nuts.

JALBHARA means "filled with water." These sandesh shapes contain rosewater in their center. The rosewater stays liquid for several days before it soaks into the harder shell.

JALEBI loops of orange dough made from a fermented flour batter. This is squeezed through a pastry tip into hot oil, then soaked in sugar syrup to give a crisp shell and soft sweet interior.

KAJU KALASH small pot-shaped sweets made by cooking ground almonds in sugar syrup until it thickens enough to set. Decorated with silver foil (varak) and saffron.

KALA JAMUN balls of milk-based dough which are deep-fried to a very dark brown, then soaked in sugar syrup. Gulab jamun are similar but softer in texture and paler in color.

KHEER KADAM each contains a tiny rossogolla and is coated in a layer of chenna and powdered khoya. These silver ones decorated with saffron were made especially for Divali.

DIVALI is the Hindu festival of light when hundreds of oil lamps are lit and fireworks are let off in the streets. It is also particularly associated with sweets. The festival takes place in October or November, on the 15th day of Kartika in the Hindu calendar and lasts for 5 days. As Divali approaches, thousands of pounds of sweets are made by the halvais (sweet-makers) of India. Extra workers are drafted in to help, temporary

SWEETS

A FONDNESS FOR SWEETS (MITHAI) IS COMMON THROUGHOUT INDIA. UNLIKE IN THE WEST THERE IS NO DISTINCTION BETWEEN SWEETS AND DESSERTS. BOTH ARE SOLD AT SWEET SHOPS AND NEITHER IS COMMONLY EATEN AT THE END OF A MEAL. INSTEAD, MITHAI REPRESENT A FORM OF GREETING, ARE USED AS RELIGIOUS OFFERINGS AND ARE SYMBOLIC OF HOSPITALITY.

Mithai vary regionally and common sweets such as barfi and laddu are available everywhere. Many places have a sweet specialty. In areas such as Bengal, the sweet capital of India, towns and small villages have their own particular varieties.

TYPES OF SWEETS

Sweets generally fit into categories based on their main ingredient, their shape, or the method of production.

BARFI are types of fudge. Their name comes from the Persian word for snow and in their original form they were probably all white. Barfi are based on khoya, a milk product, and are very sweet. Those with ground nuts or flour in them have a grainier texture than the regular milk (dhoodh) versions. SANDESH, based on chenna mixed with sugar, are one of the finest Indian sweets. The name means "news" and the sweets were originally sent to friends by messenger as a means of enquiring after them. Sandesh can be made in a variety of textures and flavors and are often pressed into decorative molds. As a specialty of Bengal, sandesh are shaped into forms such as conch shells or fish, which are representative of that area.

HALVA have a thick, pudding-like texture and are based on ingredients such as semolina, grated carrots, besan flour and legumes. Sweet-makers in India are called halvais.

ROSSOGOLLAS were the invention of Nobin Chandra Das in 1868. They are Kolkata's (Calcutta) most famous sweet. They are now made by the Das family at their factory in the city. First, paneer is made by separating milk into curds and whey and draining off the whey. The paneer is then pushed through an extruder to get rid of any excess moisture. Sugar is added to make chenna and the mixture is rolled into balls by hand.

stands are set up and sweet production goes into overdrive. Every corner of every shop is utilized, including the basement and roof. Sweets are lavishly decorated using gold and silver leaf, nuts, dried fruit and saffron. Trays, each holding a different type of sweet, are piled high. The sweets are sold by weight or packaged into fancy gift boxes. Sweets are bought as gifts for friends and relatives and also to use as religious offerings.

LADDU are named for their ball shape rather than their ingredients. They are made with a besan flour or coarse flour dough which is pressed into patties, deep-fried, then crumbled and shaped into balls with sugar, ghee, spices and nuts. There are many variations, some of which are made with puffed rice mixed with sugar and often nuts.

DEEP-FRIED sweets are fried in oil and then soaked in sugar syrup such as jalebi and imarti (loops of orange dough).

MILK-BASED sweets and desserts range from Bengali specialties such as rossogollas and kheer (rice pudding) to southern dishes such as payasam (sago or sevian puddings).

MILK-BASED SWEETS

Milk is often used in sweet-making. It is either boiled for prolonged periods until it thickens, or is converted to a type of fresh cheese (paneer) by coagulating it with lemon juice.

RABRI or RABADI is milk at a quarter of its original volume, eaten as a thick, creamy pudding, or as a sauce for sweets such as ras malai.

KHOYA, a fudgy solid mass, is milk at an eighth of its original volume. It is the main ingredient in many milk-based sweets.

CHENNA is paneer sweetened with sugar and is the ingredient on which rossogolla and sandesh are based.

MALAI is the Hindi word for cream. Malai varies in thickness.

DECORATIONS

Indian sweets are required not only to taste good but also to look fabulous. They are often colored with pink, yellow or green, studded with nuts or golden raisins, or covered with a gossamer-fine layer of gold or silver leaf (varak). Though everyday sweets are not as fancy, those sold around festival times are made more elaborate with extra decorations.

FLAVORINGS

Saffron, cardamom, rose essence, kewra (pandanus), khus (fragrant grass), coconut, pistachio and almond are the most common flavors. Unrefined sugars such as gur or jaggery also add flavor and are often preferred to refined sugar.

The balls vary in size depending on whether they are to be sold loose (larger) or tinned (smaller). The rossogollas are cooked in large vats of simmering sugar syrup, each vat heated by a special system based on steam. When the rossogollas are spongy and cooked through they are either left to cool in the syrup or put straight into cans. The factory uses 250 to 400 gallons of fresh milk every day for its sweet-making.

KULFI WITH FALOODA ice cream made with reduced milk and flavored with cardamom and nuts. Falooda are noodles flavored with saffron and cooked in sugar syrup.

MOTHI CHUR LADDU made from tiny balls of fried besan flour mixed with sugar syrup and crushed nuts, these have a crisp, crunchy, crumbly texture and are a specialty for weddings.

SHAHI RABRI a pudding made by boiling milk for several hours until it thickens. This is then sweetened and garnished with pistachio nuts. Sold in individual bowls at sweet shops.

CHANDA KALA a sweet version of the savory samosa, these are filled with a sweet cream mixture and will be deep-fried before serving. Other versions are filled with coconut.

GULAB JAMUN gulab means rose and these are deep-fried balls of chenna or milk powder mixed with ghee soaked in rose-flavored sugar syrup. These are served either warm or cold.

PEDA is a fudge-like mixture, based on khoya. Many are flavored with almond, orange or rose essence and decorated with nuts. A particular specialty of the Punjab and Uttar Pradesh.

PISTA ROLLS are made from a paste of ground almonds and sugar and wrapped around a filling of chopped pistachio nuts. These are decorated with a layer of silver leaf (varak).

RAS MALAI are chenna balls which are cooked in sugar syrup and then floated in a rich cream (rabri) sauce. Some versions include nuts or are flavored with saffron or cardamom.

BARFI

BARFI is a popular Indian sweet usually made with khoya. Mixtures vary—some are similar to sandesh and set quite hard, others are softer and may include nuts such as cashew *(far left)* and flavorings such as saffron *(center left)*. Ajmer barfi *(center right)* is made by cooking milk until it caramelizes. Some barfi, such as the dried fruit and nut barfi *(far right)* specialty of Hyderabad, may not be milk-based.

CASHEW NUT BARFI

3 1/3 cups cashew nuts
6 cardamom pods
2 cups powdered milk
2 tablespoons ghee or butter
1/4 teaspoon ground cloves
3/4 cup sugar
2 sheets edible silver leaf (varak),
(optional)

SERVES 12

PLACE a small frying pan over low heat and dry-roast the cashew nuts until browned all over. Cool and chop in a food processor or with a knife. Remove the cardamom seeds from the pods and crush them in a spice grinder or pestle and mortar. Line a 10 x 7 inch baking pan with waxed paper.

COMBINE the powdered milk and cashew nuts in a large bowl and rub in the ghee until completely mixed in. Stir in the cardamom and cloves.

COMBINE the sugar and 1 cup of water in a heavy-bottomed saucepan and heat over low heat until the sugar melts. Bring to a boil and simmer for 5–7 minutes to make a sugar syrup. Quickly stir the sugar syrup into the cashew mixture—if you leave it too long it will stiffen—and spread the mixture into the baking pan (the mixture should be about 5/8 inch thick). Smooth with a greased spatula. Place the silver leaf on top by inverting the sheets onto the surface and peeling off the paper backing. Allow to cool, then slice into diamond shapes. Serve cold.

Carefully lay sheets of silver on the barfi and pull off the backing paper. If you touch the silver with your hands it will stick to them.

PAYASAM

1/2 cup sago
2 tablespoons ghee
2/3 cup chopped or slivered almonds
1 cup golden raisins
2 oz. sevian, broken into 1 inch
pieces
4 cups milk
1 cup light brown sugar
3 tablespoons golden syrup or
dark corn syrup
1 teaspoon ground cardamom
1/4 teaspoon ground cloves
1 teaspoon rosewater (optional)
2 tablespoons grated coconut
(page 283)

SERVES 6

COOK the sago in 4 cups simmering water, stirring occasionally, for 20–25 minutes, until the sago is clear, then drain. Rinse and drain the sago again.

HEAT the ghee in a heavy-bottomed frying pan over low heat, brown the nuts and golden raisins and remove. Fry the sevian in the same pan until light brown. Add most of the milk and simmer the sevian until soft, stirring as it cooks. Add the sago and remaining milk. Stir with a fork, add the sugar and golden syrup and simmer, stirring constantly.

ADD a little milk if necessary as the payasam thickens, then add the cardamom, cloves and rosewater and stir to a pourable consistency. Stir in two-thirds of the nuts and golden raisins. Serve immediately or chill. Garnish with the coconut and remaining nuts and golden raisins.

PAYASAM

Roll the gulab jamun into smooth balls. When they have fried to a deep golden brown, add them to the flavored sugar syrup.

GULAB JAMUN

LITERALLY TRANSLATED TO MEAN ROSE-FLAVORED PLUM, GULAB JAMUN IS AN EXTREMELY POPULAR INDIAN SWEET MADE BY SOAKING FRIED BALLS OF CHENNA IN SYRUP. A PINCH OF GROUND CARDAMOM CAN BE ADDED TO THE DOUGH FOR EXTRA FLAVOUR.

SYRUP
2 cups sugar
4–5 drops rosewater

GULAB JAMUN
1 cup low-fat powdered milk
2 tablespoons self-rising flour
2 teaspoons fine semolina
2 tablespoons ghee
4 tablespoons milk, to mix
24 pistachio nuts (optional)
oil for deep-frying

MAKES 24

TO MAKE the syrup, put the sugar in a large heavy-bottomed saucepan with 3$\frac{1}{2}$ cups water. Stir over low heat to dissolve the sugar. Increase the heat and boil for 3 minutes to make a syrup. Stir in the rosewater and remove from the heat.

TO MAKE the gulab jamun, combine the powdered milk, flour, semolina and ghee in a bowl. Add enough milk to make a soft dough, mix until smooth, then divide into 24 portions. If using the pistachio nuts, press each piece of dough in the center to make a hole, fill with a pistachio, then roll into a ball. If not using pistachios, just roll each piece into a ball.

FILL a karhai or deep saucepan a third full with oil. Heat the oil to 300°F (a cube of bread will brown in 30 seconds) and fry the balls over low heat until golden brown all over. Remove with a slotted spoon and transfer to the syrup. When all the balls are in the syrup, bring the syrup to boiling point, then remove from the heat. Cool and serve the gulab jamun at room temperature.

SHRIKHAND

THIS IS YET ANOTHER MILK-BASED RECIPE. IT IS TRADITIONALLY MADE BY STRAINING YOGURT AND FLAVORING IT WITH SAFFRON AND CARDAMOM TO GIVE A THICK, RICH, CREAMY DESSERT.

$\frac{1}{2}$ teaspoon saffron strands
3 cardamom pods
1$\frac{1}{2}$ cups plain yogurt (page 280)
3 tablespoons sugar
a few toasted sliced almonds

SERVES 4

SOAK the saffron in 1 teaspoon boiling water. Remove the cardamom seeds from the pods and coarsely crush them in a spice grinder or pestle and mortar.

PUT the yogurt, sugar, cardamom and saffron in a bowl and beat until well mixed. Divide among four bowls and refrigerate before serving. Serve with toasted almonds sprinkled on top.

SHRIKHAND

APRICOTS IN CARDAMOM SYRUP

A KASHMIRI SPECIALTY BEST MADE FROM DRIED KASHMIRI APRICOTS WHICH HAVE LOTS OF FLAVOR. THE SILVER LEAF MAKES THIS A SPECIAL DESSERT BUT DOES NOT HAVE TO BE USED. IT CAN BE SERVED WITH CREAM OR YOGURT TO TEMPER THE SWEETNESS.

1²/₃ cups dried apricots
3 tablespoons sugar
3 tablespoons slivered, blanched
  almonds
¹/₂ inch piece of ginger, sliced
4 cardamom pods
1 cinnamon stick
4 pieces edible silver leaf (varak),
  (optional)

SERVES 4

SOAK the apricots in 3 cups of water in a large saucepan for 4 hours, or until plumped up.

ADD the sugar, almonds, ginger, cardamom and cinnamon to the apricots and bring slowly to a boil, stirring until the sugar has dissolved. Reduce the heat to a simmer and cook until the liquid has reduced by half and formed a thick syrup. Pour into a bowl, then refrigerate.

SERVE in small bowls with a piece of silver leaf for decoration. To do this, invert the piece of backing paper over each bowl. As soon as the silver leaf touches the apricots it will come away from the backing and stick to them.

KHEER

THIS IS THE INDIAN VERSION OF RICE PUDDING AND IS MADE ON THE STOVETOP INSTEAD OF IN THE OVEN. IT IS EXOTICALLY DELICIOUS, RICH AND CREAMY, WITH THE CARDAMOM AND ALMONDS GIVING IT A DISTINCTIVE TEXTURE AND FLAVOR.

³/₄ cup basmati rice
20 cardamom pods
10 cups milk
¹/₃ cup sliced almonds
³/₄ cup sugar
¹/₄ cup golden raisins

SERVES 6

WASH the rice, then soak for 30 minutes in cold water. Drain well. Remove the seeds from the cardamom pods and lightly crush them in a spice grinder or pestle and mortar.

BRING the milk to a boil in a large heavy-bottomed saucepan and add the rice and cardamom. Reduce the heat and simmer for 1¹/₂–2 hours, or until the rice has a creamy consistency. Stir occasionally to prevent the rice from sticking to the pan.

DRY-FRY the almonds in a frying pan for a few minutes over medium heat. Add the sugar, almonds and golden raisins to the rice, reserving some almonds and raisins. Mix, then divide among bowls. Serve warm, garnished with almonds and golden raisins.

KHEER

An advertisement for dairy products.

SALT LASSI

LASSIS ARE A VERY POPULAR DRINK IN INDIA. THEY ARE MADE BY BLENDING YOGURT WITH A FLAVORING WHICH CAN BE EITHER SALTY OR SWEET. BOTH THESE VERSIONS ARE COOLING, REFRESHING AND PERFECT TO DRINK WITH A CURRY.

1 teaspoon cumin seeds
$2^1/_2$ cups plain yogurt (page 280)
$^1/_2$ teaspoon salt

SERVES 4

PLACE a small frying pan over low heat and dry-roast the cumin seeds until browned and aromatic.

BLEND the roasted cumin seeds (reserve a few for garnish) with the yogurt, salt and $1^1/_4$ cups of water, either by hand or in a blender, and serve in tall glasses. If you would like the lassi a little colder, add about eight ice cubes to the blender, or stir them into the blended lassi. Garnish with the reserved cumin seeds.

MANGO LASSI

1 lb. ripe mango
1 cup chilled milk
1 cup plain yogurt (page 280)

SERVES 4

CHOP the mango to a pulp with a knife or in a blender, add a pinch of salt and push through a nylon strainer with the back of a spoon. Discard any fibers. The remaining syrup should be thick but should not contain any stringy bits of pulp. Refrigerate until cold.

BLEND the mango with the milk and yogurt, either by hand or in a blender. If you would like the lassi a little colder, add 8 ice cubes to the blender, or stir them into the blended lassi.

IF YOU want to use green unripe mangoes, cook them with 1 cup sugar and a little water and add 2 cups milk to the lassi, instead of yogurt and milk.

MANGO LASSI

ALMOND SARBAT

1¹/₃ cups freshly ground almonds
2 lb. sugar
12 cardamom pods
almond extract, to taste
5–6 drops rosewater (optional)

MAKES 1 CUP

PUT the almonds, sugar and 1 cup of water in a large, heavy-bottomed saucepan and cook over low heat, stirring constantly until the sugar dissolves. Grind the cardamom with 1 tablespoon water in a pestle and mortar or spice grinder. Add to the almond syrup. Stir the mixture, removing any impurities from the top. Cook until the syrup thickens. Remove from the heat, strain through a strainer lined with cheesecloth, and allow to cool.

ADD the almond extract and rosewater, if using, and serve in long glasses, with water, over lots of crushed ice.

Brightly colored bangles on sale in the market in Hyderabad.

FALOODA

SWEET DRINKS, INDIAN MUSLIM IN ORIGIN, ARE OFTEN DRUNK DURING THE MONTH-LONG RAMADAN FAST. IN THIS ROSEWATER DRINK, THE SUGAR IS AN ENERGY SOURCE THAT IS HIGHLY RECOMMENDED WHILE FASTING. FALOODA CAN ALSO BE MADE WITH FALOODA NOODLES INSTEAD OF THE AGAR JELLY.

ROSE SYRUP
1 cup white sugar
2 teaspoons rosewater,
  or to taste
pink food coloring

FALOODA
2 teaspoons agar-agar
yellow food coloring
2 tablespoons basil seeds
1 tablespoon confectioners' sugar
4 cups milk, chilled
6 tablespoons ice cream
  or whipping cream
pistachios, chopped (optional)
almonds, chopped (optional)
mint leaves (optional)

SERVES 6

TO MAKE the rose syrup, put the sugar and 1 cup of water in a large, heavy-bottomed saucepan, bring to a boil and boil for 2 minutes. Add rosewater, to taste, and enough coloring to make a pink syrup. Cool.

TO PREPARE the falooda, dissolve the agar-agar in 1 cup boiling water in a small saucepan. Cook over medium heat, stirring constantly for 15 minutes. Add a little yellow food coloring. Pour into a large, flat dish and refrigerate until set. Turn out onto a cutting board and slice into thin strips (these should be thin enough to be sucked up a straw).

SOAK the basil seeds in a little water for 1 hour, then drain. Stir the confectioners' sugar into the milk.

TO PREPARE six glasses of falooda, pour 2 tablespoons rose syrup into each large glass. Add a helping of falooda and 2–3 teaspoons basil seeds to each and top with the sweetened, chilled milk and 1 tablespoon cream or ice cream. Garnish with nuts and mint leaves if you wish.

FALOODA

MASALA CHAI

1 inch piece of ginger
2 inch piece of cinnamon stick
4 peppercorns
3 cloves
3 cardamom pods
1 tablespoon black Indian tea
1 cup milk
3 tablespoons sugar

SERVES 6

DRY-ROAST the ginger under a broiler for 1 minute on each side. Put the spices and ginger in a pestle and mortar or spice grinder and roughly crush them. Put the spices, tea and milk in a saucepan with 4 cups water and bring to a boil. Leave for 3 minutes, then add the sugar, to taste.

STRAIN off the grounds (the easiest way is to put the whole lot through a coffee plunger or very fine strainer), then pour the tea from one pitcher to another in a steady stream. You need to hold the pitchers far apart and repeat the process until the tea begins to froth. Serve while still hot, in glasses.

MASALA COFFEE

MASALA COFFEE

THIS IS THE KERALAN CAPPUCCINO, A TRADITIONAL WAY OF MAKING COFFEE, SEEN ON EVERY STREET CORNER. THE COFFEE-MAKER, OFTEN CLAD IN A CHECKED SARONG, IS THE FOCUS OF THE VILLAGE AFTER WORK AND COFFEE IS A MUST FOR STIMULATING TALK AS THE WORLD PASSES BY.

2 cups milk
2 tablespoons sugar
1 inch piece of ginger
2 tablespoons freshly ground
  Keralan or other coffee
5 cardamom seeds, pounded
1 cinnamon stick
cocoa powder

SERVES 4

PUT the milk and sugar in a heavy-bottomed saucepan, bring to a boil over low heat and keep at a low simmer.

DRY-ROAST the ginger under a broiler for 1 minute on each side, then pound it a little in a pestle and mortar to crush it and release the juices. Add to the milk with the coffee, cardamom and cinnamon. Cover and allow the flavorings to steep in the heat for 3 minutes.

STRAIN off the grounds (the easiest way is to put the whole lot through a coffee plunger or very fine strainer), then pour the coffee from one pitcher to another in a steady stream. You need to hold the pitchers far apart and repeat the process until the coffee begins to froth. Serve while still hot, garnished with a sprinkling of cocoa.

BASICS

Rinse the rice very thoroughly under cold running water until the water running through it is completely clear.

RICE

BASMATI IS A FRAGRANT, LONG-GRAIN RICE THAT GETS ITS UNIQUE FLAVOR FROM THE SOIL IN WHICH IT IS GROWN. WE HAVE COOKED IT BY THE ABSORPTION METHOD BUT, IF YOU PREFER, YOU CAN ADD THE RICE TO A SAUCEPAN OF BOILING WATER AND BOIL THE RICE UNTIL READY.

2 cups basmati rice

SERVES 6

RINSE the rice under cold running water until the water running away is clear, then drain well.

PUT the rice in a heavy-bottomed saucepan and add enough water to come about 2 inches above the surface of the pan. (If you put your index finger into the rice so it rests on the bottom of the saucepan, the water will come up to the 2nd joint.) Add 1 teaspoon of salt and bring the water quickly to a boil. When it boils, cover and reduce the heat to a simmer.

COOK for 15 minutes or until the rice is just tender, then remove the saucepan from the heat and rest the rice for 10 minutes without removing the lid. Fluff the rice with a fork before serving.

BOILED ROSEMATTER OR PATNI RICE

ROSEMATTER IS EATEN IN SOUTHERN INDIA AND PATNI IN CENTRAL AND WESTERN INDIA. BOTH LOOK RED AND SPECKLED BECAUSE THE RICE HAS BEEN PRECOOKED IN ITS HUSK, LEAVING SOME BRAN AND HUSK STUCK TO THE GRAIN. COOK THEM AS WE HAVE, RATHER THAN BY THE ABSORPTION METHOD.

2 cups rosematter or patni rice

SERVES 6

RINSE the rice under cold running water until the water running away is clear, then drain well.

BRING a large, heavy-bottomed saucepan of water to a boil and add 1 teaspoon of salt. When the water is at a rolling boil, add the rice and bring back to a boil. Keep at a steady boil for 20 minutes, then test a grain to see if it is cooked. Drain the rice and serve.

ROSEMATTER RICE

PANEER

INDIAN CHEESE, CALLED PANEER OR CHENNA WHEN COMBINED WITH SUGAR, IS AN UNRIPENED CHEESE MADE BY COAGULATING MILK WITH LEMON JUICE, THEN ALLOWING TO DRAIN TO LET THE CURDS AND WHEY SEPARATE. IT IS THEN PRESSED INTO BLOCKS.

12 cups milk
6 tablespoons strained lemon juice, or vinegar

FOR THE CHENNA
1 teaspoon sugar
1 teaspoon maida or all-purpose flour

MAKES 1 LB.

TO MAKE the paneer, pour the milk into a large heavy-bottomed saucepan. Bring to a boil, stirring with a wooden spoon so that the milk doesn't stick to the bottom of the saucepan. Reduce the heat and stir in the lemon juice, then keep over low heat for a few more seconds before turning the heat off as large bits of curd start to form. Shake the saucepan slowly to allow the curds to form and release the yellow whey.

IF the curds are slow to form, put the saucepan over low heat again for a few seconds. This helps with the coagulation.

LINE a colander with cheesecloth so that it overlaps the sides. Pour off the whey, collecting the curds gently in the colander. Gently pull up the corners of the cheesecloth so that it hangs like a bag, twist the cloth so that the whey is released, then hold the "bag" under running water to wash off the remaining whey, twisting some more to remove the excess liquid.

ALLOW the bag to hang from the faucet for several hours so the weight of the curds releases more liquid and the cheese compacts. To remove more liquid, press the bag under a heavy weight, such as a tray with some canned food piled on top, for about 1 hour. This will form a firm block of paneer. When the block is firm enough to cut into cubes, the paneer is ready for use.

TO MAKE chenna, remove the cheese from the bag and knead the paneer well with the palms of your hands until it is very smooth. Combine the paneer with the sugar and maida, kneading the sugar in until it is fully incorporated.

Once curds have formed, drain everything through a cheesecloth-lined strainer. Squeeze out excess liquid and drain for several hours.

TAMARIND PASTE

5 oz. tamarind block, broken into
  small pieces

MAKES 1 1/4 CUPS

PUT the tamarind in a bowl, pour in 1 cup of very hot water and soak for 3 hours or until the tamarind is soft. (If you are in a hurry, simmer the tamarind in the water for 15 minutes. Although this is efficient, it doesn't give as good a result.) Mash the tamarind thoroughly with a fork.

PUT the mixture through a strainer and extract as much of the pulp as possible by pushing it against the strainer with the back of a spoon. Put the tamarind in the strainer back in the bowl with another 1/2 cup of hot water and mash again. Strain again. Discard the fibers left in the strainer. The paste can be frozen in 1 tablespoon portions and defrosted as needed.

TAMARIND PASTE

GINGER JUICE

2 inch piece of ginger

MAKES 2 TABLESPOONS

POUND the ginger in a pestle and mortar, or grate with a fine grater into a bowl. Put the ginger into a piece of cheesecloth, twist it up tightly and squeeze out all the juice.

GINGER JUICE

YOGURT

YOGURT OR CURDS ARE EATEN WITH OR IN NEARLY EVERY INDIAN MEAL IN SOME FORM OR OTHER.

YOGURT ACTS AS A TENDERIZER IN MARINADES, THICKENS SAUCES AND MAKES REFRESHING DRINKS.

2 1/2 cups milk
2 tablespoons plain yogurt

MAKES 2 1/2 CUPS

BRING the milk to a boil in a heavy-bottomed saucepan, then allow to cool to lukewarm. Stir in the yogurt, cover and leave in a warm place for 8 hours, or overnight. The yogurt should be thick. If it is too runny, the milk was probably too hot for the starter yogurt; if it is too milky, the yogurt was probably not left in a warm enough place to ferment. From each batch, use 2 tablespoons to make the next batch.

WHEN the yogurt is set, put it in a strainer lined with a piece of cheesecloth and allow to drain overnight. This will give a thick yogurt which does not contain too much moisture.

GRATED COCONUT

GRATED COCONUT IS BEST WHEN IT IS FRESH. DRIED OR DESICCATED COCONUT CAN ALSO BE USED BUT IT NEEDS TO BE SOAKED, THEN CHOPPED MORE FINELY OR GROUND TO A PASTE, OTHERWISE IT WILL BE FIBROUS. IF YOU CAN BUY A COCONUT GRATER, THE JOB WILL BE MUCH EASIER.

1 coconut

MAKES 5–6 CUPS

DRAIN the coconut by punching a hole in two of the dark, colored eyes. Drain out the liquid and use it as a refreshing drink. Holding the coconut in one hand, tap around the circumference firmly with a hammer or pestle. This should cause the coconut to split open evenly. (If the coconut doesn't crack easily, put it in a 300°F oven for 15 minutes. This may cause it to crack as it cools. If it doesn't, it will crack easily when hit with a hammer.)

IF YOU would like to use a coconut grater (hiramne), the easiest ones to use are the ones where you sit on one end, then scrape out the coconut from each half on the serrated edge, catching it in a large bowl. If you don't have a coconut grater, pry the flesh out of the shell, trim off the hard, brown, outer skin and grate either by hand on a box grater or chop in a food processor. Grated coconut can be frozen in small portions until it is needed.

Crack the coconut by tapping it around the circumference with a heavy object. It will open neatly.

COCONUT MILK AND COCONUT CREAM

COCONUT MILK IS NOT THE LIQUID WHICH IS FOUND INSIDE THE COCONUT, WHICH IS THE JUICE OR WATER, BUT IS MADE BY SOAKING THE GRATED COCONUT FLESH IN WATER AND THEN SQUEEZING IT. THE FIRST SOAKING AND SQUEEZING GIVES A THICKER MILK, SOMETIMES CALLED CREAM.

1 grated coconut

MAKES 1/2 CUP COCONUT CREAM AND 1 CUP COCONUT MILK

MIX the grated coconut with 1/2 cup of hot water and allow to soak for 5 minutes. Pour the mixture through a strainer that is lined with cheesecloth, then gather the cheesecloth into a ball to squeeze out any extra liquid. This will make a thick coconut milk.

REPEAT the process with another 1 cup of water to make thinner coconut milk.

COCONUT MILK AND
COCONUT CREAM

PANCH PHORON

PANCH PHORON

PANCH PHORON IS A FIVE-SPICE MIX USED TO FLAVOR VEGETABLES AND LEGUMES. THE MIX IS FRIED

AT THE BEGINNING OF A DISH, OR FRIED AND ADDED AS A FINAL SEASONING (TARKA).

1 teaspoon cumin seeds
1 teaspoon fennel seeds
1 teaspoon fenugreek seeds
1 teaspoon brown mustard seeds
1 teaspoon kalonji (nigella seeds)

MAKES 1 TABLESPOON

GRIND all the spices to a fine powder in a spice grinder, a pestle and mortar, or with a grinding stone. Store in a small airtight container until you need it.

GARAM MASALA

GARAM MASALA MEANS "WARMING SPICE MIX." IT CAN BE A MIXTURE OF WHOLE OR GROUND SPICES.

RECIPES ARE NUMEROUS BUT THEY ARE ALL AROMATIC, RATHER THAN "HOT" MIXES.

8 cardamom pods
2 Indian bay leaves (cassia leaves)
1 teaspoon black peppercorns
2 teaspoons cumin seeds
2 teaspoons coriander seeds
2 inch piece of cinnamon stick
1 teaspoon cloves

MAKES 3 TABLESPOONS

REMOVE the seeds from the cardamom pods. Break the bay leaves into small pieces. Put them in a spice grinder or pestle and mortar with the remaining spices and grind to a fine powder. Store in a small airtight container until needed.

GARAM MASALA

CHAAT MASALA

CHAAT MASALA IS A SALTY, TANGY SEASONING USED IN POPULAR SNACKS SUCH AS BHEL PURI. IT CAN

BE TOSSED THROUGH DRY SNACK MIXES OR SPRINKLED ONTO FRUIT AND VEGETABLES AS A SEASONING.

4 tablespoons coriander seeds
2 tablespoons cumin seeds
1 teaspoon ajowan
3 tablespoons black salt
1 tablespoon amchoor powder
2 dried chiles
1 teaspoon black peppercorns
1 teaspoon pomegranate seeds

MAKES 10 TABLESPOONS

PLACE a small frying pan over low heat and dry-roast the coriander seeds until aromatic. Remove from the pan and dry-roast the cumin seeds, then separately, the ajowan. Grind the roasted mixture to a fine powder with the other ingredients, using a spice grinder or pestle and mortar. Store in an airtight container.

CHAAT MASALA

THE TWO main tea-producing areas in India are Assam *(left page)* and the Nilgiris *(right page)*. In Assam, the tea gardens are situated along a flat valley and the bushes are interspersed with shade trees. In the Nilgiris, they are on the rolling foothills. However, both areas have a high rainfall, a prerequisite for growing tea. Tea is picked by hand, with only the bud and top leaves being plucked. One section of the

TEA

TEA FROM CHINA WAS SO IMPORTANT TO EUROPE BY THE 18TH CENTURY THAT WHEN TRADE IN TEA STOPPED DURING THE OPIUM WARS, THE BRITISH DECIDED TO GROW CHINESE TEA IN INDIA. THEY THEN FOUND A NATIVE TEA ALREADY GROWING IN ASSAM.

The first tea garden in India was established in 1835 and India quickly became the world's biggest producer of tea and a nation of tea drinkers. Tea is made from the fresh leaves of the *Camellia sinensis or Camellia assamica* tree native to both south-west China and Assam in the far north-east of India. The leaves can be processed in different ways. Green tea is dried before fermentation and black tea is fermented before drying. In India, black tea (chai) is the most common.

MAKING TEA

The process of turning fresh green tea leaves into black tea is called "making." Making tea by either the CTC or the Orthodox method refers to the way the leaves are cut or rolled. CTC means "crush or cut, tear, curl"—the leaves are fed through a cutter before they are fermented and dried. This gives a fine, granular tea. Orthodox refers to the method of rolling the leaves (only the best are used) on a rolling table to give whole leaf or broken leaf tea. Both methods break down the veins in the leaves and start the fermentation process. Orthodox tea is considered to have superior flavor and CTC tea to have more strength. The two are often blended to give a strength and flavor balance.

MAKING ASSAM TEA

THIS BATCH of CTC tea is being made at Chubwa Tea Estate in Assam. First the top two leaves and a bud are hand-picked from the bush tops. At the factory, they are tipped out onto withering troughs and left for 12–18 hours so that some moisture is lost and the fermentation process is triggered. The withered leaves are then conditioned by feeding them through a CTC (crush, tear, curl) or rotovane machine to turn the leaves into "mal." Orthodox tea, which has whole leaves, is made by feeding the leaves through a rolling machine *(right)* instead.

This twists and rolls up the leaves. Both methods release the juices in the leaves by breaking down the leaf cells. For CTC tea, the mal is then fed on a conveyor belt through a rotary sifter in a single layer. This helps it form into granules and gets rid of any unwanted fiber. The mal is then fed through a fermenting machine which blows cold, humidified air through it. This induces an oxidization process which develops the color, strength and flavor of the tea. When the mal reaches a coppery color and has the correct nose (aroma) it is passed

through a vibro fluid bed drier which is heated to 255–265°F. The mal is "fired" for up to 20 minutes. This stops the fermentation process. The tea has now become a blackish-brown. The mal is then passed through a sorter fitted with different mesh sizes. This sorts the tea into seven different grades (sizes). Each grade is kept separate and then packed into paper sacks, tea chests or bags. After each batch is made (three are made in a day), the factory is washed and cleaned thoroughly so each batch of tea does not contaminate the next batch.

GLOSSARY OF INDIAN FOOD AND COOKING

agar-agar Also known as China grass, this is a setting agent made from certain types of seaweed. It is sold as strips, sheets, flakes or powder, dissolves in boiling water, and unlike gelatin will set at room temperature. Available from supermarkets, health food shops and Indian food shops.

ajowan (ajwain) A spice that looks like miniature cumin seeds and has a similar aroma but stronger flavor. Use sparingly.

amaranth (marsa) A leafy green or green and dark red vegetable. It has a peppery flavor and can be substituted with spinach in recipes. Available at Indian food shops.

amchoor/amchur powder (khatai) A fine beige powder made by drying green mangoes. It is used as a souring agent or meat tenderizer in Indian cooking. It is an essential flavor in chaat masala (page 284). Available at Indian food shops.

asafoetida (hing) This yellowish powder or lump of resin is made from the dried latex of a type of fennel. Asafoetida has an extremely pungent smell which has earned it the name "devil's dung." It is used to make legumes and beans more digestible and Hindu Brahmins and Jains use it instead of garlic and onions which are forbidden to them. Asafoetida is always fried to tame its aroma. It comes in small airtight containers and is available from Indian food shops.

atta Sometimes called chapati flour, this is made from finely ground whole durum wheat. Sometimes has a proportion of white flour added, labeled as 80/20 or 60/40. Atta is much finer and softer than whole wheat flour so if you can't find it, use half whole wheat and half maida or all-purpose flour instead.

banana flower (kere kafool/mocha) This is the purple, teardrop-shaped flower of the banana plant.The purple leaves and pale yellow buds which grow between them are discarded. Only the inner pale core is eaten. This needs to be blanched in boiling water to remove any bitterness. Wear rubber gloves to prepare banana flower as it has a gummy substance, which can stain your fingers. Available from Indian food shops.

banana leaves Large green leaves which can be used as a wrapping (dip in boiling water to soften them) for foods, or as a plate to eat off. Young leaves are preferable. Available from Indian food shops.

basil seeds (subja) These tiny black seeds of a type of wild Indian basil are soaked in water until they swell. When soaked, they are surrounded by clear jelly. They have no flavor and are used for texture in drinks like falooda (page 271). Buy at Indian food shops.

besan flour Also known as gram flour, this is a yellow flour made from ground Bengal gram or chickpeas. It has a nutty flavor and is used as a thickener in curries, as well as in batters, dumplings, sweets and breads.

bitter melon Also known as bitter gourd, karela or warty melon, this looks like a pale cucumber with a warty skin. The flesh is bitter and needs to be blanched or degorged, then married with strong flavors.

black-eyed beans (lobhia) Also called black-eyed peas, these are actually dried cow peas and are also known as chowli dal when split. They are buff-colored beans with a small dark eye on one side. They need to be soaked overnight or cooked before use. Avoid dark or wrinkled beans as these are old.

black salt (kala namak) A rock salt mined in central India. Available as black or dark brown lumps, or ground to a pinkish grey powder. Unlike white salt, it has a tangy, smoky flavor. Buy at Indian food shops.

buttermilk (chaas) The mildly sour liquid left when milk is churned to butter. Commercial buttermilk is made from fermented skim milk and is not "live" as real buttermilk would be.

cardamom (elaichi) Dry green pods full of sticky, tiny brown or black seeds which have a sweet flavor and pungent aroma. If you need ground cardamom, open the pods and grind the seeds. Pre-ground cardamom quickly loses flavor. Use pods whole or crushed. Brown cardamom has a peppery flavor not suitable for sweet dishes.

cayenne pepper A very hot red chili powder made from sun-dried red chiles.

chaat masala Seasoning used for various snacks known as chaat (which means "to lick" in Hindi). The spice blend uses a variety of flavorings including asafoetida, amchoor, black salt, cumin, cayenne, ajowan and pepper. (See page 284.)

chana dal (gram lentils) These are husked, split, polished, yellow Bengal gram, the most common type of gram lentil in India. They are often cooked with a pinch of asafoetida to make them easier to digest.

chenna Sweetened Indian cheese, used in sweet dishes. Found in the refrigerated section in supermarkets and Indian food shops. To make your own, see page 279.

chickpeas (chana) Chickpeas come white (kabuli/kubli) or black (kala). The white garden is worked on at a time to make sure that the tea bushes are kept to the same height. A stick is laid out along the bush and the leaves above it are picked. The tea is collected three times a day. The baskets are emptied, then the leaves are briefly sorted through to get rid of any twigs, then weighed at the collection points throughout the garden. The leaves are then delivered to the factory to be made into tea.

TEA-PRODUCING AREAS IN INDIA

ASSAM lies beneath the foothills of the Himalayas. Assam tea is produced seasonally in first and second flushes. The second flush produces "tippy" tea which means the black tea has plenty of young gold tips. Assam tea is known as "orange" tea due to its brown and gold color. Assam teas are full-bodied, with a strong, rich taste which tends to linger in the mouth.

THE NILGIRIS these hills form part of the Western Ghats in the south of India. Tea produced here has a bright color and astringent quality and is picked at all times of the year.

DARJEELING, a rich tea produced in the foothills of the Himalayas, has a "muscatel" flavor. Sometimes described as the champagne of teas, it is produced in limited quantities. Darjeeling tea is often sold as tea from a single garden.

OTHER AREAS in India where tea is grown include the Dooars in Bengal, and the Kangara valley in Himachal Pradesh where green tea is produced.

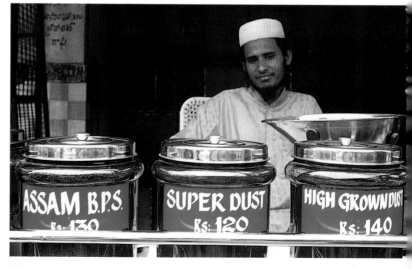

INDIA produces approximately 1 billion pounds of tea a year. Half of this is exported and the rest is drunk in India. Chai is made by boiling tea with milk and sugar to make a strong, sweet brew.

TEA TASTING

EVERY BATCH of tea made is tasted and all tasting is done using the same method. Fresh, non-chlorinated water is brought to a boil, 2.5 g of tea is put in a clean lidded cup, the water is added and the tea infused for exactly 5 minutes. It is then decanted into a cup and the leaves shaken into the lid. The tea is sucked into the mouth off a spoon, then spat out to judge flavor. The leaves are inspected visually.

TEA AUCTION

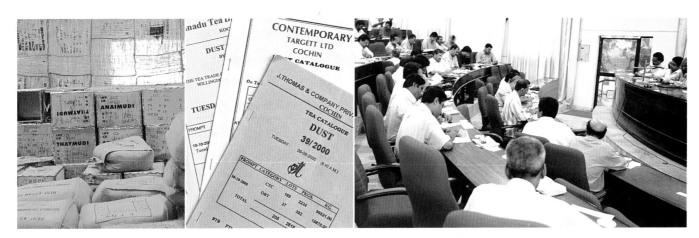

TEA IS AUCTIONED by the Tea Trade Association as shown here in Kochi (Cochin). Each tea garden has a nominated broker who stores the tea in a designated warehouse, gives a valuation, prints the catalogue and makes samples available to the buyers for tasting. The tea is auctioned to the highest bidder. Tea gardens can pack and sell their tea under their own brands, at their own price, or send it to auction.

TEA GRADES

TEA IS SOLD by grades, which refer to the leaf size. Orthodox teas are made from whole, rolled leaves or pieces of rolled leaf. CTC teas are made from cut leaves of various sizes. Orthodox grades range from flowery pekoe through orange pekoe *(left)* and broken orange pekoe fannings *(center left)* to dust. CTC teas range from pekoe through broken orange pekoe *(center right)* to pekoe dust *(right)*.

chickpeas are actually a tan color and the black ones are dark brown. Usually sold whole, but also sold split, dried chickpeas need to be soaked for 8 hours in cold water before use. They will double in size. Canned ones can be used but need to be added at the end of the cooking time as they are already very soft.

chiles (lal mirch/hari mirch) Red and green chiles are widely used in Indian cuisine. Recipes generally give a color, rather than a variety. Many varieties are grown in India and are used in a regional or seasonal context. Kashmiri chiles are dark red and mild, Goan chiles are short and stubby and mundu chiles are round. Small dhani (bird's eye chiles) are the hottest.

chiles, dried (sabat lal mirch) Dried whole chiles of various shapes, sizes and heat levels. Sometimes soaked to soften them. Remove the seeds if they are very hot.

chili flakes Dried, coarsely ground chiles with the seeds included; usually hot.

chili powder A wide variety of chiles are dried and crushed to make chili powders. Some, such as Kashmiri chili powder and paprika, are used for color, whereas others like cayenne are used for heat. Don't use chili powder indiscriminately. The amount used can be varied, to taste, so start with a small amount and determine how hot it is.

cilantro (hara dhaniya) Fresh cilantro leaves are used both in recipes and also as a colorful garnish. Buy healthy bunches of green leaves. Avoid any which are yellowing.

cloves (laung) The dried, unopened flower buds of the clove tree. Brown and nail-shaped, they have a pungent flavor, so use in moderation. Use whole or ground.

coconut (nariyal) The fruit of a coconut palm. The inner nut is encased in a husk which has to be removed. The hard shell can be drained of juice and cracked open to extract the white meat which is jellyish in younger nuts and harder in older ones. Dried coconut meat is known as copra. The method for cracking coconuts is shown on page 283.

coconut cream This is made by soaking freshly grated coconut in boiling water

and then squeezing out a thick, sweet coconut-flavored liquid. It is available canned. To make your own coconut cream, see page 283.

coconut milk A thinner version of coconut cream, made as above but with more water or from a second pressing. Available canned. To make your own, see page 283.

coconut milk powder A powdered form of coconut which when mixed with water makes coconut milk or cream. Sold in supermarkets or Indian food shops.

coriander (dhaniya) seeds The round seeds of the coriander plant. The seeds have a spicy aroma, are widely used in Indian cooking and are common in spice mixes such as garam masala. To intensify the flavor, dry-roast the seeds until aromatic, before crushing them. Best freshly ground for each dish. Available whole or ground.

creamed coconut A solid block of coconut cream which needs to be reconstituted with water, or can be added straight to a dish to give a strong coconut flavor. Slice pieces off the block as required.

cumin (jeera) seeds The green or ochre, elongated ridged seeds of a plant of the parsley family. It has a peppery, slightly bitter flavor and is very aromatic. To intensify the flavor, dry-roast the seeds before crushing them. Best freshly ground for each dish. Available whole or ground. Kala jeera are a black variety.

curry leaves (kadhi patta/meetha neem) Smallish green aromatic leaves of a tree native to India and Sri Lanka. These give a distinctive flavor to south Indian dishes. They are usually fried and added to the dish or used as a garnish at the end.

dal (dhal) is used to describe not only an ingredient but a dish made from it. In India, dal relates to any type of dried split pea, bean or lentil. The cooking times vary as do the texture and flavor. A dal dish can be a thin soup or more like a stew. All dal should be rinsed before use.

degchi A cooking pot, often brass lined with tin, which has no handle. It has a thick bottom and straight sides like a saucepan.

drumsticks (sahjan) Long, dark green, ridged fibrous pods from the horseradish tree. Drumsticks, so called because of their rigidity, need to be cut into pieces before being cooked. The inner pulp, the only part eaten, is scooped out with a spoon or scraped out with your teeth. Select uniformly slim pods. Sold in Indian food shops.

fennel (saunph) seeds The dried seeds of a Mediterranean plant, fennel seeds are oval, greenish yellow, with ridges running along them, and look like large cumin. Used as an aromatic and a digestive. To intensify the flavor, dry-roast the seeds before crushing them. Available whole or ground. Best freshly ground.

fenugreek (methi) seeds Not a true seed, but a dried legume. Ochre in color and almost square, with a groove down one side, fenugreek has a curry aroma (it is a major ingredient in commercial curry powders) and is best dry-roasted for a few seconds before use. Don't brown them too much or they will be bitter.

garam masala A northern Indian spice mix which means "warming spice mix," it mostly contains coriander, cumin, cardamom, black pepper, cloves, cinnamon and nutmeg. There are many versions and you can buy pre-ground mixes or make your own (page 284). Garam masala is usually added to meat dishes as a final seasoning.

ghee A highly clarified butter made from cow or water buffalo milk. Ghee can be heated to a high temperature without burning and has an aromatic flavor. Vegetable ghees are also available but don't have the same aromatic qualities. You can substitute clarified butter, or make your own ghee by melting unsalted butter in a saucepan, bringing to a simmer and cooking for 30 minutes to evaporate out any water. Skim any impurities from the surface, then drain the ghee off, leaving the white sediment behind. Allow to cool.

ginger (adrak) The rhizome of a tropical plant which is sometimes referred to as a "root." It is sold in "hands." Fresh young ginger should have a smooth, pinkish beige skin and be firm and juicy. As it ages, the skin toughens and the flesh becomes more fibrous. Avoid old ginger which is wrinkled as it will be tough. Choose pieces you can snap easily. Ginger is measured in inches and this means pieces with an average-sized width. Variations in size will not adversely affect the flavor of the dish. Ginger is also available dried and ground.

green banana (kela) Cooking banana, also known as plantain, which looks like a large, unripe green banana.

green unripe mango (kacha am) A variety of mango widely used for cooking in Asian countries. Available from Indian food shops.

hilsa (elish) A much-prized fish, this is a type of shad with sweet flesh and lots of tiny bones. Hilsa are caught when they enter fresh water to spawn. Large herrings or firm white fish can be used instead.

Indian bay leaves (tej patta) These are the dried leaves of the cassia tree. They look somewhat like dried European bay leaves but they have a cinnamon flavor. They are used mainly in Bengali cuisine and cuisine of the north of India and are available from Indian food shops.

jaggery (gur) Made from sugar cane, this is a raw sugar with a caramel flavor and alcoholic aroma. Jaggery, which is sold in lumps, is slightly sticky and varies in color depending on the juice from which it is made. Jaggery can also refer to palm sugar. Light brown sugar can be used as a substitute.

kalonji (nigella seeds) Small teardrop-shaped black seeds with an onion flavor, used both as a spice in northern India and as a decoration for breads such as naan. It is used in panch phoron (page 284).

karhai/kadhai A deep wok-shaped cooking dish. Heavy cast iron ones are best for talawa (deep-frying) and carbon steel ones for bhoona (frying). There are decorative ones which are best for serving, not cooking.

Kashmiri chili powder Made from ground red Kashmiri chiles which have a deep red color but little heat. A mild, dark red chili powder can be substituted.

kokum The dried purple fruit of the gamboge tree which is used in southern Indian, Gujarati and Maharashtran cuisine to impart an acid fruity flavor. Kokum looks like dried pieces of purple/black rind and is quite sticky. It can be bought from Indian food shops and is sometimes called cocumful. A smoked version which is called kodampodli is also available. Kokum needs to be briefly soaked before use.

maida All-purpose white flour used for making naan and other Indian recipes. All-purpose flour is a suitable substitute.

masoor dal (red lentils) When whole (known as matki or bagali) these are dark brown or green. When split, they are salmon in color. The split ones are the most common as they cook more easily and do not usually need soaking as the whole ones do.

methi (fenugreek leaves) The leaves of young fenugreek plants, these are used as a vegetable and treated much like spinach. They have a mildly bitter flavor. Strip the leaves off the stems as the stalks are often tough. Spinach leaves can be used but will not give the same flavor. Available fresh or dried, from Indian food shops.

moong dal Split and skinned mung beans, which are pale yellow. The dal does not always need to be soaked. Whole mung beans (sabat moong), also called green gram, must be soaked before use.

mustard oil (sarson ka tel) Made from pressed brown mustard seeds, this is a strongly flavored oil which is used in Bengali and Punjabi cooking. The oil is usually preheated to smoking point and then cooled to temper its strong aroma.

mustard seeds (rai) Yellow, brown and black mustard seeds are used in Indian cooking, especially in Bengal. Brown and black are interchangeable. The seeds are either added to hot oil to pop, to make them taste nutty rather than hot, or are ground to a paste before use in which case they are still hot. Split mustard seeds are called mustard dal.

oil (tel) Several types of oil are used in Indian cuisine, depending on where the dish comes from. An Indian pantry should contain several oils for different uses. Cold-pressed or refined peanut (groundnut) oil is used in northern and central India and is a good all-purpose oil (use only the refined version for deep-frying). Sesame oil made from raw sesame seeds is used in the South, and mustard oil in the Punjab and Bengal. These oils impart flavor to the dishes in which they are used. Coconut oil is also used in the South where coconut is a major flavoring. It fries well but is very high in saturated fats.

okra (bhindi) Also known as ladies' fingers, these are green, fuzzy, tapered pods with ridges running down them. When cut they give off a mucilaginous substance which disappears during cooking.

panch phoron (panch phora) Meaning five spices, this mix is used in Bengali and Bangladeshi cuisine. It contains fennel, brown mustard, kalonji, fenugreek, and cumin seeds in equal amounts. It can be used whole or ground. (See page 284.)

paneer A fresh cheese made by coagulating milk with lemon juice and allowing it to drain. Paneer is usually pressed into a block and can be found in the refrigerated section in supermarkets and Indian food shops. To make your own, see page 279.

pappadam (poppodom, papad, appalam) These are quite thin wafers made from a paste of lentil (gram) flours, rice flour or even tapioca or sago flour, which is rolled out very thin and then sun-dried. Pappadams come in different sizes and flavors. Northern Indian ones often have chili flakes or spices added. To fry pappadams, heat 1 inch oil in a frying pan until very hot, add the pappadams one at a time and press them down into the oil with a spatula until they expand and lighten in color. To flame-roast them, hold a pappadam in some tongs above a gas flame until it expands in size, curls and gets flecked with bubbles (toast both sides). Fried pappadams will stay crisp for about two hours.

paprika (deghi mirch) A reddish orange powder made from ground sweet peppers grown in Kashmir. Usually sweet rather than hot, paprika is used for color. It needs to be fried to get rid of any raw flavor. Spanish or Hungarian paprika can be substituted.

pine nuts Small cream seeds from Neosia pine cones which grow in the Himalayas. In Kashmir, they are a staple and are used whole and ground. Any pine nut may be used.

pomegranate seeds (anardana) Sun-dried whole or ground sour pomegranate seeds, used to add a sour, tangy flavor to north Indian dishes. They are also used as a garnish. Available from Indian food shops.

pomfret (rupchanda, chamna) A silvery seawater fish with tiny black spots. Pomfret is expensive and hard to find outside India, although it is sometimes available frozen. Sole, flounder, leatherjacket or John Dory fillets can be substituted.

poppy seeds (khus khus) In India, white poppy seeds are used rather than the European black or grey ones. They are used either whole or ground. The ground poppy seeds are used to thicken dishes like korma. Whole ones are often roasted and used in spice mixes. Don't use black poppy seeds as a thickener or the color of your dish will be greyish.

puffed rice (moori, mamra, kurmura) Rather like popcorn, puffed rice is made by exploding dried rice out of its husks by dropping the grains onto hot sand. It is used in snacks such as bhel puri, or rolled in jaggery to make sweets. Available from Indian food shops.

rice (chaaval) Rice grain types and sizes vary across India. Much of the rice which is eaten is grown locally and it is nearly always white and polished. Popular long-grained rices include basmati, a particularly fragrant rice used for special occasions (it is expensive); patna, with a more rounded grain, is eaten in the North; and gobindavog is used in Bengal. Rices with some husk left on, which gives them some red coloration, include red patni, grown in central and western India, and rosematter, grown in southern India. You can use whichever variety you like best.

rice flour (chaaval ka atta) Finely ground rice which is used for making dosas. A coarser grind called idli-rava is used for idlis. Buy at Indian food shops.

rice sticks (rice vermicelli, chaaval ke sev) Made from rice flour, these noodles are very thin. They are used for sweets or savory snacks and need to be softened in boiling water. Other Asian rice vermicelli can be used as a substitute.

roasted chana dal Bengal gram which have been roasted so they puff up and get a porous, crunchy texture. Used in snacks. Buy in bags from Indian food shops.

rohu A black, silvery carp with one central bone and firm flesh. It cuts into steaks very well. Any firm-fleshed fish can be substituted.

rosewater (ruh gulab/gulab jal) Made from rose essence and water, this is used to perfume sweets, desserts and drinks. It has aroma but no flavor. Use sparingly.

saag A generic term for leafy greens.

saffron strands (kesar/zaffran) The dried stigmas of a crocus flower. The strands give an intense yellow color and musky aroma. Only a few are needed for each dish. Indian saffron grows in Kashmir. It needs to be soaked in liquid before use.

sago (sabudhana) Small dried balls of sago palm sap which are used for milky desserts and savory dishes. Cooked sago is transparent and soft with a silky texture.

semolina (sooj, rava) A fine, coarse or medium grain made from processed wheat with the wheat germ removed. It swells when cooked to give a creamy, textured effect. Used for sweets and upama.

sev Very fine noodles, used in bhel puri, made from besan flour. Sold at Indian food shops.

sevian These are very fine noodles made from wheat flour. They have a cookie-like flavor. Sold at Indian food shops.

silver leaf (varak) Very thin, edible sheets of silver. They have no flavor or aroma and come in boxes or books between sheets of tissue paper. Always apply the silver to the food from the backing sheet and then pull off the backing sheet. If you touch the foil it will stick to you. Silver leaf does not go on in an even layer because it is so fragile.

split peas (matar dal) Split dried peas which need to be soaked before they are cooked and have a slightly chewy texture. Green and yellow ones are available.

tamarind (imli) A souring agent made from the pods of the tamarind tree. Sold either

as a block of pulp, fibrous husk and seeds, as cleaned pulp, or as ready-prepared tamarind paste or concentrate. If using the pulp, see page 280 to make your own paste.

tandoori food coloring A bright red powder which is used to color tandoori dishes. Add to tandoori pastes to color them.

tarka This is a seasoning process, either the first or last step, used in Indian cookery. Spices and aromatics are fried in oil to flavor the oil, then the flavored oil is stirred into the dish, most commonly at the end of cooking.

tava A specially shaped hotplate used in India to cook breads. Some are flat, others are slightly convex or concave. Keep oiled to stop them going rusty. Nonstick ones are also available.

toor dal (toovar dal) Also called yellow lentils, these come oiled and plain. Oiled ones look slightly greasy and need to be soaked in hot water to remove the oil. Soak the dal for a few hours before cooking.

turmeric (haldi) Dried turmeric, sold whole or ground, is a deep yellow color. It has a slightly bitter flavor and a pungent aroma. Turmeric is used for both color and flavor.

urad dal The split variety (chilke urad) is a cream color with black skin. The skinned variety is cream. Urad dal does not usually need to be soaked. The dal is used when making dosa and idli batters and it becomes glutinous and creamy when cooked.

vinegar (sirka) Made from fermented alcohol, vinegars based on sugar cane molasses (dark) and coconut (clear) are used, mainly in Parsi, Anglo-Indian and Goan food. If unavailable, substitute balsamic or white vinegar.

whole black gram (sabat urad) This whole urad dal has a black skin. Usually it has to be soaked or precooked before use.

yogurt (dahi, doi) Yogurt in India is made with whole milk and is a thick, set yogurt. If you use commercial yogurt in recipes instead of making your own, you may need to drain the yogurt in cheesecloth first to remove any excess liquid. See page 280 for home-made yogurt instructions.

INDEX

BIBLIOGRAPHY

Achaya, K.T. *A Historical Dictionary of Indian Food.* Oxford University Press, 1998.

Baljekar, Mridula. *Secrets from an Indian Kitchen.* Pavilion Books Limited, 2000.

Banerjee, Satarupa. *Book Of Indian Sweets.* Rupa and Co, 1994.

Bharadwaj, Monisha. *The Indian Kitchen.* Kyle Cathie Limited, 1996.

Bladholm, Linda. *The Indian Grocery Store Demystified.* Renaissance Books, 2000.

Bradnock, Robert and Roma. *Footprint India Handbook.* Footprint Handbooks, 1999

Davidson, Alan. *The Oxford Companion to Food.* Oxford University Press, 1999.

Gupta, Minakshie Das and Bunny, Jaya, Chaliha. *The Calcutta Cook Book.* Penguin Books, 1995.

Jaffrey, Madhur. *A Taste of India.* Pavillion Books Limited, 2000.

Kaimla, Maya. *Savouring the Spice Coast of India.* HarperCollins, 2000.

Kingman, Rani. *A Taste of Madras.* Interlink Books, 1996.

Lonely Planet. *India.* Lonely Planet Publications. Pty Ltd, 1999

Marks, Copeland. *The Varied Kitchens of India. Cuisines of the Anglo-Indians of Calcutta, Bengalis, Jews of Calcutta, Kashmiris, Parsis, and Tibetans of Darjeeling.* M. Evans and Company, Inc., 1986.

The Rough Guide. *India.* Rough Guides Ltd, 1999

Sinclair, Charles. *International Dictionary of Food and Cooking.* Peter Collin Publishing Ltd, 1998.

Singh, Dharamjit. *Indian Cookery.* Penguin Books, 1970.

Solomon, Charmaine. *Encyclopedia of Asian Food.* William Heinemann, 1996.

Stobbart, Tom. *The Cook's Encyclopedia.* Grub Street, 1998.

Veerasawmy, E. P. *Indian Cookery.* Arco Publications, 1964.

Westrip, Joyce. P. *An ABC of Indian Food.* Prospect Books, 1996.

Wickramasinghe, Priya. *Leith's Indian and Sri Lankan Cookery.* Bloomsbury Publishing Plc, 1998.

THE FOOD OF INDIA

Published by Murdoch Books®

© Text, design, photography and illustrations Murdoch Books® 2002.
All rights reserved. Published 2002

ISBN 1-55285-370-5

Publishing Manager: Kay Halsey
Food Editor: Lulu Grimes
Design Concept: Marylouise Brammer
Designer: Susanne Geppert
Editor: Wendy Stephen
Photographers: Jason Lowe (location); Alan Benson (recipes)
Stylist: Sarah de Nardi
Stylist's Assistants: Rekha Arnott, Julie Ray, Sonia Grieg
Recipes: Priya Wickramasinghe, Carol Selva Rajah
Additional Recipes: Kuvel Sundar Singh, Lisa Harvey, Margaret Grimes, Ajoy Joshi, Rekha Arnott, Radha Jayaram
Map: Rosanna Vecchio

Publisher: Kay Scarlett
Production Manager: Kylie Kirkwood
Chief Executive: Juliet Rogers

PRINTED IN CHINA by Leefung-Asco Printers Ltd.
No part of this publication may be reproduced, stored in a retrieval system or transmitted in any form or
by any means, electronic, mechanical, photocopying, recording or otherwise without the prior written
permission of the publisher. Murdoch Books® is a subsidiary of Murdoch Magazines Australia Pty Ltd.

Murdoch Books® Australia
GPO Box 1203, Sydney, NSW 1045
Phone: (612) 4352 7000   Fax: (612) 4352 7026

Murdoch Books® UK
Ferry House, 51– 57 Lacy Road, London SW15 1PR
Phone: (020) 8355 1480   Fax: (020) 8355 1499

IMPORTANT: Those who might be at risk from the effects of salmonella food poisoning
(the elderly, pregnant women, young children and those suffering from immune deficiency
diseases) should consult their GP with any concerns about eating raw eggs.

ACKNOWLEDGMENTS

The Publisher wishes to thank the following for all their help in making this book possible:

The Oberoi Group: Victoria Hobbs, Aleysha Allan; Taj Hotels and Palaces: TATA Tea Ltd: Mr S.M. Kidwai, Mr Shamsher
Singh Dogra, Kiran Desai; Spices Board of India: V. Jayashankar, Dr. P.S.S.Thampi. James Finlay: Mike Jones.
Ian Hemphill. Ajoy Joshi, Arun Ramrakha.

Kerala: Joerg Drechsel and Txuku Iriarte Solana, K.P.Francis, Joseph Jescil, Ram Prem, Saju, Sony, Stephen, Suresh,
Rajesh, Eldhose, Malabar House Residency, Kochi; Mr Lakshmanan, Ramkumar Menon, Mr Kalyanraman, Tata Spices
Centre, Kochi; Mr Angelos, Mr Balakrishan, Tata Tea Bag Unit, Kochi; George Netto, TATA Tea, Munnar; Mr Devanand,
Jacob, Spices Board of India, Kochi; Spice Village, Periyar; High Range Club, Munnar; Mylamdumpara Spice Research
Station. Chennai: Alex Baja, B. Balaji, Sanjeev Khan,Taj Coromandel, Chennai. Hyderabad: G. Pulla Reddy, Hyderabad;
Sanjukthaa Roy, Taj Krishna, Hyderabad. Calcutta: Rabindra Nath Das (late) and family, K.C. Das Private Ltd, Calcutta; Ranvir
Bhandari, Oberoi Grand, Calcutta. Assam: Mr and Mrs Prabal Choudhury, Mr and Mrs A. Bhattacharya, S. Rafique, A. Dutta,
Loni Borpatra Gohain, Chubwa Tea Estate; Mr and Mrs Bordoloi, A. Kapur, G. Bora, S. Das, R. Hazarika, Powai Tea Estate,
Assam. Delhi: Ashima Lal Sharma, Ramneek Lamba, Oberoi, New Delhi; Bengali Sweet House, Delhi; Haldiram, Delhi.
Mumbai: Anil Kaul, Oberoi Mumbai; V.R.Joglekar, Mumbai Port Trust.